THEODORE ROETHKE

THEODORE ROETHKE

AN INTRODUCTION

TO THE POETRY

KARL MALKOFF

COLUMBIA UNIVERSITY PRESS

NEW YORK & LONDON

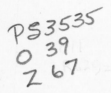

For

MARCIA GORDON MALKOFF

JOHN UNTERECKER

Foreword

Shortly before he died, Theodore Roethke interrupted a public reading of his poems to remark that he was happiest when he was working in "long forms"—sequences of related lyrics. Though he did not go on to say that he was also concerned to construct relationships between the sequences themselves, a careful appraisal of the body of his work shows that such a plan must have been very much in his mind. For, in spite of the fact that his subject matter changes from early celebrations of the varied natural world to late accounts of the terrors of incoherent landscapes, patterns of recurrent imagery and groups of recurrent themes link poem to poem, sequence to sequence.

When I say "link," I do not mean to imply that the linkage is in the nature of an obvious progression. The links are generally unobtrusive and the progress is often made in terms of reversals. Indeed, Roethke's related poems sometimes resemble Blake's—marriages of heaven and hell, innocence and experience. Poem and following poem, sequence and following sequence seem to be carrying out an internal warfare, though perhaps the design should more accurately be described as a Hegelian series of oppositions: conflicts that resolve themselves in brief reconciliations from which new conflicts spring. Roethke's image for this progress is that of a salmon laboriously struggling upstream to die at its spawning place, the place of its birth.

Overall patterns, of course, occur in the work of many men; yet Roethke exposes his own in peculiarly personal ways. His poems are the product of a man who discovers in the external world a mirror for the emotional battles that rage within his mind, the triumphs and defeats that help define his soul. It is for this reason, I think, that most of us are initially unaware of the great technical skill that has gone into their composition. We are so alive to the protagonist's terror, delight, and ecstasy that we are only vaguely conscious that that terror, delight, and ecstasy are projected through a very deliberate art, that the whole structure by which we have been moved—from the bare statements of the early poems to the witty aphorisms of the late ones—has been most ingeniously fitted together. The body of Roethke's poetry is extraordinarily articulate.

It takes a most sensitive critic to explore articulate work. Happily, Mr. Malkoff is not only sensitive, he is also eloquent, sensible, and modest. His focus is always on the poetry. His project is always to help us understand what Roethke is doing and to help us see why he is doing it.

In this age of criticism, when a flood of ingenious and specialized studies threatens to engulf all poetry, there is a special need for books of the sort that Mr. Malkoff has written, books that are designed not to impress other critics but rather to be helpful for the interested reader. In saying that Karl Malkoff has written a most helpful book, I am, therefore, giving it my highest endorsement. It is valuable because in good, clean prose it shows us how to read Theodore Roethke's intricate, rich poetry.

Preface

At the time of his death in 1963, Theodore Roethke had received recognition as an important American poet. Since then, his reputation, and interest in his work, have steadily increased. His selected prose and a volume of criticism about his work have already appeared, and a new edition of his collected poems is in process; the business of evaluating his stature is well under way. Essential to any such evaluation is a comprehensive survey of the poet's work, one which concentrates not on the merits or faults of individual poems, but which places each poem in the context of the poet's total development. The results of such a study are particularly rewarding in the case of a poet like Roethke, who created a world in terms of a consistent and obsessive symbolism, which links poems and often makes them dependent on each other for full understanding.

In this study, both form and content will be considered; for Roethke, the means of expression is as important as the perception of reality for which it is the vehicle—it is part of that perception. However, since Roethke is a difficult, sometimes "oracular" poet, the emphasis will necessarily be on explication of the text. Some critics, especially British critics, have insisted that Roethke does not really "mean" anything, that he has written low-grade nonsense verse. Without limiting the rich suggestiveness of Roethke's symbolism, I hope to be able to show that his poetry always means "something," and usually a great many things.

Following his continuous search for a direct expression of reality, Roethke's poetic techniques developed hand in hand with his thought; the organic growth of his work provides a convenient, and "natural," basis of organization for studying it —that is, in terms of the new perspectives which inform each successive volume. I have limited myself to his "serious" verse, since his "lighter" poetry and "children's" poetry do not shed much light on his total development and could only form a digression in a preliminary study of this sort. And I have given Roethke's uncollected poetry little specific attention, except while considering his earliest work, where it provides a glimpse of the poet learning his trade.

I am greatly indebted to the critics who have preceded me in the study of Roethke, and to John Matheson's valuable bibliography. I would particularly like to thank Mrs. Beatrice Roethke and Stanley Kunitz for the time and assistance they gave me, Professors William York Tindall and John Unterecker, who read my work and provided crucial criticism, and my wife, Marcia, whose insight into Roethke's work was as important a contribution as her continual moral support. I am grateful to John Collins of the University of Washington Press for making available to me a prepublication copy of Roethke's selected prose. Finally, a list of those who have kindly given permission to quote verse cited in the text follows the index.

City College of New York   KARL MALKOFF
February, 1966

Contents

FOREWORD, by John Unterecker v

PREFACE vii

ABBREVIATIONS x

1 The Greenhouse Land 1
2 An Epic of the Eyes, 1930–1941 18
3 News of the Root, 1942–1948 44
4 Out of the Slime, 1949–1951 63
5 The Ghostly Dance, 1952–1953 110
6 Being and Nonbeing, 1954–1958 124
7 The Dark Time, 1959–1963 172
8 A Man Learning to Sing 220

BIBLIOGRAPHY 227
INDEX 237

Abbreviations

FF *The Far Field.* New York, Doubleday, 1964.

LS *The Lost Son and Other Poems.* New York, Doubleday, 1948.

OH *Open House.* New York, Knopf, 1941.

SP *On the Poet and His Craft: Selected Prose of Theodore Roethke.* Ralph J. Mills, Jr., ed. Seattle, University of Washington Press, 1965.

WW *Words for the Wind: The Collected Verse of Theodore Roethke.* New York, Doubleday, 1951; Bloomington, Indiana University Press, 1961.

CHAPTER 1

The Greenhouse Land

The "lost world" of childhood experience plays a crucial part in the work of many contemporary writers. This is particularly true in the case of Theodore Roethke, who derived much of his poetic power and originality from his attempt to interpret adult life in terms of a permanent symbolism established in childhood. Roethke was born in Saginaw, Michigan, on May 25, 1908.[1] His father and uncle owned one of the largest and most famous floricultural establishments in the area at that time. There were twenty-five acres, most of them under glass, in the town itself; and beyond that, farther out in the country, the last stretch of virgin timber in the valley; and finally, a wild area of second-growth timber which the Roethkes con-

[1] The most important biographical comments on Roethke are: Ciardi, "Theodore Roethke: A Passion and a Maker," p. 13; Kunitz, "Theodore Roethke," pp. 21–22; Heilman, pp. 55–64. Roethke's main autobiographical statements are: "Open Letter" in Ciardi, Mid-Century American Poets, pp. 67–72; in Kunitz, Twentieth Century Authors, pp. 837–38; "Roethke Remembers" ("Some Self-Analysis" and "On 'Identity'"), Show, V (May 1965), 11–15. These essays, along with the previously unavailable "An American Poet Introduces Himself and His Poems" (BBC broadcast, July 30, 1953, Disc # SLO 34254), are conveniently reprinted in the recently published Mills, On the Poet and His Craft: Selected Prose of Theodore Roethke (hereafter abbreviated as SP).

verted into a small game preserve. As a child, Roethke would tag after his father as he made his rounds, or wander alone among shoots that dangled and drooped in the silo-rich dark of a root cellar, playing in a pulpy world of beetles, worms, and slugs. Growing older, his relation to the greenhouse world became more active; work and play were combined in hacking at black hairy roots under concrete benches, gathering moss in the swampy field at the edge of the forest, or triumphantly climbing to the roof of the fragile greenhouse. In short, all the joys and fears of growing up were experienced as part of this kingdom of dynamic plant life; and so, it is not surprising that in later years the greenhouse became for Roethke the focus of most childhood memories, his "symbol for the whole of life, a womb, a heaven-on-earth." [2]

But although the womblike greenhouses were dark and protective, they must have had threatening aspects as well, for Roethke later revised this description in favor of greater complexity. "They were to me, I realize now, both heaven and hell, a kind of tropics created in the savage climate of Michigan, where austere German Americans turned their love of order and their terrifying efficiency into something truly beautiful." [3]

Symbol of creation and the strict imposition of order upon chaos, on the one hand, of the protective, fertile womb, on the other, the dual nature of the greenhouse corresponds to Roethke's feelings toward his father and mother respectively. Otto Roethke, "a Prussian through and through," [4] was strong

[2] Ciardi, *Mid-Century American Poets,* p. 69.
[3] "An American Poet Introduces Himself and His Poems," *SP,* pp. 8–9.
[4] "The Saginaw Song," *Encounter,* XVIII (Jan. 1962), 94.

and firm, the personification of *Ordnung;* but this strength was, for his son, a source of both admiration and fear, of comfort and restriction. His father's mixture of tenderness and brutality comes across clearly in Roethke's "My Papa's Waltz." [5] There he describes how Otto, a bit drunk, would roughly waltz him around while his mother looked on disapprovingly, and he himself was both afraid and joyful. On another, soberer occasion, Theodore, who was seven years old at the time, saw his father bring two poachers to a halt with rifle bullets, and then, leaving his gun behind, walk over and slap them both across the face, these men who had broken the natural order.[6]

Roethke's references to his father, no matter what emotional coloring they are given, have one thing in common: they always convey a sense of awesome, godlike power. This is the man who made the flowers grow, a rainbow at his thumb as he held the watering can; this is the man who established law and enforced it. In Roethke's case, the use of the father as symbol of God (as in "The Lost Son," *WW*, 79–85) is more than an artificially conceived literary image: it is charged with experience.

Roethke's mother, the former Helen Marie Huebner, appears less frequently, and in less specific terms, through the poet's work, than his father. She is, however, the central figure in one of Roethke's important series of contemplative poems, *Meditations of an Old Woman.* "The protagonist is modelled, in part, after my own mother, now dead, whose favorite reading was the Bible, Jane Austen, and Dostoevsky—in other

[5] *Words for the Wind,* p. 53 (hereafter abbreviated as *WW*).
[6] See "Otto," in *The Far Field,* pp. 56–57 (hereafter abbreviated as *FF*).

words a gentle, highly articulate old lady believing in the glories of the world, yet fully conscious of its evils." [7] Although this is not a childhood recollection, there is a definite sense of continuity between this quiet, literate old woman, and the young mother who, with the nurse, used to sing Theodore to sleep with nursery rhymes in English and German.

Praise to the End!, another of Roethke's sequences, in which he attempts to recapture his childhood world, is filled with representations of this young mother, but they are generalized and archetypal, rarely as individualized as those of the father. Conceivably, since the mother is shown at the apex of an Oedipal triangle, Roethke never learned to deal with the sexual connotations of specific memories. [8] In any case, however simplified the image of the mother may be in Roethke's poetry, it is necessary to keep in mind that she was a complex figure to her son, and often usurped the father as an establisher of values. "My mother," wrote Roethke, "insisted upon two things —that I strive for perfection in whatever I did and that I always try to be a gentleman." [9] And Roethke had also told friends "the story of a brutal fist fight from which he dragged himself home bruised and bleeding, and how it was his mother who refused to let him into the house, ordering him to go back and thrash the boy who had just thrashed him." [10]

Roethke attended Arthur Hill High School. There he wrote a speech for the Junior Red Cross which became part of an

[7] "Theodore Roethke Writes . . ." *SP*, p. 58.

[8] See Roethke's awareness of the link between the figure of the mother and sexual attractiveness in woman, in the last stanza of "The Saginaw Song."

[9] "Some Self-Analysis," *SP*, pp. 4–5.

[10] Ciardi, "Theodore Roethke: A Passion and a Maker," p. 13.

international campaign and was translated into many languages. But in spite of the glow of this success, chief among many similar prize-winning achievements, he intensely disliked the high school, the town itself, and (with the exception, at times, of the land owned by his father and uncle) that entire area of Michigan. Like many adolescents, Roethke was very much disturbed by the hypocrisy of the adult world, by the venom of small-town gossip, its pettiness, its sugary destructiveness. Roethke ended by being convinced that the most "respectable" and "human" members of the community were the gangsters and bootleggers who operated out of Saginaw at that time. He would go to all lengths to have a drink with one of his idols; for Roethke, in spite of his genuine affection for the small and helpless of the world, had great, perhaps excessive, respect for power and for those who wielded it.

Roethke received his A.B. from the University of Michigan in 1929, and attended Michigan Law School and Harvard before finally earning his M.A. at Michigan in 1936. He seems to have disliked all of these schools impartially, but it was at Harvard that Roethke showed his poetry to Robert Hillyer, and received encouragement—"Any editor who wouldn't buy these is a damn fool!" [11]—crucial to his career. It was at this point that he abandoned all ideas of a future in law or advertising. He was studying law, and had already written advertising copy which had been used in a national campaign—his first love, after all, had been prose. However, soon after the meeting with Hillyer, Roethke's poetic career was fully under way, and by the mid 1930s he was contributing regularly to numerous periodicals.

[11] Kunitz, *Twentieth Century Authors,* p. 838.

From 1931 until 1935, Roethke was an instructor at Lafayette College, and from 1936 to 1943 he was at Pennsylvania State College (becoming assistant professor in 1939). At both schools, he not only taught English, but coached the tennis teams as well. This should serve to remind us of another aspect of Roethke's personality. He wrote of flowers, of the delicate and small things of the world, he sang the spirit as he found it manifested in man and nature; but he himself was anything but delicate—he stood six feet three inches tall and weighed well over two hundred pounds—and he was very much aware of his own physicality. In tennis, or in any game, he was a fierce competitor, quite likely to sulk and storm if he lost. He was a big bear of a man. But that is only a partial truth; he was not slow, and, if he was not light-footed, neither was he totally clumsy. In later years, for example, when Roethke was at the University of Washington, there was once a fire in the waste basket in the English office that left everyone else flatfooted and gaping while Roethke ran for an extinguisher and put the fire out. If Roethke was a bear, he was a dancing bear, not only in physical movement, but in his life as a whole. By the alchemy of his poetry he transformed a gross and ugly material world into an image of the spirit; he created something graceful out of an awkward reality.

By the time Roethke was thirty, the pattern of his life as poet and teacher was set; but the real struggle had only begun. Throughout his adult life, Roethke was subject to periodic breakdowns within a broader cycle of manic-depressive behavior. His torment was compounded, at least for many years, by the need to cover up these breakdowns in order to survive in the academic community, and he suffered an acute sense of

[handwritten marginalia: broad enumeration of Roethke's poetry and what it was to serve]

humiliation and defilement as a result of both the illness itself
and the position in which it put him. However, he was ultimately able to make of this liability one of his chief assets.

Early poems treat the breakdowns from an objective point
of view; they are talked about and intellectualized rather than
directly experienced. In particular, Roethke says he is going
to salvage what he can, and use the illness to move beyond
himself, to a greater awareness of reality.[12] Now these poems
do not succeed as representations of Roethke's experience because they lack particularity, they are vague rather than universal; but Roethke is not here interested in exploring the
nature of insanity itself, but rather the relation of periods of
insanity to normal life. He has not yet learned to turn this concern into good poetry, but this point of view is at the heart of
his later work. Insanity, for Roethke, is not a phenomenon
divorced from life; it is rather incorporated into it. It is an
aspect of experience from which one can perhaps learn a good
deal more than from one's routine existence.

In later poems, such as "The Pure Fury" (*WW*, 158–59),
"The Renewal" (*WW*, 160–61), and "The Exorcism" (*WW*,
176–77), the mental anguish is not simply talked about, but
is directly experienced. Roethke manages this with the aid of
vastly improved techniques; but the great power of these
poems is ultimately due to the vision of insanity as an integral
part of life implicit in his earliest work. The anxiety experienced during a psychotic episode, the dissociation of personal-

[12] See "Statement," *Commonweal*, XXVII (Dec. 31, 1937), 261. Other
poems concerned with what is apparently the same period of stress are
"Lines upon Leaving a Sanitarium," *New Yorker*, XIII (March 13, 1937),
34, and "Meditations in Hydrotherapy," *New Yorker*, XIII (May 15,
1937), 107.

ity, become in Roethke's hands not states of mind peculiar to
the insane, but rather more intense perceptions of the human
condition as it is experienced by any man.

There is an equally important corollary to this. If insanity
involves more acute as well as distorted perceptions of reality,
then, in certain areas, the insane man holds a privileged position; he is in the forefront of human consciousness partly by
virtue of his insanity, and, if he can control the tools of language, he can write the poetry of prophecy, he can give to the
rest of mankind the insight necessary to change one's life so
that it will be more in accord with reality than our mind-dull-
ing society allows. In his last years, Roethke was convinced
that there was a close relationship between genius and insanity, and he saw himself in the company of those poets who
turned their madness into verse.[13] "What's madness," asked
Roethke, in one of his final poems, "but nobility of soul/ At
odds with circumstance?" (*FF*, 79) This nobility, according to
Roethke, is a product of heightened awareness; it is the tragic
vision of life which transforms a meaningless sequence of
events into something greater than itself.

In 1941, Roethke's first volume of poems, *Open House*, was
published. (The name, and the very existence, of the title
poem were suggested by Roethke's close friend, Stanley
Kunitz.) The forty-nine poems represented only a little more
than half of the poet's published work. In later years, even
most of these began to "creak," and Roethke preserved only
seventeen of the poems of his first eleven years of writing in
Words for the Wind. Nonetheless, the book was well received,

[13] In "Heard in a Violent Ward" (*FF*, 62), Roethke grouped himself
with William Blake, Christopher Smart, and John Clare.

and its apparent conventionality made possible the near uni-
versality of praise never accorded his more controversial later
work. Roethke used traditional lyric forms, his content tended
to be intellectual rather than sensuous; poets such as the
metaphysicals, Auden, Léonie Adams, and Elinor Wylie loomed
in the background as reasonably well assimilated influences.
Although we can now look back on this work and trace the
origins of what were to become Roethke's major themes (e.g.,
the tension between flesh and spirit, the exploration of the
self as a search for identity), there was little indication to
someone reading his poems at the time of what was to follow.

In 1943, Roethke started teaching at Bennington. Two of the
circumstances of his stay there are of note: he no longer taught
tennis; and one of his students was Beatrice Heath O'Connell,
whom Roethke met again several years later and ultimately
married.

In 1947, Roethke arrived at the University of Washington
(where he taught until his death) as associate professor. The
next year, he was made full professor; and his second book,
The Lost Son and Other Poems, was published. It contained
several lyrics in the mode of *Open House,* but the greenhouse
poems at the beginning, and the four long developmental
poems at the end, were startlingly new, for contemporary
poetry as well as for Roethke. The notion that the world of
plants might be used as an emblem of human growth was
traditional, but not until the greenhouse poems had anyone—
not even D. H. Lawrence—combined this with Roethke's concentrated sensuality of imagery and adept manipulation of a
subterranean, Freudian universe. The long poems were even
more original. Using a framework provided by Freud and

Jung, Roethke presented the development of the individual
not by means of rational discourse, but in terms of the imagery
and symbolism of the natural world, of the world of myth and
legend, and the prerational consciousness from which it springs.

In 1951, Roethke published *Praise to the End!*, a sequence of
developmental poems built around the nucleus of the last four
works of his previous volume. So successfully did Roethke
achieve his goal of finding an adequate symbolism with which
to communicate the process of individuation directly, that he
found himself in the practically unique position of having in-
stituted, perfected, and finally exhausted a genre. Grumbling
critical voices were beginning to make themselves heard; but
the disapproval came largely from England, which was busy
lowering the reputation of other nondiscursive poets, such as
T. S. Eliot and Dylan Thomas. In general, acclaim was re-
sounding.

One of the most important years of Roethke's life was 1953.
He brought out *The Waking*, which received the Pulitzer
Prize; he began the readings in philosophical and religious
works which were to play so important a part in his later
poetry; and, on January 3, he married Beatrice O'Connell.

The Waking included a selection of poems from *Open
House*, almost all of *The Lost Son*, and the entire *Praise to the
End!* There were also several new poems, in one of which
Roethke announced a new source of inspiration: "I take this
cadence from a man named Yeats;/ I take it, and I give it
back again . . ." (*WW*, 120) Unquestionably, a certain Yeatsian influence was present in the stanzaic forms, the use of
slant rhymes, the lyrical expression of public, philosophical
themes. But while the critics were only too glad to believe

that Roethke had borrowed something from Yeats, many were reluctant to admit that he had given anything back. The question of whether or not Yeats's influence was properly assimilated will be taken up later in this study. In any case, these reservations were not pronounced enough to prevent Roethke from receiving the Pulitzer Prize in 1954. Awards were not new to Roethke; he had, for example, received from *Poetry* the Eunice Tietjiens Prize (1947) and the Levinson Award (1951). But this, his first recognition on a popular and national scale, was vastly important to a man whose competitive instincts were not limited to the tennis court, who had committed himself fully to the struggle for recognition, and who, only a few years before his death, was able to refer to himself sardonically as "the oldest younger poet in the U.S.A." [14]

Roethke's marriage seems to have been for him a kind of joyous reawakening. His feelings toward his wife are represented in his poetry from the beautiful epithalamion, "Words for the Wind" (*WW*, 147–50), written during the honeymoon visit to Auden's villa on an island off Naples, through the playful fear of Beatrice's anger in "Her Wrath" (*FF*, 47); but his final word was the moving "Wish for a Young Wife" (*FF*, 48), his prayer that she live without hate or grief after his death.

The various other aspects of Roethke's life should not be allowed to overshadow the fact that he earned his living as a teacher. However, his concern with teaching went much further than that; he compared good teaching to the dance—a significant experience that cannot be recaptured—and was always concerned with ways of improving his own performance. "The Teaching Poet," an essay, clearly reveals the sympa-

[14] Quoted by Stanley Kunitz in "Theodore Roethke," p. 22.

thetic, sensitive nature of his approach.[15] But far more telling than this was the almost universal regard he received from his students: they considered him a great teacher.

As for the faculty, Roethke felt that it should contain more "screwballs"; he certainly seemed one himself, especially during his high periods, and he was not always an easy person to get along with. He could rage unnecessarily against a particular teacher in private. But he was immensely (and honestly) glad when someone had received recognition for achievement, and his public praise for the department as a whole was endless. He was, insists his chairman, more profoundly concerned about the department than most of those who took their "good citizenship" for granted.[16]

Roethke's feelings toward those with whom he worked, and those with whom he competed, were, to say the least, ambivalent. Sometimes, his rage and hate would grow to intolerable levels; he finally came to publish wave after wave of invective in frenzied, Joycean prose, using the pseudonym Winterset Rothberg. In "Last Class," he attacked the members of "Hysteria College," the mindless, impenetrable students, the isolated, passionless faculty.[17] "A Tirade Turning," published posthumously, contains a similar storm of language, directed this time against Roethke's peers: critics, teachers, and poets.[18] But the significant fact is that the tirade does after all turn, the outburst of hate leads to love: "Behold, I'm a heart set free, for I have taken my hatred and eaten it." Identifying his present competitors with the cousins with whom he competed as a

[15] *SP*, pp. 44–51.
[16] Heilman, pp. 61–62.
[17] *SP*, pp. 96–104.
[18] *Encounter*, XV (Dec. 1963), 44–45 (*SP*, pp. 151–54).

boy in Saginaw, Roethke dissipates his rage. It is poetry used as therapy. Possibly, as John Ciardi has suggested, this process is behind much of Roethke's good verse: "This is poetry as a medicine man's dance is poetry. The therapy by incantation. Roethke literally danced himself back from the edge of madness." [19]

In this manner, then, a ranting, dancing bear, Theodore Roethke approached the last, great years of his career. *Words for the Wind,* which still must be considered his most important single volume, was published in England in 1957, and in this country the following year.[20] It contained *The Waking* in its entirety, and an equally long selection of new poems. In Love Poems and Voices and Creatures, the psychological quest for the self is given new depth and meaning in philosophical and religious terms. Existentialist thinkers such as Kierkegaard, Buber, and Tillich, and both western and oriental mystics, become the starting points of frenzied metaphysical lyrics. The Dying Man is Roethke's most direct tribute to Yeats, a brilliant sequence of poems that seem to be in Yeats's style, and yet are unmistakably Roethke's; no man who was simply imitating could have written them.

The book concludes with five—four in the British edition—longer poems, collectively entitled Meditations of an Old

[19] Theodore Roethke: A Passion and a Maker," p. 13. The notion that the balance of sanity may be maintained through the process of creation is by no means a new one; for example, Carl Jung made the same analysis of James Joyce's relation to his writing. But to what extent this hypothesis is true, or even meaningful, is still a question of psychological rather than literary debate.

[20] However, a new edition of Roethke's collected poems, including previous books and sixteen new poems, has been compiled by Mrs. Roethke and Stanley Kunitz for publication in 1966.

Woman. These poems, avoiding rational discourse, like those of *Praise to the End!*, are organized psychologically, in terms of association of imagery, and musically, in terms of alternating themes. The Meditations are the search for the self with new implications, the search for an identity that transcends the temporal limits of the material world; like all of Roethke's more powerful work from this point on, they are pervaded by a growing awareness of imminent nonbeing, of the fact of approaching death. T. S. Eliot has often been cited as having influenced the structure, and, to some extent, the content of these poems. At this suggestion, Roethke was highly indignant (as he was not when Yeats was invoked). Perhaps he was protesting too much. But certainly with regard to content, the points of direct contact with Eliot seem to indicate, as we shall learn, a direct opposition rather than imitation.

There is, however, one sense in which Roethke would not have minded being compared to Eliot; he too had the "auditory imagination," and frequently insisted that his verse was above all meant to be heard.[21] For some years, Roethke had been giving poetry readings whenever he could, and experimenting with recordings. The strain on him was enormous, but he always managed to put on a good show. His major recording, the only one widely available, is *Words for the Wind*, readings of a selection of poems from that book.[22]

Words for the Wind earned for its author both the National Book Award and the Bollingen Prize. It had even become the Christmas selection of the Poetry Book Society when it appeared in England, and Roethke was overjoyed at finally hav-

[21] See "Some Remarks on Rhythm," *SP*, p. 80.
[22] Folkways FL9736, New York, 1962.

ing been accorded that degree of recognition there. There was even more adverse criticism than before, most of it from English poets provoked by Roethke's larger exposure on that side of the Atlantic, and a number of cries of "pseudo-Yeats"; but both criticism and praise were louder than ever before, which itself gave weight to Roethke's claim to acceptance as a major poet. In addition, he was at the center of what Carolyn Kizer called the "School of the Pacific Northwest," a school united not so much by form or intellectual content as by "the feeling area" of their work and by a sense of artistic community.[23] Yet, for a man like Roethke, the apparent security of his position could in an instant give way to limitless extremes of anxiety. Each new successful poem was viewed with terror as possibly the last of its kind. Each comment in which a contemporary was praised could be interpreted as a slight to his own stature. So the struggle did not cease; it barely paused. At times appearing so confident he would bully his friends and guests, at times filled with self-loathing and self-depreciation, he danced on.

Some of his last years were spent at the house of Morris Graves, while Graves painted in Ireland; some were spent at the home the Roethkes later bought at nearby Puget Sound. There was another trip to Italy, which Roethke did not like, partly because of his inability to master Italian or any other foreign language, and a trip to Ireland which, because of his

---

[23] Kizer, pp. 18–19. Some of the poets in this group are Kizer, Kenneth Hanson, Richard Hugo, William Stafford, David Wagoner, Carol Hall, James Wright, Carol Christopher Drake, Robert Kriezer, Errol Prichard. The first five are the *Five Poets of the Pacific Northwest*, ed. R. Skelton (Seattle, University of Washington Press, 1964), in a book dedicated to Roethke.

easy adaptability to the pubs, he liked to excess. It was at a neighbor's pool, near the house at Puget Sound, that Roethke died of a heart attack on August 1, 1963. He was only fifty-five years old, but he had been sick for some time. The film made shortly before his death, *In a Dark Time* (Poetry Society of San Francisco, 1964), shows him old beyond his age, and the poems of his last years are filled with premonitions of death.

The Far Field appeared posthumously in 1964, including most of the poet's serious verse since *Words for the Wind*.[24] This volume, which received the National Book Award in 1965, is devoted to the perfection of old forms rather than to the development of new ones. North American Sequence is a series of long contemplative poems, in the mode of Meditations of an Old Woman, with the author this time using himself as persona. Psychological and religious imagery are interwoven in this final revery in search of the self, in search of transcendent identity. The Love Poems once again have a Yeatsian touch, but this time in the vein of lyrics such as *Words for Music Perhaps,* rather than the more abstract philosophical poems. Mixed Sequence, for the most part less concentrated in its diction, provides an essential change of pace. And the last part, Sequence, Sometimes Metaphysical, is the culmination of the volume, and of Roethke's career. The sequence begins by describing a mystic experience (in "In a Dark Time," *FF*, 79), and then explores its implications for the poet's life. Psychology and theology, madness and mysticism, have drawn very close together in this last phase of Roethke's

---

[24] *I Am! Says the Lamb,* a book of children's poetry, with a reprinting of the greenhouse poems, had appeared in 1961. And *Party at the Zoo,* a children's fantasy in poetic form, was published in 1963. However, these volumes fall beyond the scope of this study.

work. The sequence is similar in intent to Roethke's early explorations of the relation of a nervous breakdown to "ordinary" life. But that is the end of the similarity. In content, Roethke has passed from platitudes to a full awareness of the complexities of the human condition; and, in technique, which makes full use of the powerful and exact archetypal imagery of the meditative poems combined with the density of meaning achieved through expert manipulation of form, Roethke is completely equal to these complexities.

With the publication of his collected poems and selected prose, most of the essential materials upon which a fair estimation of Roethke's poetic worth must be based have become available. Allan Seager is preparing a biography, and several full-length studies of Roethke, including a collection of essays edited by Arnold Stein, are published or underway. This present study is intended as a beginning of the detailed examination of the full scope of Roethke's serious verse necessary to its fair evaluation.

CHAPTER 2

An Epic of the Eyes
1930 – 1941

The poetry of Theodore Roethke begins, as it ends, with the metaphysical. But while the last poems, intensely personal explorations of the nature of being in the world, are metaphysical in the broadest sense of the word, much of his earliest work can be more specifically classified: he wrote in the tradition of witty, strong-lined poetry established by John Donne, George Herbert, Henry Vaughan, and other seventeenth-century English poets.

This is not in the least surprising when one considers the intellectual and literary climate at the time Roethke was learning his trade. In 1921, Grierson's anthology, *Metaphysical Poetry, Donne to Butler,* and T. S. Eliot's famous essay, "The Metaphysical Poets," had converted the "metaphysical revival," actually in process since the turn of the century, into a major movement. Before 1930, I. A. Richards and William Empson had provided the groundwork for a criticism, which, emphasizing the tension between intellectual content and form, seemed best suited to deal with the complexities peculiar to metaphysical verse. There were few poets who were not to some extent influenced.

However, Roethke's association with the metaphysicals was by no means simply a matter of chance, the unthinking acceptance of the dominant fad in poetic techniques. For Roethke, as for his seventeenth-century predecessors, poetry was born of the paradoxical nature of human existence. Like Donne, he was torn by the split between flesh and spirit; like Herbert, he was tormented by the near impossibility of faith; like Vaughan, he sought the eternal in the temporal. Roethke's similarity in technique is clearly rooted in a similar perception of reality.

We might suspect that the contemporaries by whom Roethke was most influenced as he began to write would also fall largely within the metaphysical tradition. And this is indeed the case, with W. H. Auden, Louise Bogan, Léonie Adams, and Elinor Wylie probably heading the list. Once again, Roethke's affinity to these poets is based on more than method; all are concerned with the tension between flesh and spirit, Auden is particularly involved in problems of faith, and the latter three inhabit a world infused with supernatural light that seems often on the point of revealing its mystical origins to probing motions of the mind.

Early Uncollected Poems

Roethke's poetic debts, perceptible as reasonably well-assimilated influences in *Open House,* can best be studied in the uncollected poems of this period, where they are glaringly obvious. Roethke was aware of what he was doing. "Imitation," he wrote, years later, "conscious imitation, is one of the great methods, perhaps *the* great method of learning to write."[1]

Let us first examine "In the Time of Change,"[2] which is of particular interest since it seems to concern the same kind of mystical experience described in "In a Dark Time," at the end of Roethke's career. First, we are given a vision of mutability: "All things must change. . . . we cannot stay/ The lovely miracle of May." Then, in a moment of mystic illumination, the poet finds himself beyond the motions of this world; even his surprise is "passionless" as he perceives "the shape of an eternity." However, whether or not Roethke actually experienced what he described, he is not completely successful in communicating the sense of that particular mode of experience; and the reason for his failure is of special interest. In this poem, there is a great deal of Vaughan, some Blake, and even a touch of Emily Dickinson. The list of presences could be extended well beyond these three, but it is already clear that "In the Time of Change" is so crowded that there is little room for Roethke. The communication of deeply felt experience in simple terms depends almost entirely on the sense of the unique personality of the poet; there is no room for second-hand emotion.

"In the Time of Change" represents an attempt to create a world of possibilities to which Roethke was sympathetic, but which he had not himself entered. Other imitations were less ambitious attempts to capture less complex perceptions of reality. "This Light,"[3] for example, was written with Elinor

---

[1] "How to Write Like Somebody Else," *SP*, p. 69.

[2] *Atlantic*, CLIX (Jan. 1937), 47.

[3] *American Poetry Journal*, XVII (Nov. 1934), 3.

Wylie and Henry Vaughan in mind.[4] The light, which will lead the poet to "eventual peace," can be thought of as one aspect of the illumination described in the preceding poem. The content of "This Light" is perhaps more monotonous than anything by Vaughan or Wylie, but the experimentation with new rhythms, which shift with the flow of light, shows that imitation is being put to good use.

"The Buds Now Stretch"[5] is a completely self-conscious effort to recreate the even more private world of a single poet, Léonie Adams. The toughening of images such as buds stretching into the light, "mellow gold" leaves, "garnered sheaths," by the use of metaphysical conceit—e.g., "that sweet vertical, the sun"—captures much of the feeling of Adams' poetry. It is useful to look at Roethke's own analysis of the way this imitation contributed to his development:

I feel it something Miss Adams and I have created; a literary lovechild. Put it this way: I loved her so much, her poetry, that I just *had* to become, for a brief moment, a part of her world. For it *is* her world, and I had filled myself with it, and I *had* to create something that would honor her in her own terms. . . . I was too clumsy and stupid to articulate my own emotions: she helped me to convince myself that maybe, if I kept at it, I might write a poem of my own, with the accent of my own speech.[6]

[4] "How to Write Like Somebody Else," *SP*, p. 64. This poem should be compared with Wylie's "O Virtuous Light," a poem whose expression of the tension between flesh and spirit apparently fascinated Roethke. Echoes of it appear throughout Roethke's early work, e.g., "Second Version," *Sewanee Review*, XL (Jan. 1932), 88.

[5] *Adelphi*, VI (April 1933), 9.

[6] "How to Write Like Somebody Else," *SP*, p. 66.

Other debts can be more briefly noted. Auden's landscape equivalents of the human mind provide the dominant imagery of such poems as "The Pause": "Two wind-blown hemlocks make a door/ To a country I shall soon explore." [7] The kind of melodramatic setting Auden gave to situations representing the adolescent attaining maturity can be found in "The Bringer of Tidings." [8] Louise Bogan dogs the heels of "Now We the Two":

> Now what of her endures? Of these,—the fine
> Fleet flesh, the live hair, the thighs,—
> Only the bones of memory.[9]

And "I Sought a Measure" illustrates the direct influence of the seventeenth-century metaphysicals, particularly Donne: "I sought a measure for your subtle being,—/ A plumbline that could accurately sound you . . ." [10] The examples for each of the poets above could easily be multiplied, and other poets added to the list; but this should be sufficient to pinpoint most of Roethke's important sources of borrowings, and to obtain a sense of the methods used by him at the start of his career.

Open House

We can begin our discussion of *Open House*, which excluded the more obviously derivative poems mentioned above, by looking at its structure. The poems are not presented in chron-

[7] *Poetry,* LIII (Dec. 1938), 141.
[8] *Ibid.*
[9] *American Poetry Journal,* XVII (Nov. 1934), 5.
[10] *Ibid.,* 4.

ological order, but the book is divided into five parts. Roethke's own remarks on how a book should be put together suggest that there are definite principles of organization: "I believe a book should reveal as many sides of a writer as is decent for him to show; that these aspects be brought together in some kind of coherent whole that is recognizable to the careful reader. This means that some poems will support other poems, either by being complements to them, or by providing contrasts." [11] Only John Holmes seems to have given the organization of *Open House* any thought, but we must pay particular attention to what he says, since he was an early friend of Roethke's, a fellow teacher at Lafayette:

> The wholeness of *Open House* demands comment. Mr. Roethke has built it with infinite patience in five sections. The first is personal pronoun; the second the out-of-doors; the third is premonition of darker things—death among them; the fourth is the purest of metaphysical wit, something very rare in our time; and the fifth contains still another side of the poet's nature, the human awareness of which he has become capable in his recent development.[12]

This is good as far as it goes; Holmes shows that there is a unity in each individual part. But he fails to indicate the unity of the work as a whole. Closer inspection will reveal that together the individual parts form what "Open House," the first poem in the volume, calls "An epic of the eyes." [13] Throughout the book, both "eye" and "I" are of supreme importance; and,

[11] "Theodore Roethke Writes . . ." *SP,* pp. 57–58.
[12] Boston *Evening Transcript,* March 24, 1941, p. 9.
[13] *Open House,* p. 3 (hereafter abbreviated as *OH*). When poems appear both in *Open House* and *Words for the Wind,* references to the latter book will be given, since it is more readily available.

in the first part in particular, the actual movement of the poet's emphasis is from "I" to "eye."

I

"Open House" announces that Roethke will explore modes of knowing the self. At once turning within, "Feud" presents a pessimistic sense of origins, which seems to belong as much to the world of myth and superstition as to modern psychology; the intuition is Freud's, the means of presentation Auden's:[14]

> Exhausted fathers thinned the blood
>
> .   .   .   .
>
> You feel disaster climb the vein.
>   . . . The spirit starves
> Until the dead have been subdued.   (*OH*, 4)

The thought of these influential dead leads to the sobering "Death Piece" (*WW*, 18);[15] then Freud and Auden are again invoked for "Prognosis," which deals not with ancestors, but with the crippling effects of one's immediate family: "Though the devouring mother cry, 'Escape me? Never—'/ And the honeymoon be spoilt by a father's ghost . . . We are not lost." (*OH*, 8)

"To My Sister" and "The Premonition" continue explorations

[14] Cf. Auden's "Family Ghosts." The use by both authors of the image of a besieged city to represent the assault on the protagonist is particularly striking.

[15] Cf. Léonie Adams' "Night Piece," Elinor Wylie's "Now That Your Eyes Are Shut," and Stanley Kunitz' "Night-Piece." Although Roethke's poem is completely his own, the similarity of theme between Roethke and the neo-metaphysical poets among his contemporaries is often remarkably close.

of the immediate family, associating adulthood and sexuality with death. In the first poem, the poet asks his sister to "defer the vice of flesh" (*WW*, 19), to avoid growing up; in the second, death and sex are united in the "hair on a narrow wrist bone" (*OH*, 9), his father's bone, as the father's reflection is lost in the flux of the water. This marks an important point in the individual's attempt at self-definition; he is threatened by emotions whose origins are obscure, which cannot be communicated or represented rationally. Clearly, for Roethke, the analytic probings of inner life are limited; the core of emotional truth cannot be reached by the process of thought turned in on itself.[16] And, with "Interlude," the poet's eye begins to focus on the outer world.

"Orders for the Day" and "Prayer" first define, and then elevate to supreme importance, the functions of the eye. "Let light attend me to the grave" (*WW*, 21), the latter poem ends. Roethke is clearly talking about something beyond the physical phenomenon of sight; for, he says, "the Eye's the abettor of/ The holiest Platonic love . . ." Roethke is in fact announcing his commitment to a view of reality in which it is possible to move from the material world to the light of the highest spiritual truth, in which there is a knowing more profound than what Blake would have called "single vision." "The Signals" (*OH*, 15) praises the flash of intuitive perception; and in the first part's final poem, "The Adamant" (*WW*, 22) becomes a symbol for the essential core of truth which remains intact in spite of all the tools of analysis.

[16] Cf. "Lines Upon Leaving a Sanitarium": "Self-contemplation is a curse/ That makes an old confusion worse." *New Yorker*, XIII (May 15, 1937), 107.

II

The lyrics of the first part have begun the "epic of the eyes." We have witnessed a progression from the poetry of analysis to the poetry of vision, from "I" to "eye." But we must not conclude that Roethke will therefore abandon his explorations of the self; he has simply shifted the grounds of his presentation. Part II does, as Holmes indicated, deal with the "out-of-doors"; but it is concerned with the landscape as an emblem of the human mind. It presupposes a correspondence between inner and outer worlds, and exploits that correspondence not only as a means of representing, but also, in a quasi-mystical sense, as a means of knowing the reality within.

The clearest illustration of this, combining a far more personalized sense of the illumination Roethke has learned to appreciate through Wylie and Vaughan with a less mechanized version of metaphysical correspondences, is "The Light Comes Brighter." After a naturalistic description of the coming of a brighter sunlight with the spring season, Roethke concludes as follows:

> The leafy mind that long was tightly furled,
> Will turn its private substance into green,
> And young shoots spread upon our inner world. (*OH*, 19)

This final image draws the entire poem into focus. By withholding it until the end, Roethke has avoided the impression of a contrived and artificial metaphor, and allows his reader to share his own sense of sudden insight. Similar, if less unexpected now, is the method of a companion poem, "Slow Season," which ends: "The blood slows trance-like in the altered vein;/ Our vernal wisdom moves from ripe to sere." (*OH*, 21)

In "Mid-Country Blow," inner and outer worlds of storm are linked, as the poet's "ear still kept the sound of the sea like a shell." (*WW*, 23) And the protagonist of "In Praise of Prairie" (*OH*, 23) observes the significant proportions of an Auden-esque landscape. Only after a firm sense of correspondence between man and macrocosm has been established does Roethke omit explicit reference to this relation. And even then the autumnal poems of "The Coming of the Cold" keep the analogy implicit in their imagery: "The late peach yields a subtle musk"; "The ribs of leaves lie in the dust"; "And frost is marrow-cold." (*OH*, 24–27) Almost without realizing it, the reader perceives in the outer world the inner association of death and sexuality.

"The Heron" seems to be a straightforward description; but careful reading reveals that the sense of correspondences is still present, this time in a more sinister way. Roethke tells us that the bird's "beak is quicker than a human hand" (*WW*, 24), establishing the relation with a swift stroke. The next image is fine and terrible: the heron "jerks a frog across his bony lip," stirring connotations of a predatory kind of sexuality. The poem concludes with a "single ripple" starting from where the heron stands. A note of recognition is touched. In "The Premonition," the image of the father flashes with sunlight in a ripple before being "lost in a maze of water." It helps to know that Roethke and his father would frequently drive several miles into the game preserve in order to watch the herons.[17] But the association of sexuality of a particularly aggressive kind, the sense of godlike, somewhat amoral power, and the

[17] Roethke in Ostroff, p. 216.

feeling of death and a transitory reality, are all present without recourse to external reference.

The last poem of part II is "The Bat"; and here any tendency one might have to consider the bat a symbol of the dark and subterranean forces of the human mind is encouraged by the concluding couplet: "For something is amiss or out of place/ When mice with wings can wear a human face." (*WW*, 25)

III

We have already seen Roethke probe the inner and outer boundaries of his existence in his search for self-definition. Those categories would seem to include, in a general way, all the limits of the self; but they do not. There still remain the limitations of nonbeing, of negation; and part III is a detailed examination of modes of nonbeing hinted at in previous sections. "No Bird" (*WW*, 26) begins with a vision of the ultimate negation, death. Then, the consuming fires of "The Unextinguished" (*OH*, 34) symbolize the periodic purging of the mind that must inevitably precede renewal, as "thought crackles white across the brain." And in " 'Long Live the Weeds' *Hopkins*," Roethke praises the beneficial aspects of negation,

> The ugly of the universe.
> The rough, the wicked, and the wild
> That keeps the spirit undefiled.   (*WW*, 27)

"Genesis" (*OH*, 36) is Roethke's version of the first law of thermodynamics, the conservation of energy, still another instance in which destruction or negation is the prerequisite of re-creation: the force wrested from the sun is ultimately contained within marrow bone. "Epidermal Macabre" (*WW*, 28) views the flesh in its aspect of negation of the spirit. And the dispersal of being, still another form of nonbeing, is the object of the incantation "Against Disaster" (*OH*, 38), while verse reminiscent of Emily Dickinson answers society's negation of the individual in "Reply to Censure." (*OH*, 39)

The conceit of a sale of furniture as the purging of the spirit, of giving up outgrown characteristics, informs "The Auction." (*OH*, 40) And "Silence" (*OH*, 41) is the last mode of nonbeing explored before the cycle is completed, with death returning to the fore in "On the Road to Woodlawn." (*WW*, 29) By this time, however, we have a new awareness of the significance of death; the sentimental insincerity, the trimmings that attempt to deny death's reality, render "the mourners' anonymous faces" less alive than the dead man's, with his "sunken eyes, still vivid, looking up from the sunken room."

IV

The inner "I," the "eye" looking outward, and now the "sunken eyes": an epic of the eyes defining the self. Part IV follows with a necessary shift in tone; rather than adding a completely new dimension to the picture of the self, Roethke is changing perspective. He approaches reality with the distance of the comic point of view; the self is all-encompassing when we are involved in it, puny when seen from without.

"Academic" (*WW*, 30) is Roethke's sardonic view of himself as teacher. And man (or woman) is placed among the other animals, rather than given a separate and special identity, in "For an Amorous Lady" (*OH*, 46): the poet's lady, delighting in both giving and receiving caresses, is classified, according to something the poet has read in a natural history book, as both mammalian and reptilian.

Throughout this part, Roethke more or less systematically parodies positions and perspectives he has held before, without, however, invalidating them. The creative hero, for example, is reduced to ineffectual "Poetaster," the "fortunate" man "whose mamma pays the bills!" (*OH,* 47) And "Vernal Sentiment" (*WW,* 31), which those intent on making Roethke a tormented puritan read as an expression of his loathing of sex,[18] is actually a gentle mocking of the earlier uses to which he had so seriously put spring landscapes, of all the noisy clatter of rebirth. The dangers of introspection are once again— humorously this time—decried in "Prayer Before Study," in which Roethke asks to be delivered "from all/ Activity centripetal." (*OH,* 49) "My Dim-Wit Cousin" (*OH,* 50) lightly goes over the hereditary terrors of "Feud"; and "Verse with Allusions" (*OH,* 51) suggests that even those who scorn the "Abstract Entities" may have something after all.

v

Part v of *Open House* places the self, now fully defined, into its social context. This is probably the least successful part of the book. For some reason, Roethke was never able to write very good poetry about society, or even about the individual's relation to society in a general sense. ("Dolor" [*WW,* 55] is a possible exception.) This should not imply that Roethke was so drawn into himself that he had no broader concerns. On the contrary, his position was quite clear, both in domestic issues,[19] and in the international affairs that drew the commit-

[18] See, for example, Southworth, p. 327.
[19] See "Random Political Reflections," an attack on Senators Glass and Byrd and Representative Dies, in *New Republic,* XCVIII (March 1, 1939), 98.

ment of other poets such as Auden, Spender, and MacLeish. In a review of *And Spain Sings: Fifty Loyalist Ballads,* Roethke wrote: "What has lifted even minor talents above themselves is a spirit of a great people who embody the heroic virtues of plain people everywhere struggling for decent life. Neither these poems nor the force that animated them will be lost upon the world." [20] If Roethke could not deal directly with the more public realms of experience, he was nonetheless very much aware of the social role of his personal poetry, and anxious to encourage the reader to open himself to the possibilities of his inner life which were being smothered by society.

Part v begins with the "Ballad of the Clairvoyant Widow," a kind of formal folk song which presents a remarkably conventional picture of the unfulfilled rich, the starving poor, the "cultural lag." It ends with an equally conventional expression of faith: "The salmon climb the river, the rivers nudge the sea,/ The green comes up forever in the fields of our country." (*OH,* 55) The cult of success is attacked in "The Favorite," where the protagonist has so consistently overcome all competition that he "longed to feel the impact of defeat." (*OH,* 58) "The Reminder" (*OH,* 59) conveys the dreariness of an affair now past; "The Gentle," a portrait of the self-defeating victim, is too melodramatic to be saved by its fine last line, "The sleep was not deep but the waking is slow." (*OH,* 60) And similarly, that "lack that keeps us what we are" is bemoaned in "The Reckoning." (*OH,* 61)

"Lull (November, 1939)" is a somewhat better poem, but it is not sufficiently detached from Auden's "September 1, 1939" to stand on its own. Where Auden says that man, beleaguered

[20] *Poetry,* LII (April 1938), 43–46.

by "Negation and despair," craves "Not universal love/ But to be loved alone," Roethke echoes:

> Reason embraces death,
> While out of frightened eyes
> Still stares the wish to love.   (*OH*, 62)

"Sale," concerned with "the taint in a blood that was running too thin" (*WW*, 32), places the "Feud" with the past in a more public context; "Highway: Michigan" (*OH*, 66) sees the factory worker only able to escape the machine when he is killed by it; and "Idyll" (*OH*, 68) shows the suburban town surrounded by the encroaching darkness of a world in chaos, which it dutifully ignores. The book ends with "Night Journey," easily the finest poem in the last part. Here, the poet, looking out from the window of a moving train, returns to the poetry of vision; and his sense of union with the land he loves is communicated once more by the binding of inner and outer worlds with fine, metaphysical wit:

> Bridges of iron lace,
> A suddenness of trees . . .
> Then a bleak wasted place,
> And a lake below my knees.
> Full on my neck I feel
> The straining at a curve;
> My muscles move with steel,
> I wake in every nerve.   (*WW*, 33)

Our survey of the structure of *Open House* has, then, revealed the following plan of organization:

I. From analytic probing to vision as a means of knowing the self.

II. The self seen in terms of the correspondence between inner and outer reality.

III. The self defined by nonbeing, by negation.

IV. The self seen from the distance of comic perspective.

V. The self in its social context.

The structure of *Open House* is far more complicated than that of any other book by Roethke. The reason for this is clear. As Roethke began to experiment with modes of expression, his poems tended increasingly to differentiate themselves in terms of form and technique. But here, confronted with the task of putting together a book of more or less traditional lyrics all concerned with the same general subject, the definition of the self, his principles of organization had to be subtler.

However, our analysis has significance beyond this first book; for in *Open House* Roethke has established the categories that will contain all of his future work. The poems of part I lead to the synthesis of analysis and vision of *Praise to the End!* and the North American Sequence; part II provides the basis of the greenhouse poems; part III becomes the confrontation of nonbeing of The Dying Man, Meditations of an Old Woman (which also contains many elements of part I), some of the Love Poems, and the Sequence, Sometimes Metaphysical; part IV contains the types of most of Roethke's lighter pieces. In fact, if we allow for the mixing of categories, particularly in the longer poems, this breakdown holds remarkably true. But there seems to be one glaring exception. What of the poems of part V? This can be explained in the light of a peculiarity of *Open House* we have not yet noted. With the exception of "The Reminder" (a part v poem), there are no love poems in the book. So that the social comment of *Open House*, which leads nowhere, and the bulk of the Love Poems of *Words for the Wind* and *The Far Field*, which seem to have no antecedents, are really all dealing with aspects of the self in its social context; clearly, the only form of social behavior that was, for Roethke, the stuff of poetry was the most personal and private of all, love.

This structural survey has provided a convenient analysis of the content of Roethke's earliest work; and we have naturally had occasion to examine incidentally certain aspects of form and technique. But these last matters deserve more direct consideration; the early poems may well contain the seeds of Roethke's later methods, as well as themes. First, let us ask whether there is any pertinent statement of stylistic intent by Roethke himself. And we will find that his review of Ben Belitt's first book, *The Five-Fold Mesh,* indeed seems to culminate in pure manifesto: "The best short poems are still being written by those writers who impose upon themselves the strictest limitations. Such poets regard inversion as a device to be handled with extreme caution; they hate adjectives; they prefer the homely to the bold, to the decorative. Sometimes their work may be arid, but it is rarely artificial; it may be rough, but it is often powerful. . . . In distrusting the naive, he [Belitt] seems to have paralyzed at least part of his sensibility." [21]

For the sake of inclusiveness, our survey has paid a good deal of attention to some of Roethke's less distinguished work. But fairness demands that we test the extent to which he ap-

[21] *Poetry,* LIII (Jan. 1939), 217 (*SP,* pp. 114–15).

plied his principles with a solider achievement, with what as tough-minded a critic as Yvor Winters has called "one of the best things in the book and in recent poetry," [22] "The Adamant":

> Thought does not crush to stone.
> The great sledge drops in vain.
> Truth never is undone;
> Its shafts remain.
>
> The teeth of knitted gears
> Turn slowly through the night,
> But the true substance bears
> The hammer's weight.
>
> Compression cannot break
> A center so congealed;
> The tool can chip no flake:
> The core lies sealed.   (*WW*, 22)

The hatred of adjectives is certainly in evidence; there are only three in the entire poem, none at all in the last stanza. "Great" and "true" are monosyllabic, and they represent essential qualities; like the adamant itself, they cannot be broken down. In contrast, even "knitted" seems complex, which it should. Language is stripped bare, there is nothing unessential.[23] Rather than inversion, we find the straightforward sen-

---

[22] "The Poems of Theodore Roethke," *Kenyon Review*, III (Autumn 1941), 515.
[23] It was, interestingly enough, Ben Belitt who first called attention to the fact that "Mr. Roethke's operative words are monosyllables; adjectives like 'spare,' 'strict,' 'pure,' 'sere,' 'ripe,' 'fine,' 'true'; nouns like 'rage,' 'shock,' 'hate,' 'poise,' 'maze,' 'care,' 'blood.' All drive strenuously towards what is most essential in his thought, and in 'Death Piece' and 'Road to Woodlawn,' they fall like blows to testify that 'the true substance bears the hammer's weight.'" Belitt, p. 463.

tence structure of everyday speech. And the central image, the machine-resisting adamant, is tough and bare rather than delicately elaborate. Roethke is talking about the ultimate inaccessibility of truth to reason, and of the essential self to analysis; but clearly the "core" is also his conception of the ideal poem, the perception of reality that can be broken down no further.

The mechanics of the central image may at first escape notice. It seems to consist simply of viewing the same process from slightly different perspectives; but these shifts of perspective are crucial. The movement is from "truth," to "true substance," to "core." We begin with abstraction, which is, after all, a tool of reason; we come next to the "true substance," a charged particular, truth embedded in reality, but still defined abstractly; and finally we arrive at the "core," the ultimate unit, which can no longer be defined except by itself. The movement is thus from philosophy to art, from allegory to symbolism.

The rhythm of "The Adamant" is of particular interest. Most lines are end-stopped; the others conform to a two-line unit. This is in marked contrast to the complex and sophisticated rhythms used by the metaphysicals, especially Donne; Roethke is after rhythmic as well as linguistic naiveté. Another effect, however, is subtler. Originally, Roethke tells us, the poem consisted of regular trimeter quatrains;[24] but by the elimination of one or two of those hated adjectives, and some rearrangement, he cut a foot out of the concluding line of each stanza, imitating the crushing action of the machine.

"The Adamant" belongs in the metaphysical tradition; it is,

[24] In the film *In a Dark Time.*

after all, built around a good metaphysical conceit. However, as his "manifesto" indicates, Roethke is here aiming at a less sophisticated, more rawly powerful effect. But even if this was the main tendency of Roethke's verse, we must nonetheless examine several variations in order to obtain a complete picture; even in his good poems, he did not always follow the "manifesto" exactly.[25]

"Epidermal Macabre," for example, easily the best of Roethke's very earliest efforts—it was first published in 1932 —falls more directly in the tradition of involved and intellectual wit. Admitting the indelicacy of rejecting the fleshy aspects of his being, the poet nonetheless expresses his loathing for "epidermal dress":

> . . . willingly I would dispense
> With false accoutrements of sense,
> To sleep immodestly, a most
> Incarnadine and carnal ghost.   (*WW*, 28)

The method of this poem is suggested by the Shakespearean lines that may well have inspired its conclusion:

> No, this my hand will rather
> The multitudinous seas incarnadine,
> Making the green one red.
>   (*Macbeth*, II.ii.60–62)

Roethke, like Shakespeare, takes advantage of the contrast between Latin and Anglo-Saxon word origins, between polysyllabic and monosyllabic words. Whole phrases are played off against each other (e.g., "stitched on bone" with "vesture of the skeleton"). Adjectives contend with their nouns, as in

---

[25] The review of Belitt's book appeared in the same year as "The Adamant," and probably reflects his views at that time.

"Epidermal dress," "carnal ghost." And the final effect is achieved by the syllabic shrinking of the last line from "Incarnadine" to "carnal" to "ghost." The poet's wit is further shown off by the accumulation of variations on the basic conceit of flesh as clothing: it appears not only as "clothes," but as "fabric," "vesture," "garment," "cloak," "veil," "dress," "rags," and "accoutrements."

"Epidermal Macabre" consists basically of closed couplets, a favorite form of Roethke's when he was writing his first poems. This associates it most closely with the vein of satire and wit in English and American poetry. We should note an important similarity between this poem and "The Adamant." The tension between flesh and spirit is essentially the same, for Roethke, as that between analysis and intuition; the former concerns the self, the latter the world. Both define the dual nature of reality.[26]

The intellectuality of the poems we have been considering should not give the impression that the more purely lyrical was beyond Roethke's early range. "To My Sister" will illustrate this, although even here we must not expect complete abandonment of the previously stated principles:

> O my sister remember the stars the tears the trains
> The woods in spring the leaves the scented lanes
> Recall the gradual dark the snow's unmeasured fall
> The naked fields the cloud's immaculate folds
> Recount each childhood pleasure: the skies of azure
> The pageantry of wings the eye's bright treasure.

[26] This dualism, which appears mainly in terms of the correspondence between inner and outer worlds in *Open House*, is much more explicit in the uncollected poems, and becomes an important theme in Roethke's later work. See, for example, "Second Version," *Sewanee Review*, XL (Jan. 1932), 88, and "Second Shadow," *Poetry*, LVII (Feb. 1941), 293.

> Keep faith with present joys refuse to choose
> Defer the vice of flesh the irrevocable choice
> Cherish the eyes the proud incredible poise
> Walk boldly my sister but do not deign to give
> Remain secure from pain preserve thy hate thy heart.

The poem, except for the shock of the concluding "preserve thy hate thy heart," seems to be straightforward nostalgia. But a closer reading shows that the conclusion has been carefully prepared for. The scent of the lanes, the naked fields, the cloud's folds: the imagery of innocent childhood itself contains sexual overtones. In addition, the latent sensuality is reinforced by internal sound echoes. This hints at an important link between the two stanzas: innocence is a kind of illusion, the refusal to choose a denial of reality.

The poet bids his sister "Cherish the eyes"; and we know that for Roethke the eye is the key to truth, the door to vision. The eye is his symbol of spiritual perception, the foe of grasping sensuality. But in spite of the witty exercise "Epidermal Macabre," Roethke ultimately accepts, as any poet must to some degree, the world of the senses. It is, in fact, by means of the senses that one perceives reality. The companion poems, "Orders for the Day" and "Prayer," make this perfectly clear; sight, embodied in the eye, is elevated above the other senses, while hands must be careful that they do not bruise the spirit. But hands have important functions; they have their place within the hierarchy, and cannot be dispensed with. "Cherish the eyes" is not free from irony; and since it is followed by reference to pride, and by the phrase "do not deign to give," we may be justified in reading it also as "Cherish the I's."

The tense maliciousness of holding back emotion, including love, is conveyed by the Freudian-slip ending, where the poet means to say "preserve thy heart," says "hate" instead, and must correct himself. The method of the poem, then, is to present a facade of sentimental lyricism which, almost without wishing to, reveals the less glittering reality it covers. We might miss it all were it not for the word "hate" in the last line, which seems out of place at first, but then becomes the key to the feelings that have been repressed throughout.[27] As in "The Coming of the Cold," by withholding the crucial phrase until the end, Roethke enables the reader to share his sense of insight.

Removal of most punctuation gives the effect of stream of consciousness, or of dream, either of which would be quite appropriate to the revelation of repressed materials. The technique is, in short, remarkably sophisticated, unique in Roethke's early work. But it is an important anticipation of the symbolic, sensuous imagery, and indirect, sometimes obscure, communication of fact, that he eventually used to explore the reality of the child's world in *Praise to the End!*

To obtain a complete picture of Roethke's technical abilities at the time of *Open House,* we must examine still another poem, "The Premonition." Walking in a field, the poet is reminded of the past, of a summer day spent trailing after his father; at that time his father had dipped his hand in the river.

> Water ran over and under
> Hair on a narrow wrist bone;

[27] Cf. "Delicate the syllables that release the repression," in "The Gentle." (*OH*, 60)

His image kept following after,—
Flashed with the sun in the ripple.
But when he stood up, that face
Was lost in a maze of water.   (*OH*, 9)

While "The Adamant" and "Epidermal Macabre" are built around metaphysical conceits, and "To My Sister" works through an accumulation of images, "The Premonition" depends upon the building up and dissolution of a single vivid image—the water running over and under hair on a narrow wrist bone—for its impact. This method suggests another literary movement that had been important in Roethke's youth: imagism.

Certainly imagism was not without its effects on Roethke; and if we can generalize about his development at all, we should point out the movement from the metaphysical to the imagistic, from the intellectual to the sensuous.[28] But Roethke's actual development is hardly so clear cut, and consists rather in a shift in emphasis than a drastic change; after all, the metaphysical and imagistic tended to merge in the poetry of the time, and it is impossible to know, for example, whether the opening lines of "The Love Song of J. Alfred Prufrock" present an "image" or a "neo-metaphysical" conceit. Clearly, these strains mingled in Roethke, whose sense of metaphysical correspondence and analogy provides a framework for what seems to be pure image.

In "The Premonition," imagist principles dominate more than is usual; but even here the direct presence of the metaphysicals is strongly felt. The central image is almost certainly

[28] In the film *In a Dark Time,* Roethke states that he often tries for the imagistic effect, but never the purely imagistic. His is not the painter's art; he wants more than picture.

taken from Donne's "The Relique," in which the lover envisions himself as being buried with a "bracelet of bright haire about the bone" (or perhaps it is "That subtile wreathe of haire, which crowns my arme" in "The Funerall," undoubtedly the same circle of hair). As a result, the "Hair on a narrow wrist bone" of Roethke's poem becomes a vision of death; or rather the allusion intensifies this vision, for the bone itself would be enough to produce this sense of mutability. The loss of the father in the rippling maze of the river, symbol of time and flux, confirms the feeling of dissolution. And closer inspection reveals greater complexity than we might have expected. As the protagonist "kept/ Close to the heels" of his father, so the father's image in water "kept following after." The boy is established as an equivalent of the father's image; and this is true in more senses than one. He is the image in so far as he is his son, and also in so far as he too partakes of his father's mortality. The premonition of the father's death leads to the still vaguer premonition of his own death.

One more characteristic of the poem should be noted: there is no regular rhyme scheme, but seven of the thirteen lines end in -er; in addition, "kept" is linked with "steps," "shallows" with the "o" sound of "bone" and the "l" sound of "ripple," as well as with "following," and "lace" looks back to "half" and forward to "maze." The cumulative effect is that of the flux and flow of the river.

We have, in a sense, come full circle to the methods of "The Adamant." Although "The Premonition" does not contain a conceit, it, like "The Adamant," achieves its effect by means of a single powerful image, modulated by subtler relationships pointed out by the means of presentation. The language fol-

lows the patterns of everyday speech and is certainly un-
adorned; there is only one adjective in the entire poem, and
that at the crucial point, for emphasis ("narrow wrist bone").

Although Roethke does not anticipate later developments in
technique nearly so decisively as he does in content, the careful craftsmanship that was to make later, more revolutionary
approaches feasible characterizes all of his early work; in poems such as "To My Sister" the use of Freud, symbolism, and
generally freer methods is already in evidence—the movement
from the indirect and intellectual to the direct and sensuous is
under way.

The reception of *Open House* in 1941 was favorable. W. H.
Auden's remarks in particular must have been extremely en-
couraging to Roethke: "A good poet can be recognized by his
tense awareness of both chaos and order, the arbitrary and the
necessary, the fact and the pattern. . . . By such a test, Mr.
Roethke is instantly recognizable as a good poet." [29] But most
prophetic of all was the criticism of Stephen Baldanza. He
liked *Open House,* but only he and Roethke himself were dis-
satisfied enough with the dominant poetic techniques of the
time to realize that Roethke had not yet found fully adequate
means of communicating the "core" of his reality, his self: "de-
spite the promise of his introductory poem, his revelation is
not complete; it embodies a caution which is at the core of his
poetic impulse. . . . Once he shows more willingness to ex-
pose his true self more courageously in form and in content
he will attain a great stature." [30]

[29] Auden, p. 30.
[30] Baldanza, p. 188.

CHAPTER 3

News of the Root
1942 – 1948

The Lost Son and Other Poems (1948), which for one of Roethke's most perceptive critics, Stanley Kunitz, is still "the great book," [1] established its author as an important poet. Unsurprisingly, it continued Roethke's probing of the self; but the techniques he used toward that end were unexpected.

The book consists of four parts: part I explores the greenhouse world of Roethke's childhood, often in microscopic detail, and with a sensuous, suggestive use of language; part II contains more traditional lyrics, in the mode of *Open House*, dealing with youthful experiences and observations of the social scene; part III investigates possible systems of metaphors for the self; and part IV presents four long poems which trace the development of the self, using the principles of part III, the kinds of experience shown in part II, and, often, the techniques of part I. These last four poems ultimately became the core of *Praise to the End!* (1951), and will best be considered within the context of that later work. In this chapter, I shall be concerned with examining the three earlier parts, which, although they can be thought of as preparations for the final

[1] Kunitz, "Theodore Roethke," p. 22.

part, are, particularly in the case of the greenhouse poems, remarkable in their own right. But first I should like to take up what seems to be an extremely curious phenomenon.

Open House is a book of traditional lyrics; far from experimental, it was criticized for being insufficiently bold. Yet, with the publication of *The Lost Son*, only eight years later, Roethke was hailed for his new techniques. What had happened? Had there been a sudden inspiration, or a reversal of direction? Current criticism has been eager to seize upon the notion of a sudden change, but there is no need to depend upon so mysterious an explanation. What seems to be a drastic revision of method is actually a perfectly logical, and rather gradual, shifting of emphasis, a development of possibilities which is, admittedly, somewhat obscured by the fact that *The Lost Son* is not chronologically arranged.[2] I have already sketched the dependence of part IV upon the previous parts of the book, but even the greenhouse poems are the result of a consistent process of thought.

In the previous chapter, I noted Roethke's tendency to abandon intellectual analysis in favor of a direct apprehension of reality.[3] As a means of achieving this end, he praised the

[2] All but one of the thirteen poems of part I were originally published between 1946 and 1948. ("Frau Bauman, Frau Schmidt, and Frau Schwartze" was not in *The Lost Son*; it was first published in 1952, added to the sequence in *The Waking*.) All but three of the twelve poems of the middle two parts were published between 1941 and 1944. The poems of part IV first appeared in the latter half of 1947 and the beginning of 1948.

[3] Kenneth Burke bases a similar observation about the greenhouse poems upon an involved discussion of Kant: "The ideal formula might be stated thus: *a minimum of 'ideas,' a maximum of 'intuitions.'* In this form it can sum up the Roethkean esthetic. (The concept would be admitted as a kind of regrettable necessity.)" Burke, p. 76. This essay, written just

observation of strict limitations, the preference of the blunt to
the elaborate, the search for the powerful and the avoidance
of the artificial. But while poems such as "The Adamant" ar-
gued against an analytic representation of reality, they were
themselves too bound up in intellect to be what they preached.
Clearly, Roethke had to go further. In 1946, he used his review of Roy Fuller's book *A Lost Season* to issue another "manifesto"; after a long paragraph of tirade (in a manner reminiscent of Joyce or Thomas) attacking a variety of "schools of
verbalizers," Roethke concludes:

> The trouble probably lies in the age itself, in the unwilling-
> ness of poets to face their ultimate inner responsibilities, in
> their willingness to take refuge in words rather than transcend-
> ing them. The language dictates; they are the used. The co-
> habitation of their images is, as it were, a mere fornication of
> residues.
>
> One can say that the poetry of the future will not come from
> such as these. Instead it will be, let us hope, lightly conscious,
> subtle and aware, yet not laboriously referential; eloquent but
> not heavily rhetorical; clear perhaps in the way that Dante is
> clear; sensuous but not simple-minded; above all, rooted deeply
> in life; passionate and perhaps even suffused, on occasion, with
> wisdom and light.[4]

I. *"The Greenhouse Poems"*

Our suspicion that Roethke has extended rather than con-
tradicted his former position is strengthened by the fact that

---

at the conclusion of the period being discussed in this chapter, is still the
best analysis of the theory of Roethke's verse.
    [4] *SP*, pp. 123–24.

we find him attacking precisely the same poetic tendencies as before: that is, all forms of exploitation of technique for its own sake, poems that have been cut off from reality in order to achieve their effects. The poet's ultimate responsibility is to his own inner self, Roethke says, stating clearly what was previously implicit in his work, and by this alone can he test the reality of his art. In a few crucial words near the conclusion of his remarks, Roethke defines the materials with which poetry can attain these ends: "sensuous but not simple-minded; above all, rooted deeply in life." We recognize here a guiding principle of the greenhouse poems, where experience is presented not as subject to intellectual analysis, but directly in terms of sensory perception. Stanley Kunitz has said that Roethke's imagination in these poems is predominantly tactile and auditory;[5] but visual and olfactory qualities rank close in importance, nor is taste completely excluded. Life is apprehended as a whole, rather than dissected.

The rooting of poetry deep in life is the logical development of Roethke's earlier work. And so is a second, related characteristic of the greenhouse poems. Roethke had previously stressed the importance of the naive as opposed to the sophisticated; and the techniques of these poems, the very choice of the greenhouse as subject, represent an extension of this search for naiveté.[6] The poems belong to the world of the child rather

[5] Kunitz, "News of the Root," p. 224.
[6] Cf. Burke, still using Kantian categories: "All told then, we can see in Roethke's cult of 'intuitive' language: a more strictly infantile variant of the Dantesque search for a 'noble' vernacular; a somewhat suburban, horticultural variant of Wordsworth's stress upon the universal nature of rusticity; and a close replica of Lawrence's distinction between the 'physical' and the 'abstract.'" Burke, p. 81.

than that of the adult; they belong to the natural world rather
than to man's artificial society (although this must be modified
by the fact that the greenhouse itself, if not its contents, is
manmade); and finally, they belong, as I have already suggested, to the physical rather than the abstract.

Childhood, nature, the physical: but there is still another
way in which Roethke strives for the naive or direct perception of reality. The obvious sexual implications of such poems
as "Root Cellar" and "Orchids" should alert the reader to the
Freudian possibilities of the entire sequence. Roots, soil, and
cellars in particular seem to provide a context for unconscious
or prerational mental processes. However, we must be careful
not to identify Roethke with those who arbitrarily seed their
poems with established Freudian symbols. True to his pre-
cepts, Roethke's poetry is deeply rooted in life. The value of
a symbol is never imposed upon it from without; the symbol
is rather the experience itself—it means itself. Instead of bor-
rowing Freudian language and imagery, Roethke investigates
its origins. In "Root Cellar" (*WW*, 39), for example, the shoots
that dangle and droop, "lolling obscenely," like snakes, clearly
qualify as Freudian symbols. But the sexual implications of
the poem are hardly dependent upon extra-literary references.
The sense of a force that cannot be contained, the lush heat,
the moisture, the grasping, caressing shoots, the creation of
life out of the dead and decaying, all provide a context for the
Freudian forms so clearly sexual in itself that the snaky shapes
seem to derive their significance from their setting.

There is a third important characteristic of the greenhouse
poems: the assumption of a correspondence between the human and vegetable worlds. This is, as we have already learned,

precisely the technique of part II of *Open House*. It is true
that Roethke now seems to be viewing his plants from a closer
distance than before; but even this does not serve to distinguish clearly the newer poems from those of Roethke's first
volume. There is no essential difference of perspective between
the lines from "The Light Comes Brighter" and "Slow Season,"
quoted above, and the following lines from "Cuttings—*later*":

> I can hear underground, that sucking and sobbing,
> In my veins, in my bones I feel it,—
> The small waters seeping upward,
> The tight grains parting at last.   (*WW*, 38)

What, then, is the difference between these lines and those
previously quoted; in what sense has there been any development at all?

First, there is the shift from emphasis upon visual perception to the direct appeal to all the senses, particularly auditory
and tactile, noted above. Second, there is in the new poems a
more dynamic presentation of the plant world. The poems from
Open House are like snapshots; only when we place two of
them side by side do we notice change and development (as
from the shoots of spring to the shoots of autumn in the two
poems cited above). But a poem from *The Lost Son* contains
a sense of growth and struggle within itself. This is, as Kunitz
has pointed out, one of the important characteristics differen-
tiating the greenhouse poems from other close observations of
plants. "What absorbs his [Roethke's] attention is not the intricate tracery of a leaf or the blazonry of the complete flower,
but the stretching and reaching of a plant, its green force, its
invincible Becoming." [7] The struggle of the cut stems to put

[7] Kunitz, "Theodore Roethke," p. 223.

down feet is called by Roethke a "resurrection of dry sticks"; "What saint strained so much," he asks. In part II of *Open House,* Roethke had simply seen the human in terms of the plant world; but now, in order to achieve his dynamic effects, he also sees the plant in human terms.

This, then, is the esthetic of the greenhouse poems: the rooting of poetry in sensuous experience, the search for naive, even prerational, modes of expression, and a more dynamic concept of the correspondence between the vegetable and the human. Each is an extension of Roethke's earlier poetic principles rather than a sudden alteration.

The greenhouse land of Roethke's father and uncle provided a setting particularly suitable to the development of these esthetic ends. But the most important reason Roethke chose to write a sequence of poems about this vegetable realm is probably far less complex: as the scene of his childhood, it was a world highly charged with experience and significance. It was, as we have seen, both fertile womb and rigid principle of order imposed upon chaos, both heaven and hell; it was nature and society, mother and father. It was all of life.

There is no reason to suppose that the poems of the sequence are arranged in so strict an order that to alter the position of any one would drastically affect its meaning, but there does seem to be a general sense of growth uniting the poems organically as well as by theme. The first five poems, for example, are explicitly concerned with the struggle to be born. In "Cuttings," "small cells bulge" until a single "nub of growth" nudges and pokes its way through the sand. (*WW,* 37) The second "Cuttings" poem picks up this strain toward becoming at a later point, at the "urge, wrestle, resurrection of dry sticks." (*WW*, 38) And the same struggle is present in "Root Cellar" (*WW*, 39), where the bulbs break out of boxes and hunt for chinks in the dark. Here, however, the image is more complex, since the root cellar is itself a dark and fertile womb, but one that is filled with a sense of destructiveness as well as fruitfulness in sexuality: the soil smells of its rotten richness, the reaching shoots provide a snaky allusion to the fall of man.

A sense of great exertion is implicit even in the title of "Forcing House." The image of life emerging from "lime and dung and ground bones—" (*WW*, 40) makes it a suitable companion poem for "Root Cellar." But contrasts between the two are more significant than the similarities. For the first time in the sequence, man's influence is felt as something more than a source of obstacles around which and through which plants manage to grow. Here man is the dynamic force, speeding growth, until there are "Fifty summers in motion at once." "Root Cellar" is filled with images of darkness, of boxes; the cellar itself is a symbol of the womb. But in "Forcing House," plants respond to the life-bringing pipes, which are, for Roethke, always associated with the image of the father:[8]

> All pulse with the knocking pipes
> That drip and sweat,
> Sweat and drip,
> Swelling the roots with steam and stench. . . .

---

[8] The most striking instance of this is the signaling of the coming of Papa by a "pipe-knock" in "The Lost Son." (*WW*, 84) The association is strengthened by a second significance of the word "pipe," which we would not be aware of without Roethke's own comment: "But 'Papa,' or the florist, as he approached, often would knock the pipe he was smoking on the sides of the benches, or on the pipes." "Open Letter," *SP*, p. 39. See also "Big Wind" (*WW*, 44), discussed below.

From the impersonal, cell-like growth images of the first two poems, through the mother and father symbols of the next two, Roethke comes finally to the child himself in "Weed Puller," the fifth of the birth poems. The struggle of the embryo to be born becomes tied up with a host of sexually charged objects, represented by the weeds. There is no need to limit meanings to birth alone; but that this is in fact one of the primary images of the poem should be clear from the wish to be born from the womb of the last lines:

> Me down in that fetor of weeds,
> Crawling on all fours,
> Alive, in a slippery grave.   (*WW,* 41)

The "slippery grave" is, of course, the womb; "fetor" suggests "foetus." (That this is indeed a punning poem is indicated by its earlier use of the word "inviolate" to describe a field of flowers; it means both "not violated" and "filled with violets.")

The emphasis of each of these "birth poems" is on the struggle which Roethke identified as the main theme of the longer poems of part IV: "each in a sense is a stage in a kind of struggle out of the slime; part of a slow spiritual progress; an effort to be born, and later, to become something more." [9] The greenhouse poems prefigure the later version of the struggle. To be sure, the poems' meanings should not be limited to this reading; they are certainly, among other things, literal descriptions of a greenhouse and the activities centered on it. But what differentiates Roethke's verse from other "flower" poems is precisely his awareness of the fight to exist as an aspect of reality shared by man and plant.

The next three poems deal with the development of a more

[9] "Open Letter," *SP,* p. 38.

self-conscious sexuality. The flowers of "Orchids" are compared to infants: but infancy here is not the age of innocence,
but rather of demanding, grasping, undisciplined sexual urges.
These musky, "devouring infants" are characterized by fingers,
lips, mouths. "Moss-Gathering," taking place away from the
greenhouse, but associated with it, shifts to the ages dominated
by auto-erotic impulses. The "gathering" itself takes place in
a landscape with clearly sexual overtones; it is followed by a
feeling of guilt at the onanistic action:[10]

And afterwards I always felt mean, jogging back over the road,
As if I had broken the natural order of things in that swampland;
Disturbed some rhythm, old and of vast importance,
By pulling off flesh from the living planet;
As if I had committed, against the whole scheme of life, a desecra-
 tion.   (*WW*, 43)

While this sense of guilt at an "unnatural" action is hardly
limited to masturbatory activities, the phrase "pulling off flesh"
provides a less ambiguous context for the uneasy emotions.

In "Big Wind," the protagonist confronts a more adult kind
of sexuality. We have had hints of this before (particularly in
the concluding lines of "Cuttings, *later*"), but never was sexual
intercourse itself so intimately related to the poem's central
metaphor; the progression from infant to childhood to adolescent awareness is here completed. The images of the poem are
mixed; the greenhouse is envisioned as a ship riding out a
storm. But those masculine steampipes are at work again (as
in "Forcing House"), "pumping the stale mixture" into the

---

[10] Onanism figures prominently in *Praise to the End!*, and is actually the
central action in the first section of the title poem. Roethke provides the
equation, onanism equals death ("Open Letter," *SP*, p. 70), but this does
not eliminate further connotations.

greenhouse; this, the violence of the storm, and the femininity of the greenhouse seem to signal the child's growing knowledge of a sexual world.

The next three poems shift the emphasis away from the child's activities to those of the tenders of the greenhouses, the manipulators of this vegetable world. "Old Florist" is the first of Roethke's representations of his father as a type of God: the florist can pick away the rotten leaves, scoop out a weed, "drown a bug in one spit of tobacco juice," "fan life into wilted sweet-peas," "or stand all night watering roses." (*WW,* 46)[11] In "Transplanting," the watching child is awed by the power of the florist's swift, sure movements, which give life to the young plants.

Placed appropriately between these two poems is the later work, "Frau Bauman, Frau Schmidt, and Frau Schwartze." (*WW,* 47; see footnote 2.) Although these ladies are not placed in a religious context, their "magical" powers, related to those of the florist, contribute to the supernatural sense of the act of creation; flying like witches, they keep creation "at ease," sew up the air with a stem, trellis the sun. With regard to meter and diction, this poem is in marked contrast to those around it. It was written in the period when the influence of Yeats was most evident in Roethke's verse. As opposed to the slow, winding, sensuous rhythms of most of the other poems, these lines are tougher, quicker, more energetic, perfectly suited to the trio of birdlike ladies.

[11] Cf. the expansion of this last line in section 4 of "Where Knock Is Open Wide." (*WW,* 65) Here, the florist's thumb has a rainbow, suggesting the covenant. See also the coming of Papa in section 4 of "The Lost Son." (*WW,* 84.)

The final three poems of the first part of *The Lost Son* concern the triumph and terror of emerging from the greenhouse
world of childhood. "Child on Top of a Greenhouse" shows the
protagonist having literally climbed to the heights, with "everyone, everyone pointing up and shouting!" (*WW,* 50) The small
child is achieving a certain recognition, a sense of identity of
his own; but this attainment is not without its uneasy conse-
quences. The chrysanthemums stare up "like accusers." There
is clearly a great deal of guilt involved in growing up. And the
terror of the situation is explicated in "Flower Dump" (*WW,*
51), which, although it does not seem so at first, is a companion poem to "Child on Top of a Greenhouse." The child
high above the shouting crowd of adults is equivalent to the
tulip of this second poem, on top of the pile, swaggering above
"the dying, the newly dead." The "dying" and the "newly
dead" are the adults; the tulip, the child, leaving "eternity"
for the world of adults, the world of awareness of death.

"Carnations," filled with "pale blossoms," "wet hemlocks,"
"that clear autumnal weather of eternity" (*WW,* 52), is indeed
a poem of death, somewhat reminiscent of D. H. Lawrence's
"Bavarian Gentians." The movement from childhood to death
may seem inordinately quick, an artificial completion of the
cycle from birth to death. But actually, we should have been
prepared for this gap. In poems such as "To My Sister" and
"The Premonition," we saw the identification of sexuality and
adulthood with death. The protagonist peers out from childhood at the emptiness beyond time; in more analytic terms, the
child, feeling himself threatened by annihilation in the process of growing up, retreats into childhood. Only the painful

probing of *Praise to the End!*, under the guidance of a father-God-analyst figure, is able to confront the impasse with which the greenhouse poems end.

There is one more matter to be taken up before considering the middle parts of *The Lost Son:* the rhythms and meters of the greenhouse poems. There was, of course, some experimentation in Roethke's earlier work (the poems of part III of *The Lost Son*, which chronologically precede the greenhouse poems, might be included in this group), but the greenhouse poems mark the first use on a large scale of free verse. This innovation is closely associated with the "esthetic" of the greenhouse poems, with which this chapter began. "If we concern ourselves with more primitive effects in poetry," Roethke wrote, "we come inevitably to consideration, I think, of verse that is closer to prose." [12] Roethke goes on to elaborate the precise means of obtaining these "primitive effects." Lines can be varied, modulated, stretched out, or shortened; the writer strives to produce "the language that is natural to the immediate thing, the particular emotion. . . . There are areas of experience in modern life that simply cannot be rendered by either the formal lyric or straight prose. . . . The writer in freer forms must have an even greater fidelity to his subject matter than the poet who has the support of form. He must keep his eye on the object, and his rhythm must move as his mind moves, must be imaginatively right, or he is lost." [13]

In the greenhouse poems, with his "eye on the object," Roethke manipulates his lines to capture the immediacy of the experience described: from the long, slow lines of the guilt-

[12] "Some Remarks on Rhythm," *SP*, p. 81.
[13] *Ibid.*, p. 83.

ridden "Moss-Gathering," through the alternately long and short weaving lines of the sensuous, snaky "Root Cellar," to the short, breathless phrases of "Big Wind," rhythm and experience are united in each of the poems.

II

In spite of some experimentation in rhythm, the poems of part II of *The Lost Son* are most like the traditional lyrics of *Open House;* this is true with regard to content as well as form, since these poems describe personal recollections as in part I of the earlier book, and comment on social problems as in part V. "My Papa's Waltz," probably the best of these poems, perfectly conveys in a few lines of regular, dancelike rhythms the father's mixture of brutality and tenderness, the boy's admiration and fear. "Pickle Belt" recalls the days when Roethke actually was employed in a pickle factory, "Prickling with all the itches/ Of sixteen year old lust." (*WW*, 54)

In his best poem of social criticism, "Dolor," Roethke describes with purposely monotonous rhythms the "Endless duplication of lives and objects" (*WW*, 55) of the office worker. And "Double Feature" picks up a similar theme, the futile attempt of empty lives to find fulfillment in fantasy. After watching a serialized melodrama, the protagonist, sensing his own smallness in the real world, is painfully able to "remember there was something else I was hoping for." [14]

[14] *The Lost Son and Other Poems*, p. 30 (hereafter abbreviated as *LS*). However, I have followed the practice established in previous chapters of citing *Words for the Wind* whenever a poem appears in both books.

In "The Return," the feeling of self-infection, so often evident in *Open House,* emerges once more. The need to escape the viciousness of this often-paced circle by probing the source of infection becomes one of the important motives of the search of *Praise to the End!* "Last Words" is a lyrical wish to escape the dullness of routine existence, anticipating in form and content the illumination of "The Lost Son." "Judge Not," for the most part an undistinguished poem, should perhaps be noted for its toying with the possibility, ultimately rejected by Roethke, that death might be the only solution to the ills of life.

The poems of part II, then, seeking to understand the self through the objective examination of past experiences, most often end in platitudes. Roethke is not effective with discursive poetry; he must seek new methods, like those of the greenhouse poems, and he must approach his materials from a new perspecitve. Part III does in fact explore a series of metaphors for the self, all of which will be used prominently in the last part of *The Lost Son,* and, of course, in *Praise to the End!*

III

"Night Crow" states, in particularly powerful form, the effectiveness of the theory of correspondences we have already seen at work in Roethke's poetry; an object in the outer world is mirrored by the inner landscape. But there is something special about the correspondence in this particular poem: the crow on the wasted tree not only represents something within the mind, it is able to evoke it as well:

When I saw that clumsy crow
Flap from a wasted tree,
A shape in the mind rose up;
Over the gulfs of dream
Flew a tremendous bird
Further and further away
Into a moonless black,
Deep in the brain, far back.   (WW, 58)

In Carl Jung's words, "We are dealing with a reactivated archetype, as I have already called these primordial images. These ancient images are called to life by the primitive, analogical mode of thinking peculiar to dreams." [15] These remarks clearly fit Roethke's poem. It represents still another attempt to make the poem a direct communication of experience, this time using Jung's concept of the collective unconscious, the racial memory held in common by all humanity.

The application of Jung's ideas to poetry with which Roethke was unquestionably familiar is Maud Bodkin's *Archetypal Patterns in Poetry*.[16] I shall quote from the first paragraph of this influential work:

The special emotional significance possessed by certain poems —a significance going beyond any definite meaning conveyed —he [Jung] attributes to the stirring in the reader's mind, within or beneath his conscious response, of unconscious forces which he terms 'primordial images,' or archetypes. These archetypes he describes as 'psychic residua of numberless experi-

---

[15] *Two Essays on Analytical Psychology* (New York, Meridian, 1956), p. 147.

[16] Stanley Kunitz, a close friend of Roethke's, cites his familiarity with the book in "Roethke: Poet of Transformations," p. 25. Both Kunitz and Mrs. Roethke have told me that Roethke also read Jung himself, but the precise extent and nature of this reading is not certain.

ences of the same type,' experiences which have happened not
to the individual but to his ancestors, and of which the results
are inherited in the structure of the brain, *a priori* determinants
of individual experience.[17]

This is the theory of "Night Crow"; it ultimately will provide
the framework for the entire *Praise to the End!* sequence. But
first, Roethke must fully explore the implications of his new
method. The atavistic imagery of "River Incident" probes still
further into the nature of the collective unconscious. The protagonist, with sea water in his veins, is taken back to his
origins, to man's origins:

> . . . I knew that I had been there before,
> In that cold, granite slime,
> In the dark, in the rolling water.   (*LS*, 38)

Once again, Jung is pertinent: "The contents of the collective
unconscious are not only the residues of archaic, specifically
human modes of functioning, but also the residue of functions
from man's animal ancestry, whose duration in time was infinitely greater than the relatively brief epoch of specifically
human existence." [18]

The fact that this regressive journey into the slime beneath
the sea is necessary is probably the most important justification for Roethke's "developmental" poems. According to Jung,
when a man encounters an obstacle with which he cannot cope,
he regresses to childhood, or even to the time before childhood—that is, to the collective unconscious—to find a new way
of dealing with his current situation.[19] This is the significance

[17] London, Oxford University Press, 1963.
[18] Jung, p. 109.
[19] *Ibid.*, pp. 86–87.

of "River Incident"; this is the therapeutic function of *Praise to the End!* Bodkin explains the process in words quite suitable to Roethke's poem (words that conceivably could have inspired it):

> Before a 'renewal of life' can come about, Jung urges, there must be an acceptance of the possibilities that lie in the unconscious contents 'activated through regression . . . and disfigured by the slime of the deep.'
>
> The principle which he thus expounds Jung recognizes as reflected in the myth of 'the night journey under the sea.' [20]

In "The Minimal," Roethke reaffirms the correspondence of small and primitive forms of life to the human mind, this time with specific reference to the healing, curing effects of these probing, Jungian explorations of the depths of the self. "Bacterial creepers" wriggle through wounds, kissing and cleaning, healing as they probe. (*WW*, 59) However, the fact that these images apply to the human mind should not overshadow Roethke's real affection for the "little sleepers," the small of the world.

Taken out of its context, "The Cycle" could be interpreted as referring to the cyclic nature of existence in the broadest sense; however, considering its particular surroundings, we might suspect that this cycle is related to Jung's theory of regression and progression. The image of dark water underneath rock and clay tends to confirm this suspicion. The cycle of the physical world corresponds to the cycle of the mind; in both cases, the descent "Under a river's source,/ Under primeval stone" (*WW*, 60), leads to renewal. And "The Waking," the

[20] Bodkin, p. 52.

final poem of part III, is indeed a poem of renewal;[21] drawing his previous imagery together, Roethke paves the way for the great poems of part IV. The river runs over stones, water flows through the protagonist's veins and sings with joy. (*LS*, 41) We emerge from the slime into the light of a summer day.

[21] This poem, which Roethke never reprinted, should not be confused with the villanelle of the same title, which first appeared in 1953, and which gave its name to *The Waking*.

CHAPTER 4

Out of the Slime

1949 – 1951

We have already seen Roethke lay the groundwork for his long "developmental" poems in the earlier parts of *The Lost Son*, particularly in part III, which dealt with Jung's theories of regression and progression, and the necessity of the descent into the primordial world of the collective unconscious.[1] Roethke's own description of the method of these poems, originally written for John Ciardi's anthology, *Mid-Century American Poets*, confirms our analysis of theoretical origins:

> Each poem . . . is complete in itself; yet each in a sense is a stage in a kind of struggle out of the slime; part of a slow spiritual progress; an effort to be born, and later, to become something more. . . . The method is cyclic. I believe that to go forward as a spiritual man it is necessary first to go back. Any history of the psyche (or allegorical journey) is bound to be a

[1] Part IV of *The Lost Son* consists of four poems: "The Lost Son," "The Long Alley," "A Field of Light," "The Shape of the Fire." Since these poems later become the first half of Part Two of *Praise to the End!*, it will be more convenient to consider them in their context in this later book than in their order of composition. Two poems of the same kind appeared in *Botteghe Oscure* ("Song," VIII [1951], 282–83; "The Changeling," X [Fall 1952], 239–41), but they never became part of the sequence. "O, Thou Opening, O," however, was added in *The Waking* (1953).

succession of experiences, similar yet dissimilar. There is a perpetual slipping-back, then a going forward; but there is *some* "progress." [2]

This is a clear paraphrase of Jung, a prose statement of the themes of part III of *The Lost Son*. But we can do more than speak in a general way of Roethke's debt to Jung; we can identify the particular archetypal pattern the poet uses to probe his spirit.[3] "The process of individuation," at the heart of Roethke's search for the self, is, according to Jung, made conscious through the method of "active imagination" in the archetype of the child-hero:

The hero's main feat is to overcome the monster of darkness: it is the long-hoped-for and expected triumph of consciousness over the unconscious. Day and light are synonyms for consciousness, night and dark for the unconscious. The coming of consciousness was probably the most tremendous experience of primeval times, for with it a world came into being whose existence no one had suspected before. "And God said: 'Let there be light!'" is the projection of that immemorial experience of the separation of the conscious from the unconscious. Even among primitives today the possession of a soul is a precarious thing and the "loss of soul" a typical psychic malady which drives primitive medicine to all sorts of psychotherapeutic measures. Hence the "child" distinguishes itself by deeds which point to the conquest of the dark.[4]

Roethke, searching for his self, was in his own life threatened by this "loss of soul"; and so Jung's analysis lends further

[2] "Open Letter," *SP*, pp. 37–39.

[3] Hilton Kramer, p. 134, was the first to point out the applicability of this archetype to *Praise to the End!*

[4] *Psyche and Symbol* (New York, Doubleday, 1958), pp. 130–31.

weight to Ciardi's description of Roethke's verse as "poetry as a medicine man's dance is poetry . . . therapy by incantation," [5] at least in so far as *Praise to the End!* is concerned.

However, we must guard against taking a too exclusively psychoanalytic view of these poems. The obvious application of Jung's theories should be used as a tool to further understanding, not to limit it. And Roethke in fact places at least as much emphasis on the spiritual as on the psychological aspects of his quest (which is perhaps why Jung was more congenial to Roethke than the Freudians). The controlling movement of the poems is certainly from darkness to light; but this is as descriptive of spiritual illumination as it is of the psychological process of individuation. We should remember that Roethke's earliest work was influenced not only by metaphysical wit, but also by a tradition of poetry that included Vaughan, Traherne, Blake, and contemporaries whose verse contained a quasi-mystical view of reality. Not only does the archetypal journey have psychological implications, but it has also been used by St. Bonaventura, Dante, Rulman Merswin, Sufi poets, Buddhists, and countless others, as symbolic of the mind's road to union with a transcendent being.

Part 1 of *Open House* began with analytic probing, but ended with sight as a symbol of a Platonic mode of knowing, with light representing a reality beyond the physical. In *Praise to the End!*, Roethke does not abandon the poetry of vision in favor of the poetry of analysis; rather, with the aid of Jung, he attempts to synthesize these two approaches to reality. Self and soul become synonymous, as Roethke attempts to resolve the tormenting duality of the material and immaterial

[5] "Theodore Roethke: A Passion and a Maker," p. 13.

worlds; he goes even further than Jung in emphasizing the spiritual aspects of psychological life.

This emphasis is made perfectly plain by the title of the entire sequence, *Praise to the End!* It is taken from a passage in Book One of *The Prelude,* by Wordsworth, which, like Roethke's own "Long Live the Weeds," hails the psychological struggles of early life that promote the ultimate growth of the spirit:

> Praise to the end!
> Thanks to the means which Nature deigned to employ;
> Whether her fearless visitings, or those
> That came with soft alarm, like hurtless light
> Opening the peaceful clouds. . . .   (I, ll. 350–354)

This is precisely the point of view from which Roethke will consider his own childhood: an exploration of the ways in which spiritual ends are achieved through psychological means, how final peace is arrived at as a result of "early miseries."

Before going on to the individual poems, it is necessary to say something about the techniques used throughout. For this purpose, one can do no better than to examine Roethke's statement in "Open Letter," which is probably the most valuable he has made about his poetry.[6] First, Roethke warns us that although these poems look "peculiar," they are really "traditional." That is, they are traditional in terms of the materials used: fairy tales, which are among the most available sources of Jungian archetypes, and provide an excellent basis for a myth of the growth of the spirit;[7] late sixteenth-

---

[6] *SP,* pp. 41–42.

[7] See especially Jung's "The Phenomenology of the Spirit in Fairy Tales" in *Psyche and Symbol,* pp. 61–112. Interestingly enough, Jung uses the fairy tale as support of the notion that "Spirit and matter may

and early seventeenth-century drama, with its models of unsophisticated but overwhelmingly powerful expressions of emotion, quite suitable to the child's world; biblical stories, such
as that of Job, which supply a source of simple parables of the
mysterious quality of life, understandable in terms of intuition
and faith rather than reason; Blake and Traherne, who, emphasizing the presence of the eternal in the temporal, are at
the center of the tradition that makes the child particularly
receptive to intimations of a truer reality; and Dürer's art,
which lends support to the allegorical possibilities of the quest
("The Knight, Death and the Devil," for example, provides the
kind of stark imagery Roethke is seeking).

But while Roethke's elements may be traditional, his method
of composition is not. Experience is rendered obliquely, he
points out; the identity of the speaker is unclear, sometimes
because there is no single identity in question, but rather a
merging of identities; language is similarly compressed; images
and symbols are telescoped, and dependent upon context for
their full meanings, which are suggestive rather than definite.
Rhythm once again is expected to contribute to the definition
of experience; Roethke is after "the spring and rush of the
child." For the most part, "the material seems to demand a
varied short line." Emphasis upon the dramatic nature of much
of the poetry serves to remind us that the formation of the
individual personality is not simply the manifestation in reality
of a predetermined spirit, but rather the result of continual
interaction between the self and others. Above all, Roethke

---

well be forms of one and the same transcendental being" (p. 67). This
is implicit in Roethke's attempt to unite spiritual and psychological
progress, in *Praise to the End!* and elsewhere.

is aiming for direct rather than analytical presentation of experience, intuitive rather than rational perception of reality, and testing of the trueness of a poem by what is most nearly universal in the poet himself. In short, the poems of *Praise to the End!* represent the consummation of an esthetic that began its development in *Open House,* and moved logically toward its extreme.

A word or two should be added about Roethke's portrayal of the workings of the mind. He is clearly concerned with the ways in which the unconscious makes itself known to the conscious; and it is in order to communicate his sense of this experience to the reader that he avails himself as much as possible of public materials, from archetypes of the collective unconscious to a common literary tradition, although this does not in the least preclude the use of private materials to provide a greater richness and sense of reality to the text. The use of compressed language, telescoped images and symbols, merged identities, and a general suggestiveness rather than definite meanings, as means of communicating awareness of the unconscious, is comparatively rare in poetry (although Dylan Thomas and many of the surrealist poets make use of dream techniques, and also attempt to use the unconscious directly). But Roethke's real antecedent is usually classified as a writer of prose, albeit a special kind of prose: I am speaking of James Joyce, with particular reference to *Finnegans Wake*.

Indeed, with regard to the primacy of the auditory imagination, the use of "dream language," and the concern with archetypal figures and patterns, the parallels between Roethke and Joyce are striking. Joyce is by far the more allusive of the two, but this difference is superficial. A fundamental distinction may be made in terms of the units of speech and thought with which they achieve their effects. For Joyce, the unit is the word; in the denser passages of *Finnegans Wake,* a single word, alone as well as in relation to other words, may carry the burden of a wealth of meaning. For Roethke, whose imagination is not as exclusively auditory as Joyce's, the unit tends to be no smaller than a completely articulated image or symbol, sometimes consisting of the equivalent of an entire poem. The result is that Roethke presents a solider surface, which can the more easily be focused in the powerful, emotionally charged line, while Joyce conveys a far more nearly perfect sense of the flux and simultaneity of mental life. Joyce can only with difficulty escape the intellectuality of his complex structure, and must, paradoxically, depend upon accumulation rather than concentration for his emotional effects. This is, of course, perfectly appropriate to the far larger scale with which Joyce was working.

The poems of *Praise to the End!* are divided into two parts; the first one contains six poems which are, for the most part, shorter, less sophisticated, and concerned with an earlier age than the eight poems of the second. Risking an oversimplification, we may say that the poems of the first emphasize the struggle to be born, those of the second, the effort, perhaps even more strenuous, to become something more.[8]

[8] This is Roethke's phrase, but not his distinction. When he wrote "Open Letter" (mid 1950), the first seven poems of Part Two had been written, and one ("Where Knock Is Open Wide") of Part One, with another ("Give Way, Ye Gates") under way. The rest of the book had not yet been definitely planned. But while the poems of Part Two go back even to prenatal "experience," these excursions are rare, and they begin at

Part One

Any attempt to verify chronological sequence is complicated by the fact that, according to the theory of regression and progression, each poem begins well before the preceding poem's end; but a kind of progress emerges when we compare the beginnings, ends, and even, sometimes, titles of poems with one another. In any case, "Where Knock Is Open Wide," dealing with birth, and even before, fully justifies its position as first poem in the book.

The title of this poem is taken from stanza LXXVII of Christopher Smart's *A Song to David:*

> . . . in the seat to faith assign'd,
> Where ask is have, where seek is find,
> Where knock is open wide.

In Smart's poem, these lines precede the glorious floods of light of the last stanzas; the knock, for Roethke, announces a spiritual awakening, an entrance into a kingdom of light. But most of the titles in *Praise to the End!* are puns, and "Where Knock Is Open Wide" can hardly be limited to Smart's context. It refers to the literal, as well as the psychological or spiritual, birth of the child; and the words of the title have further connotations of conception, and of the sexual act itself, both of which are pertinent to the content of the poem.[9]

least in adolescence; they are attempts to find the spiritual self. Part One, however, concentrates on childhood, and the basic formation of personality; they describe a more literal being born, a more psychological kind of development.

[9] Cf. Dylan Thomas' "Before I Knocked." There are echoes of Thomas, and this poem of his in particular, in "Where Knock Is Open Wide."

The first section of "Where Knock Is Open Wide" is worth
particular study, not only because it establishes the crucial
imagery for the entire poem, and to a certain extent the sequence, but also as a demonstration of the application of
Roethke's theories of composition. The section opens with
quatrains consisting of two-beat lines; a kitten can bite with
his feet, we are told, but Papa and Mama have more teeth.
Although the presence of Papa and Mama at the poem's start
seems appropriate, the analogy of a kitten's claws and parents'
teeth at first has little more meaning than a nonsense rhyme.
But an attentive reading yields a good deal more. The second
stanza, with its speculations about cows having puppies, provides a context of sexual curiosity and sexual confusion. (*WW*,
63) "Foot" has well established phallic connotations in psychoanalytical literature, and Roethke's awareness of this is
made clear in "Praise to the End!" where "What footie does is
final." [10] (*WW*, 98) Biting would then seem to have a sexual
meaning; in fact, we can tentatively identify the first two
stanzas as the child's hazy image of sexuality, particularly of
his parents' sexual activities.

Stanza three slows the poem's rhythm by lengthening lines.
Here, the child, asking his parents to sing him a "sleep-song,"
is young enough for us to assume that these are rather articulate transcriptions of his thoughts than his actual words. The
last line, "A real hurt is soft," while it may very well concern
the child's relation to his parents, seems also to relate to the
sexual act suggested above, as an attempt to justify the ap-

[10] See, for example, Jung, *Two Essays on Analytical Psychology* (New
York, Meridian, 1956), p. 93.

parent aggressiveness of intercourse. Then, the "sleep-song" is sung:

> Once upon a tree
> I came across a time,
> It wasn't even as
> A ghoulie in a dream.
>
> There was a mooly man
> Who had a rubber hat
> And funnier than that,—
> He kept it in a can.   (WW, 63)

It brings to mind Joyce's *Portrait of the Artist as a Young Man,* which begins, "Once upon a time and a very good time it was there was a moocow coming down along the road and this moocow that was down along the road met a nicens little boy named baby tuckoo . . ." [11] However, as in Joyce, Roethke's nursery story is far more significant than it first seems.

Our initial reaction may be to identify the speaker as one of the parents, but this is not completely accurate. The story has meanings and associations for the child apart from those the adult finds there, and it is the child's version that we are given. An opening phallic suggestion is followed by a sense of time beyond time, of reality beyond dream. The "mooly man" seems a combination of father and milk-giving mother. The "rubber hat" kept in a "can" is a reasonably accurate image of sexual intercourse of several kinds; and if we are to take the "rubber" seriously, as well as the possibility, which we shall take up next, that this is an imagined version of the child's own begetting, it is indeed a "funny" situation. And the next stanza

[11] *Portable James Joyce,* ed. H. Levin (New York, Viking, 1955), p. 245.

does indeed seem to link the sexual activities of the entire section (which here comes to a close) with the begetting of the protagonist, somewhat in the mode of Sterne's *Tristram Shandy:*

> What's the time, papa-seed?
> Everything has been twice.
> My father is a fish.

The concern with time is reiterated, for this is the protagonist's entrance into time, and it is beyond even dream in the sense that he could not have perceived the act in any way. The source of insight is explained in the line "Everything has been twice." The regressive probing of memory into the world of the collective unconscious reveals human experience beyond birth; it even probes beyond human existence, in the atavistic image of father as fish. (The father as fish is also clearly the "papa-seed," that is, the sperm.) [12] In terms of spiritual enlightenment, this regressive memory was associated by Jung with perceptions of certain transcendent states of consciousness, and with dreaming back, in which an awareness of life beyond the temporal limits of the individual is an important characteristic.[13] In any case, whether by means of Jungian collective unconscious, or eastern mysticism, the protagonist of Roethke's poem envisions his own begetting, associating it with a tenderly aggressive form of sexuality.

Should there be any doubt in the reader's mind about the validity of this reading, there is, in this particular case, a way of checking our findings. For the entire incident is repeated

[12] Cf. Vardaman's "My mother is a fish," in Faulkner's *As I Lay Dying* (New York, Modern Library, 1946), p. 398.
[13] Jung, *Two Essays,* p. 202.

in a later poem, "Praise to the End!," which, when it is taken together with the lines we have been studying, leaves little doubt about what is happening:

> Rock me to sleep, the weather's wrong.
> Speak to me softly, frosty beard.
> Sing to me, sweet.
>
> Mips and ma the mooly moo,
> The likes of him is biting who,
> A cow's a care and who's a coo?—
> What footie does is final.
>
> My dearest dear my fairest fair,
> Your father tossed a cat in the air,
> Though neither you nor I was there,—
> What footie does is final.
>
> Be large as an owl, be slick as a frog,
> Be good as a goose, be big as a dog,
> Be sleek as a heifer, be long as a hog,—
> What footie will do will be final.   (WW, 98)

This section, an incantation to assure the growth of the protagonist's sexual organs, is similarly introduced by a plea for a sleep-song. This time, father and mother are identified as "frosty beard" and "sweet" respectively. The "mooly moo" is again involved with "him," and whatever they are doing is characterized by biting; the cat is once more tied up with the sexual imagery. As before, this is not the story the boy was told, but an association from it, or from bedtime in general. And now we do not have to speculate as to whether the protagonist is envisioning something he did not actually see; he explicitly tells his own "footie" that neither of them was there, but the act was quite final anyway, as his own existence testifies, and there is promise that he too will be capable of such finality.

We can be fairly certain, then, that the first section of "Where Knock Is Open Wide" is concerned with the child's conception. The second introduces images of birth—"Her neck has kittens"—and death—"My uncle's away,/ He's gone for always." (*WW*, 64) Characteristically, a cat is associated with sexuality and birth. The death of the uncle prefigures the death of the father; and the child's denial of the importance of the first event anticipates his denial (by means of the father's lingering ghost) of the reality of the latter.

The dream, or rather nightmare, imagery of the third section, with its ghost that cannot whistle, seems to dwell upon the death of the uncle; but it is also likely that some of the child's terror springs from a source of which the reader is not yet aware. Fish and worm suggest, to be sure, the fishing trip of the next section; "Fish me out" is, in fact, the boy's anguished plea. But the fish, we should remember, also *is* the father; and the worm, whose most prominent characteristic is its mouth, is one of the devouring kind, and not one that is to be devoured.

The "happy hands" at the section's end may be those of the mother comforting her waking son, those of the father in the dream, or those of the child himself; we cannot at this point be certain. The rhythms of this section are in contrast to the comparatively steady movement of the rest of the poem; the diminishing lines, the shift from slow to swift flow, mirror the mounting tensions of the dream.

The fourth section describes the fishing trip the young boy takes with his father; this combination of fishing and father is the probable subject of the preceding section, where it appeared in fragmentary form, as a dream. The father, sparing a caught fish at his son's request, is seen in his God-like aspect. In fact, the child associates with this trip the father's similar godlike powers in the greenhouse setting, as we see him watering roses, a rainbow at his thumb. Roethke in this way sets up a vision of an idyllic state which stands for both the child together with his father, and the child at one with God. Then comes the climax of the poem: "That was before. I fell! I fell!" (*WW*, 65) The appearance of a "worm," which soon becomes "snake," supports this reference to the Fall of Man. The child, like Adam, has lost paradise because of sin; and here too, as in Genesis, sin seems related to knowledge of sex. The child, aware to some extent of his parents' sexual activities, and, according to Freud, inevitably desiring his mother and fearing his father's retribution, assumes the guilt for his father's death.

However, "I fall!" has another important meaning; as in John Donne's "First Anniversary," the "fall" may be an image of birth itself, as well as of original sin. ("How witty's ruine!" wrote Donne.) And so the fall stands for literal birth, and, in the mode of Vaughan, Traherne, Blake, and Wordsworth, birth is a falling away from oneness with God. This identification of father with God brings out the Christian implications of the image of father as fish.

In the poem's final section, father and God are further united by the boy in his effort to understand what has happened; thinking of his father, he tells his mother that God lives somewhere else. In this very first poem of *Praise to the End!*, the falling away from God in birth, and the loss of the father in death, have made the protagonist a "lost son." Acknowledging the new responsibilities that accompany his awareness of separation from both father and God, the child feels he has become "somebody else." (*WW,* 66)

In the fifth section we also find a possible explanation of the mysterious "happy hands" of the third: "Don't tell my hands." The hands alone were happy before; here, they alone seem ignorant of what has happened. These two qualities are hardly incompatible. In earlier poems, the hands have been Roethke's symbol of flesh as opposed to spirit; in *Praise to the End!* they take on additional connotations of grasping for money and of masturbatory activities.[14] The hands, then, may be the child's own, representing flesh unaware of new spiritual responsibilities, of new spiritual identity.

However, if we move beyond the limits of "Where Knock Is Open Wide," the significance of "hands" becomes—without contradicting our tentative conclusions—more complex; Roethke often uses materials before they are fully explained, but the explanation is usually contained within the sequence as a whole, and individual poems become clearer with successive readings. In this case, the crucial meaning of "hands" is revealed in a phrase in "Praise to the End!": "Father, forgive my hands." (*WW,* 97) The religious and sexual contexts of this prayer emphasize its pertinence to the poem under consideration. The child has just masturbated, and is asking God's forgiveness; but he is also asking his father's forgiveness, and the reason for this is made clear when the masturbatory fantasy is revealed. It is precisely the fantasy we discussed in con-

---

[14] Cf. "The Lost Son": "I have married my hands to perpetual agitation,/ I run, I run to the whistle of money." (*WW,* 83) See also "Praise to the End!" discussed immediately below.

nection with the child's vision of his parents' sexual relations. The source of the hands' guilt is then the notion that masturbation is a sin against the father; and the unwillingness to "tell my hands" becomes symbolic of the child's attempts to deny his feelings of guilt.

In spite of the fact that more space has been devoted to "Where Knock Is Open Wide" than will be possible for most of the other poems of *Praise to the End!*, its meanings are far from fully explored. Nonetheless, it should be sufficiently clear that most of the main themes of the entire sequence— birth, death, sexual guilt and confusion, separation from father and God (the "lost son" motif)—are explicitly considered in the first poem. The method of these poems will indeed be cyclic: the reliving of significant experiences, with a difference.

"I Need, I Need" is an appropriate title for a poem that picks up the child's development at the first stage after birth. The child is completely dependent upon his mother for existence; he is in what Freudians would call the "oral" phase, and the poem does in fact begin with the child's wish to "taste" his mother, with the life of the mouth in general. (WW, 67) Roethke is probably not consciously following Freud's stages of development; but his imagery, like Freud's stages, comes from the observation of universal aspects of experience. The emphasis in this poem is accordingly upon the mother, just as it was on the father in the previous one. However, quick shifts in time bring the events of "Where Knock Is Open Wide" into focus, and the father becomes supremely important through his absence. "Do the dead bite?" the child asks, recalling the imagery of death and sex, the fishing scene of the first poem.

The second section is a dramatization of the interaction of

the self and others at an early age; two children, jumping rope, recite jingles at each other.[15] Of particular interest is the phrase, "The Trouble is with No and Yes." (*WW*, 68) Whether at the time he wrote this poem Roethke was familiar with the works of Jacob Boehme, who "rooted all in Yes and No," ("The Pure Fury," *WW*, 158) is far from certain. But something similar to the idea that everything, including the individual personality, comes into existence as the result of the tension of opposites (in this case, the self and others) is probably intended. The "Trouble" is that in so far as the individual is aware of these contending opposites, his own will becomes involved in the result, and he is faced with the responsibilities of choice.

The brief third section returns once again to thoughts of the dead father. The father, as both father and God, appears to the child as "a beard in a cloud." (*WW*, 69)[16] His absence cannot be made up for by the mother's affection; her love helps the "sun" (son), but not enough.

As earlier in the poem the child longed for the breast of the mother, now, with the mother unable to protect him from the terrors of his new situation, he longs to be gathered up by a larger, all-embracing source of comfort; he seeks his symbolic mother, the earth, the natural world. The world of nature is still magical for the child ("When you plant, spit in the pot," *WW*, 69); it is alive, even to the stones, and the young boy is part of it. The water of the dew is as soothing as the drip of the faucet of the first section. But the poem ends ominously:

---

[15] See "An American Poet Introduces Himself and His Poems," *SP*, p. 10, for Roethke's comment.

[16] Cf. "frosty beard" in "Praise to the End!" (*WW*, 98)

"I know another fire./ Has roots." Fire, associated with the
birth of kittens in "Where Knock Is Open Wide," has traditional sexual implications. As infantile sexuality seemed to
cause the fall from union with the father, or God, the growing
sexual urges now threaten to expel the child from an Eden-
like state of union with nature. The process of individuation, as
threatening as it is hopeful, is well under way; the problem,
seemingly beyond solution, is to attain and keep a separate
identity, while remaining united to the natural world.

"Bring the Day!" carries the child farther along his frightening, yet joyful, path. There is increasing disillusion, less of a
sense of magic in nature: "Hardly any old angels are around
any more" (*WW*, 71); as in Henry Vaughan's "Religion," there
is the sense of a golden age of the spirit lost to man because of
disobedience. Significantly, along with this loss of magical
existence, the child experiences a more self-conscious awareness of sexuality in the "innocent" world of nature: the herrings
are awake and singing to each other, whispering and kissing.
This corresponds to the child's growing awareness of his own
expanding sexual capacities, expressed in the language of
Blake and Thomas:

> When I stand I'm almost a tree
>
> . . . .
>
> The worm and the rose
> Both love
> Rain.   (*WW*, 71)

The child is now on the threshold of life; experience replaces
innocence as "spiders sail into summer." It is time to begin.

In "Give Way, Ye Gates" the struggle toward individuality

is taken up more aggressively; the child is now less dependent upon others than before, and he is that much less threatened by separation from them, although the amount of dependency and threat still operating should not be underestimated. This stage of the child's development would probably fall into the Freudian's anal-aggressive category; but for Roethke, aggressiveness and hand are much more closely associated: "The mouth asks. The hand takes." (*WW*, 74) This poem suitably begins with a more violent, and more advanced, version of the phallic promise of the previous poem: "Believe me, knot of gristle, I bleed like a tree;/ I dream of nothing but boards . . ." (*WW*, 72) The implications of the child telling his soft bone about dreams of stiff boards are quite clear. The child is no longer a kitten but a "cat after great milk and vasty fishes." (The yearning for both mother—milk—and father—fish—is implicit in the imagery.)

The "Mother of blue," suggesting the Virgin, continues the stream of religious reference that seems to be running through the poems. But the child's fantasies still have, for the most part, psychological rather than religious overtones: "We're king and queen of the right ground./ I'll risk the winter for you." (*WW*, 72) This seems to be an Oedipal fantasy, cast in the mythological terms of primitive ritual, in which the child is risking annihilation for possession of the mother. But in another sense, he is leaving the perpetual spring of childhood and union with nature for the world of adulthood, sexuality, and death.

The second part of the second section returns to the imagery which opened the poem, as the child addresses himself as a "tree beginning to know." (*WW*, 72) And the stage is set for an eloquent restatement of a familiar theme: the complex relationships of the image of the father, the world of nature, and the child's sexuality:

> And the ghost of some great howl
> Dead in a wall.
> In the high-noon of thighs,
> In the springtime of stones,
> We'll stretch with the great stems.   (WW, 73)[17]

Linked with the ghost (symbol of the father and of sexual guilt) is a barrier, the wall, representing the limits reality imposes upon the self "at the business of what might be." From these conflicts, the future self is built, "the instant ages." The third section is a kind of farewell to the time of union with nature; the child, addressing himself, must now dwell in "another" body, that is, his own rather than nature's. The diminishing rhythms of the fourth section pay tribute to the now distant origins of the self, the barely remembered pond at the depths of the mind.

In "Sensibility! O La!" the child's sexual awakening comes to completion; the alien "serpent," "John-of-the-thumb," is alive and jumping. The first section contains a fantasy of the beloved as Venus rising from the waves; the language is borrowed, for the protagonist is dealing with a world he has not yet mastered. The second section confirms bodily maturity: the shape of "long flesh" is here to stay: "I'm a twig to touch,/ Pleased as a knife." (WW, 75)

But the final section of the poem indicates that some of the

[17] Cf. "The Wall," the third section of The Dying Man:
> A ghost comes out of my unconscious mind
> To grope my sill. . . .
> The wall has entered: I must love the wall.   (WW, 188)

child's new confidence is premature; an important barrier to his development has not been overcome: "There's a ghost loose in the long grass!/ My sweetheart's still in her cave." (*WW*, 76) The persistence of the ghost begins to recall less cryptic lines in the poet's earlier verse: "The spirit starves/ Until the dead have been subdued" ("Feud," *OH*, 4); "And the honeymoon be spoiled by a father's ghost." ("Prognosis," *OH*, 7) In this nightmare, the boy finds that his mother is still dominating his vision of sweetheart (who is trapped in the womblike cave), and that as a result his father's ghost has been aroused.[18] The mother herself has been transformed into a frightening witch, before the child, with an effort of will mirrored in the gasping rhythms of the poem's last lines, forces himself from his dream. The "I am," closing the poem, insists not only that the dream is over, but that the self is intact as well.

If we were to classify "Sensibility! O La!" according to Freudian stages of development, we would place it in the Oedipal phase; and we would expect the next period to be latency, in which the newly developed sexual urges are sublimated and controlled. This is precisely the process implied in the title of the next poem in the sequence, "O Lull Me, Lull Me." Sexual imagery is very much toned down compared to the preceding poems; the figure of the mother appears only obliquely, in a reference to the moon. The young boy takes stock, as if to consolidate his gains: he is "an otter with only one nose" (*WW*, 78), his sexuality, like the otter's body, sub-

[18] Although the first poem of the sequence contains a vision of the father's death, it does not necessarily follow that he is dead throughout, since a strictly chronological order is not being used. The father need not be dead for his "ghost," the boy's projection of his spirit, to be significant.

merged, but very much there; he is more than he was when he was born. He is "ready to whistle," suggesting a tentative triumph over the persistent ghost, since, as we learned at the very start of the sequence, "A ghost can't whistle." (*WW*, 65)

Part Two

Part Two of *Praise to the End!* begins with what is perhaps the most important poem in this volume, "The Lost Son." It is a kind of epitome of the entire sequence and, as such, very much deserves the extensive critical attention it has received (including Roethke's own valuable comments in "Open Letter"). But before examining it in detail, we should take note of some of the ways in which the poems of Part Two in general differ from those of Part One.

The earlier poems deal with the formation of the individual in a fundamental, psychological sense; while the later poems recapitulate much of this material, they emphasize not the struggle for mere existence, but rather the struggle for a *significant* existence. Having emerged as an organism alive in the world, the protagonist must learn how to live harmoniously with the rest of creation; he must learn to transcend the apparent paradox of his dual (physical and spiritual) nature, and find his relation to reality as a unified being. The perspective from which each of the new meditations begin is that of an older person, past adolescence, exploring the nature and origins of his self, meeting a present spiritual crisis by probing his past, according to Jung's theories of regression and progression. The verse is therefore often more sophisticated than

in the earlier poems, which deal with the process of individuation from the point of view of the child trying to understand
what he is becoming rather than the adult trying to understand
what he has become; but there are frequent intentional lapses
back to the speech and thought of the younger child, for the
purpose is the reexperiencing of the past.

"The Lost Son," unlike any of the other poems of *Praise to
the End!*, has titles for each of its sections. The first, which presents the spiritual crisis that provoked the meditation, is called
THE FLIGHT. It is, in Roethke's words, "a terrified running away
—with alternate periods of hallucinatory waiting . . . ; the
protagonist . . . is hunting like a primitive, for some animistic
suggestion, some clue to existence from the sub-human." [19]
Fishing in "an old wound" (*WW*, 79), the repository of mental
scars,[20] the protagonist probes not only the private unconscious,
but the "sub-human" of the collective unconscious as well.
Roethke does not tell us the cause of this regressive flight, but
the poem itself suggests a reason: the crying of the dead at
Woodlawn. The father's ghost again threatens the lost son;
and the end of this section of the poem suggests that it is
specifically the boy's masculinity that is being threatened. The
image of otter as submerged sexual impulses, in a particularly
phallic form, is picked up from the last poem of Part One.
(*WW*, 81) The pattern should be familiar to us by now, for
we have seen it repeated continually as the child has grown
toward adulthood: the fear of latent sexuality becomes objec-
tified in the father's ghost; guilty for his probably incestuous
desires, the son feels cut off from his father, and, with the

[19] "Open Letter," *SP*, p. 38.
[20] Cf. the "wound" in "The Minimal." (*WW*, 59)

father dead, guilt is even more intense. In a religious sense, man is cut off from God by sin, by the very fact of his birth.

The slow, steady rhythms of THE PIT are in marked contrast to the alternation of tension and relaxation of the first section. The protagonist's regressive search has brought him back to an image of the womb; the scene is that of the first green-house poems, particularly "Root Cellar" and "Weed Puller." The mole stunning the dirt into noise seems to be a symbol of the impregnating male stirring the womb to life. The lost son has once again returned to the scene of his begetting, to the "slime of a wet nest" (*WW*, 81) from which he must emerge.

The third section, THE GIBBER, consists of "frenetic activity," followed by "almost erotic serenity," and finally a "rising agitation . . . rendered in terms of balked sexual experience, with an accompanying 'rant,' almost in the manner of the Elizabethans, and a subsequent near-blackout." [21] The "fre-netic activity" of the first three stanzas is crucial; in brilliantly concise imagery, Roethke has placed a clear analysis of the lost son's anxiety at the center of his poem:

> At the wood's mouth,
> By the cave's door,
> I listened to something
> I had heard before.
>
> Dogs of the groin
> Barked and howled,
> The sun was against me,
> The moon would not have me.
>
> The weeds whined,
> The snakes cried,

[21] "Open Letter," *SP*, p. 38.

> The cows and briars
> Said to me: Die.   (WW, 82)

The scene at the wood's mouth will be the setting—probably Dantesque—for attacks of anxiety throughout Roethke's work;[22] the cave's door seems to be the womblike symbol for the regressive journey rather than a Platonic reference (although both may be intended.) The dogs of the groin barking and howling are clearly the guilt-producing sexual urges; the sun is the father who has turned against the son, the moon is the mother who rejects the son's love. And the final stanza is a reliving of the child's expulsion from the state of union with an Eden-like natural world; the wages of sin is death.

In the "serene" lines that follow, there is one specific biblical reference ("Hath the rain a father?" Job 38: 28); but the imagery of the entire passage is taken from chapter 38 of Job, as are the questions about the origins of life in THE PIT. The alienation of Job from his Father is an important symbol of the poem's meaning; the protagonist's father appears here in his most frightening aspect. In terror, the child is seen attempting to commit a masturbatory sin against the scheme of things, the "time-order";[23] and with this sin is associated an acceptance of society's materialistic view of reality, still another violation of the natural order: "I have married my hands to perpetual agitation,/ I run, I run to the whistle of money." (WW, 83) This mixture of sexual and commercial imagery suggests an unsuccessful attempt to sublimate the sexual urges in equally sterile modes of action. The frantic activities and

[22] Cf. especially with "The Pure Fury" (WW, 158), "The Exorcism" (WW, 176), and "In a Dark Time." (FF, 79)

[23] Cf. "Moss-Gathering." (WW, 43)

fragmentary images must be focused before relief can be obtained; and this is precisely the function of the next section, THE RETURN.

Here we find a vision of the coming of " 'papa'— the papa on earth and in heaven are blended—there is the sense of motion in the greenhouse, my symbol for the whole of life, a womb, a heaven-on-earth." [24] This section sums up the movement of the entire poem, of the entire sequence: from darkness to light, from the unconscious to consciousness, from chaos to order, from the hell of the fire-pit to the coming of the heavenly Father, from exhaustion to renewal of potency with the coming of steam through the hot, moist pipes;[25] in this moment of rebirth, the entire greenhouse is stirred to life, morning replaces night, as warmth and "Ordnung" flood the world, and roses and chrysanthemums turn toward the light. The cycle of masturbation and renewed potency seems to provide a biological symbolism for spiritual rebirth. Onanism, for Roethke, is a violation of the natural order, a kind of death; it is a rejection of one's individuality, since it is a retreat from the establishment of one's personality in the real world. The renewal of potency then becomes a rebirth of possibilities of biological assertion of the self.

On a psychological level, the fear of paternal retribution, which formerly appeared obliquely, in obscure symbols, is traced to its origins, and dissipated by being revealed as irrational; the figure of God is no longer the dark and inscrutable tester of Job, but the giver of warmth and light, the source of order and life. (In the actual psychoanalytical process,

---

[24] "Open Letter," *SP*, p. 39.
[25] For meaning of pipes, see footnote 8, page 51, above.

transference would make a father-figure of the analyst, and this additional meaning seems to have been intended by Roethke.)[26] Seen no longer darkly, but face to face, the father inspires love rather than fear.

Obviously, a psychoanalytic interpretation of the poem is closely related to its images of spiritual growth; the early identification of father with God provides for an easy merging of these figures. But in the final section of "The Lost Son," a spiritual or religious theme seems to detach itself from the limitations of a biological base, and take on independent meaning and existence.

"In the final untitled section," [27] Roethke says, "the illumination, the coming of light suggested at the end of the last passage occurs again, this time to the nearly-grown man. But the illumination is still only partly apprehended; he is still 'waiting.'" [28] However, Roethke tells us nothing at all about the nature of the illumination. Does it proceed from the light of rational understanding; or does its glow have a mystical source, is it a flash of perception transcending reason and the senses? The crucial last stanzas of the poem are far from perfectly clear on this point, but they provide indications. Light moves over the field, then stops. The wind also stops, and then the mind moves, "not alone." It is silent.

> Was it light?
> Was it light within?
> Was it light within light?

[26] Stated by Roethke in a broadcast from Berkeley, Cal.

[27] In *Words for the Wind* (1958), the last section appeared for the first time with a title of sorts, the first line italicized and in parentheses: (*It was beginning winter.*)

[28] "Open Letter," *SP*, p. 39.

Stillness becoming alive,
Yet still?

A lively understandable spirit
Once entertained you.
It will come again.
Be still.
Wait.   (WW, 85)

The fact that the mind moves, "not alone," does indeed suggest the unitary consciousness; and the image of light within
light brings to mind the final canto of Dante's *Paradiso*. The
building of the rhythms to a climax, and their subsequent diminishing, seem to indicate the expansion of consciousness
associated with extrovertive mystic experience.[29] Perhaps more
convincing is the fact that this entire section is an elaboration
of the coming of light that accompanied seeing the father face
to face.

Many critics have seen in these lines a direct allusion to
Eliot's "still point of the turning world" ("Burnt Norton");
and their case is strengthened by the similarity of the beginning of the fifth section to the opening lines of "Little Gidding."
But there is no need to insist on this, since there are many
paths by which one may arrive at a mystical or quasi-mystical

[29] An extrovertive mystic experience involves the individual's perception of the unity of the world he sees, and of himself as part of that
unity. This should be distinguished from introvertive mystic experiences,
which involve a similar paradoxical unity of the individual's consciousness with something greater than itself; but this unity, unlike extrovertive unity, is nonsensuous as well as nonintellectual. This distinction, or
its equivalent, is made by most writers on mysticism. The above terminology in particular is used by W. T. Stace in *The Teachings of the Mystics* (New York, New American Library, 1960), pp. 15–26, and *Mysticism
and Philosophy* (Philadelphia, Lippincott, 1960), pp. 62–122.

approach to reality; Roethke himself may well have come by way of Vaughan, Traherne, Blake, and their tradition. The protagonist of "The Lost Son" has been seeking a means of regaining his childhood sense of union with nature, without losing the individuality of his adult identity. Threatened by complete annihilation in the absorbing embraces of maternal nature, as well as by complete isolation from paternal God, the son can only survive in the vision of oneness-in-separateness of the father bringing order and distinctness to the undifferentiated womb of the greenhouse; he is trying to ground his existence in the light of mystic perception. At this point, however, illumination is incomplete; there is by no means a final mystic union. And even if we can agree that Roethke is concerned with the mystic consciousness, his attitude toward this mode of experience often seems ambivalent. This "attitude" is a subject to which we shall often have occasion to return in the course of this study, and we must withhold our attempts at a conclusion regarding it until a much later point.

"The Long Alley" begins on the banks of a snakelike river, with its connotations of renewed sexual guilt and the fall from paradise; the protagonist has evidently lost most of the gains that led to the imperfectly apprehended vision at the close of "The Lost Son." As before, sexuality and sin are associated with death; but this time the source of destruction is represented by the industrial society that defaces and destroys its natural surroundings by polluting the waterways and the air. This desecration of the natural order is ironically justified by the "sulphurous water" as proceeding "from the glory of God." (*WW*, 86) We must remember, however, that in Roethke the outer landscape often corresponds to an inner state of mind.

And here, the dead fish floating in the snaky waters indicates
that the familiar guilt toward the father is again at work; the
boy's "crime" this time appears to be the acceptance of the
materialistic view of reality symbolized by the factory. In
"The Lost Son," we saw the association of commercial imagery,
the grasping for money, with masturbation; and society's materialism has in common with masturbation an unwillingness
to stand outside oneself and recognize the vitality and possibility in all of existence.

The feeling of separation from the natural world, the confinement of the soul by the materialistic philosophy, is further
developed in the second section: "The soul resides in the horse
barn./ Believe me, there's no one else, kitten-limp sister."
(*WW*, 86) The meaning of these lines may be clarified by one
of Blake's "Proverbs of Hell" (from *The Marriage of Heaven
and Hell*): "The tygers of wrath are wiser than the horses of
instruction." The soul is locked in the horse barn by the false
limits set up by reason, which dismisses an important part of
reality; the tyger, embodiment of passion (in contrast to the
rational horses), has been reduced to an ineffectual "kitten-
limp sister." That this is also an image of impotence seems
clear: "There's no joy in soft bones." (*WW*, 87) Struggling
toward illumination, the protagonist is confined by the nar-
cissisms of masturbation (biological-psychological) and materialism (spiritual): the protagonist ends by returning "the
gaze of a pond." (*WW*, 87) The imagery of confinement is
continued in the nursery rhymes of the third section: "My
love's locked in/ The old silo." (*WW*, 88) (Love must here be
understood in both sexual and spiritual terms.) The section
ends with a moment of self-realization, which paves the way

for renewed illumination. Detaching the head of a match (symbol both of masturbation and placing sulphur in the water) is seen as defeating the purpose of the cat (the protagonist); this is not the way to kill fish.

In the fourth section, having reestablished a sense of harmony with nature, the boy calls to the flowers and becomes a part of their world, surrounded by "light airs" and leaves. (*WW*, 89) Repetition of words and phrases conveys the intense excitement of this illumination; the angels, lost to the child in "Bring the Day!," are once more part of his world. The phrase "Nuts are money," in the fifth section, indicates an abandonment of society's artificial order for that of the natural world. The protagonist, no longer in need of his subhuman persona (the cat), asks that the dogs (of the groin?) be called off. The fish (father) have the breath of life brought to them by the wind; the lakes (mother) will be happy. And the son exchanges his paws for hands; they are again happy hands. The taking of the fire, with which the poem ends, is an acceptance of sexuality without guilt, uniting spiritual and material existence in a transcendent reality. As Blake said, "Man has no Body distinct from his Soul; for that call'd Body is a portion of Soul discern'd by the five Senses, the chief inlets of Soul in this age." (*Marriage*)

The stagnant water with which "A Field of Light" begins announces still another regressive journey to the slime, to the depths of the unconscious. The protagonist self-consciously seeks the source of his guilt against the father, against God, as he asks the angel within him whether he has ever cursed the "sun." (*WW*, 90) This time, the kissing of "the skin of a stone," that is, the recognition of the essential unity of being of even the inanimate world and the self, precedes the vision in the field of light:

I could watch! I could watch!
I saw the separateness of all things!
My heart lifted up with the great grasses;
The weeds believed me, and the nestling birds.
There were clouds making a rout of shapes crossing a windbreak
    of cedars,
And a bee shaking drops from a rain-soaked honeysuckle.
The worms were delighted as wrens.
And I walked, I walked through the light air;
I moved with morning.   (WW, 92–93)

There are several important points to be noted about this masterfully constructed passage. It begins with an emphasis on vision; the protagonist insists that he can see the separateness of all things. And yet, his heart is lifted up with the great grasses, there is communion with plant and animal life, he moves with the morning. As in "The Lost Son," where the mind moved "not alone," we seem to be involved in the paradoxical unity-in-separateness of the mystic's perception of reality. The protagonist retains his separate identity, but feels at one with the natural world.[30] And indeed, the rhythms of

[30] Roethke comments on this passage: "It is paradoxical that a very sharp sense of the being, the identity of some other being—and in some instances, even an inanimate thing—brings a corresponding heightening and awareness of one's own self, *and,* even more mysteriously, in some instances, a feeling of the oneness of the universe." "On 'Identity,'" *SP,* p. 25. Similarly, W. T. Stace cites Meister Eckhart—"Here all blades of grass, wood and stone, all things are One"—and comments, "There is no doubt that what Eckhart means is that he sees the three things as distinct and separate and yet at the same time not distinct but identical." *Teachings of the Mystics,* p. 16. Stace also quotes Boehme: "In this light my spirit saw through all things and into all creatures and I recognized God in grass and plants."

this passage, flowing to a peak, and then ebbing, seem a more complex version of the imitation of expansion of consciousness of "The Lost Son." Whether the experience described is meant to be an actual mystic experience, or, as is more likely, an intuition of the nature of existence that falls short of actual unitary consciousness, Roethke's protagonist clearly perceives an intimate relationship between himself and the natural world.

From the light of the field, "The Shape of the Fire" takes us back into the darkness of the womb. According to a former pupil of Roethke's, the line "An old scow bumps over black rocks" (*WW*, 93) is the mother's heartbeat as experienced by the embryo.[31] And phrases such as "Mother me out of here," and "In the hour of ripeness, the tree is barren," suggest both the wish to be born and the birth itself. The entire poem, and much of Roethke's work in general, is summarized in the concise, aphoristic verse of the third section:

> The wasp waits.
>> The edge cannot eat the center.
> The grape glistens.
>> The path tells little to the serpent.
> An eye comes out of the wave.
>> The journey from flesh is longest.
> A rose sways least.
>> The redeemer comes a dark way.   (*WW*, 95)

At first, this symbolism seems arbitrary, and some of it may very well be. But when viewed in the context of Roethke's work, the lines turn out to be suggestive and indefinite rather than impenetrable. The waiting wasp, possibly one of the

---

[31] Cited by Burke, p. 95.

"great lords of sting" (*WW*, 77) of "O Lull Me, Lull Me," seems ominously to threaten retribution; the sting may well be sexual. The phrase "The edge cannot eat the center" is partially explained by a line from a later poem, "First Meditation": "But the rind, often, hates the life within." (*WW*, 193) The dying body often hates the spirit within, and wishes to consume it, but it cannot; the spirit is able to endure. The center may also refer to the child, the new life, within the mother, and in this connection the glistening grape seems to be the child ready to be born, the ripe fruit of the opening section. The serpent crawling blindly may be either father begetting, or son being born. And the eye coming out of the wave is the act of creation itself, the coming of order to chaos, of vision to blindness, of form to flux. The long journey from flesh is both the act of being born, physically, and reborn, spiritually.[32] And the rose, traditional symbol of the mystic, present to herald the coming of Papa in "The Lost Son," is at the center of the mutable world; it is its "still point," its escape from flesh. The dark path of the redeemer is, to say the least, a suggestive image. It is: the path traveled both by the procreating father and by the new-born son; the movement from darkness to light of spiritual illumination; the source of faith in despair; the regressive journey that leads to self-understanding. It is the picture of life as the dynamic product of contending opposites, of a reality rooted in Boehme's Yes and No: only in the mystic light of illumination can the essential oneness of contraries be known.

The poem moves by processes that should by now be famil-

[32] Cf. "Those who rise from flesh to spirit know the fall," in "The Vigil." (*WW*, 123)

iar, from sexuality to the coming of spiritual light. In this case,
the fire seems to take part in the transformation; the boy speaks
with the fire, which appears to answer him in a "lewd whisper."
(*WW*, 95) But the proverbs that come from the tongue of the
flame, although basically sexual in meaning, offer a way from
flesh to spirit. And the evocation of the cool, silent light that
floods the last section of "The Shape of the Fire," miraculously capturing the calm tension of the moment of illumination, completes the metamorphosis of the hot flame's flickering
light:

> . . . light falls and fills, often without our knowing,
> As an opaque vase fills to the brim from a quick pouring,
> Fills and trembles at the edge yet does not flow over,
> Still holding and feeding the stem of the contained
> flower.   (*WW*, 96)

"Praise to the End!" recapitulates crucial materials and
brings the sequence to a kind of climax. The woods of "The
Lost Son" are now dark and more explicitly Dantesque; masturbation imagery, while still oblique, is no longer an undercurrent but the dominant theme. The boy addresses his "soft
mocker," and asks why he has "swelled like a seed"; then,
having relieved his "bone-ache," he says, "Father, forgive my
hands." Finally, describing the poem as a whole as well as its
initial act, the protagonist reminds us that "All risings/ Fall."
(*WW*, 97) Roethke explains that "a particular (erotic) act
occurs, then is accounted for by nonsense songs out of the
past."[33] The relation of masturbation to the child's fantasy of
his parents' sexual activities, described in these "nonsense
songs," has already been discussed in connection with the

[33] "Open Letter," *SP*, p. 40.

similar action of "Where Knock Is Open Wide." Between act and explanation is a nostalgic apostrophe to the protagonist's sexual organs of former times, his "bonny beating gristle," praising the happy life before the awareness of sexual guilt and responsibility; the style is distinctly that of Dylan Thomas, as we are told how the young child romped "down the summery streets of my veins,/ Strict as a seed, nippy and twiggy." (*WW*, 97)

The feeling of renewal after impotence, this time caused by "an exact fall of waters" (*WW*, 98), begins, as usual, with stones, and the breath of the wind. The boy, now thirteen years old, has a dream in which a bony image of the resurrection is combined with a vision of Jesus as fisherman giving new life to a fish (tossing it back, as the father did in "Where Knock Is Open Wide"). And the poem reaches its climax as the boy cries: "I feel more than a fish./ Ghost, come closer." (*WW*, 100) Having come to terms with the dead, no longer threatened by the father's ghost, the protagonist is ready to become the father, to assert his self.

But in this case, the final illumination does not take place; instead of moving forward with his new triumphs, the child turns back; all risings, fall. "I've crawled from the mire, alert as a saint or a dog;/ I know the back-stream's joy, and the stone's eternal pulseless longing." (*WW*, 100) The first sentence, reminiscent of "Cuttings, *later*" (*WW*, 38), seem clearly to indicate the journey from the slime. However, close examination reveals that the phrase is ambivalent; sexual guilt has been the protagonist's major problem, but neither saint nor dog has solved it in human terms. The dog lacks the will to sin and the self-consciousness necessary for guilt; the saint does not come to terms with sexual desires, but suppresses them entirely. The back stream now seems an ominous location, for we become aware that the feeling of union with the natural world is not accompanied this time by a feeling of human separateness: "I lost my identity to a pebble." (*WW*, 100)

For the first time in Part Two of *Praise to the End!*, the final section of a poem ends with emphasis on regression rather than progression: "I have been somewhere else; I remember the sea-faced uncles." (*WW*, 100) The protagonist is being drawn into the impersonality of the collective unconscious, rejecting the process of individuation in the final death wish, "Lave me, ultimate waters." The child-hero has been defeated, it seems, by the powers of the dark. But the very last line, hinting once more at light, suggests that this defeat is not permanent. As Roethke has commented, the protagonist ultimately rejects his onanistic death wish; "In terms of the whole sequence, he survives. . . . His self-consciousness, his very will to live saves him from the *annihilation* of the ecstasy." [34]

As the protagonist nears the achievement of his goal, the establishment of his self and of its relation to reality, his struggles intensify. This seems to have been the cause of the relapse at the end of "Praise to the End!"; and this is certainly the burden of the opening lines of "Unfold! Unfold!" "Eternity howls" in the crags of the cliffs that fling the hero back. These "last crags" are most difficult; the benefits of the field, place of light and illumination, are not easily separated from the threat

[34] "Open Letter," *SP*, p. 40.

of annihilation in empty eternity. The continued regressive explorations "back through those veins" are almost unendurable;
but there is no other choice. (*WW*, 101)

Encouraged by a "whelm of proverbs" issued by the adult
world, by the figure of the analyst, Mr. Pinch, the protagonist
makes a final effort at exploration of the unconscious.[35] The
time of the crossing of the soul, he has told us, using the
traditional Buddhist metaphor for the path to salvation,[36] is at
hand. Last time, he was so far back he "nearly whispered myself away"; he was "privy to oily fungus and the algae of standing waters." (*WW*, 102) And it is indeed tempting to remain
in this regressive state: "Easy the life of the mouth," before
awareness, before responsibility, before individuality. But the
dead are there to help; in the first stanza, they seem to be the
collective dead, the archetypal occupants of his conscious, but
here one voice, one "dead tongue"—which will be revealed as
the father's—is singled out as the spur necessary to goad the
lost son back on the path of revelation. And the poem's final
section contains the deepest insight into the mystical nature of
reality the protagonist has yet had:

> Sing, sing, you symbols! All simple creatures,
> All small shapes, willow-shy,
> In the obscure haze, sing!
>
> . . . .

[35] Mr. Pinch may be taken from the character in Dickens's *Martin
Chuzzlewit* or from Pinch in Shakespeare's *The Comedy of Errors;* this
character attempts to cure the "Insane": "I charge thee, Satan, hous'd
within this man,/ To yield possession to my holy prayers." (IV.iv. 56-57)

[36] See, for example, *The Teachings of the Compassionate Buddha,* ed.
E. A. Burtt (New York, New American Library, 1955), p. 118.

> A house for wisdom; a field for revelation.
> Speak to the stones, and the stars answer.
> At first the visible obscures:
> Go where the light is.   (*WW*, 102–3)

This is a clear restatement of the Hermetic doctrine of correspondences: *quod superius, sicut quod inferius.* In the great
chain of being, stones correspond to stars, the visible to the
invisible. The house, the place for study representing the con-
fining qualities of reason, leads to a limited kind of wisdom;
but the true revelation of the nature of reality must come in
the field, Roethke's place for mystic illumination, where one
can be in direct contact with the natural world. But in order
to avoid "the annihilation of the ecstasy," the mystic vision
must be expansive, separateness must be maintained even in
unity.

The doctrine of correspondences is of the greatest importance
in Roethke's poetry;[37] its insistent recurrence makes its origins
a point of legitimate interest. Most critics have assumed that
Roethke is an heir to the French symbolists.[38] But Roethke,
who did not read French, indicates no indebtedness to that
school in his essays; we must turn elsewhere for the main
theoretical basis of Roethke's techniques. This still leaves a
good many possibilities; but Roethke himself, writing of the
"steady storm of correspondences" of "In a Dark Time," gives

---

[37] See especially "Her Becoming" (*WW*, 202–203) and "In a Dark
Time." (*FF*, 79)

[38] Kenneth Burke writes: "The duality, in the apparent simplicity, of
his method probably leads back . . . to the kind of order statuesquely
expressed in Baudelaire's sonnet, 'Correspondences,' " p. 83. Other critics have followed this, insisting, as Burke does not, on the specifically
French source.

us a kind of hint, calling it "that term out of mystical literature," [39] rather than associating it with any particular poetic
tradition. This still leaves many possibilities. However, certain
other characteristics of Roethke's vision of reality suggest the
German mystic Jacob Boehme as the most significant of the
helping dead who thrash in the thicket, as the father-figure of
"Unfold! Unfold!" [40]

First, the doctrine of correspondences was prominent in the
work of Boehme most available to Roethke, *The Signatures of
All Things:* [41] "The whole world, exterior and visible, with its
essence, is but a sign or an appearance of the world that is
interior and spiritual; everything that is interior and latent has
an exterior correspondent." Second, Boehme, like Roethke, was
extremely fond of the plant world as the source of metaphor
for the mysterious Becoming of the universe: "Yes it opened
itself to me, from Time to Time, as in a Young Plant; . . .
The self then becomes conscious of the living reality of that
World of Becoming . . . in which the little individual life is
immersed." [42] (Boehme, like Roethke, often referred to himself as a tree.) [43] Third, Boehme's most famous illumination

[39] In Ostroff, p. 217. The tradition that runs from Boehme to Swedenborg to Blake is suggested.

[40] Although the dead, or ghost, as an individual, is usually the father,
Roethke regarded several figures in the past as spiritual fathers. See, for
example, The Dying Man (*WW*, 187–90), where father and Yeats are
merged.

[41] London, 1912. However, the book is now out of print; I am quoting
from Berdyaev's essay in *Six Theosophic Points and Other Writings* (Ann
Arbor, University of Michigan Press, 1958), p. viii. (In the original, the
reference is to III.2.)

[42] Quoted by Underhill in *Mysticism* (New York, Meridian, 1955), pp.
257–58.

[43] See *Confessions of Jacob Boehme,* ed. W. S. Palmer (London, Me-
thuen, 1920), *passim.*

took place in a field, the locus of Roethke's floods of light, the place for revelation.[44] And finally, Boehme's extrovertive mysticism, based on the theosophical doctrine of correspondences, emphasizes the multiplicity as well as the unity of reality, the separateness as well as the oneness of things. Hans Martensen expresses the classic distinction:

> Practical mysticism . . . often manifests hostility to nature. . . . Theosophy, on the contrary, is eagerly attracted towards nature, and Boehme often says how pleasant it is to wander among the flowers on a fine summers day, because it is then clearly perceptible how everything sprouts and grows, blooms and emits fragrance in the living and all-replenishing power of God. As the mysticism of the mind, Theosophy is attracted, not only to the *microcosm* of the soul, but to the *macrocosm,* to the universe and the universal life in all its multiplicity, but in all this multiplicity it beholds only one.[45]

There is no reason to insist that Roethke actually read Boehme before his period of great interest in and study of philosophical and religious works (which began shortly after the publication of these poems), although this is certainly possible. But in any case, the comparison with Boehme should shed further light on the nature of Roethke's approach to reality.

This approach is perhaps best characterized by the phrase "The eye perishes in the small vision" (*WW,* 102), which precedes the revelation of "Unfold! Unfold!" This brings to mind William Blake, whose indebtedness to Boehme is far more certain than Roethke's (and whose works may have led Roethke to Boehme): "May God us keep/ From single vision

[44] See Underhill, p. 256.
[45] *Jacob Boehme,* ed. Stephen Hobhouse (London, Rockliff, 1949), p. 16.

& Newton's sleep!" ("Letter to Thomas Butts, 22 Nov. 1802")
And the next poem in the sequence, "I Cry, Love! Love!," taking its title from Blake's *Visions of the Daughters of Albion,*
emphasizes the mystic, or intuitive, mode of perception as the
way to a true vision of reality. Like Blake, Roethke disparages
the possibilities of the rational faculties, calling reason a
"dreary shed, that hutch for grubby schoolboys!" (*WW,*
104)[46] Blake is here a "thingy spirit," emphasizing the presence of the eternal in the concrete. Another illumination
occurs and Roethke, calling on "willie" to walk in the wind,
proclaims "once more a condition of joy." [47] The dry bones of
resurrection are then alluded to, and finally the stones, which
always seem to accompany Roethke's descriptions of mystic
intuition, appear.

But in the third section, there is a sudden exhaustion; the
protagonist hears "the owls, the soft callers, coming down
from the hemlocks." The diminishing rhythms allude to the
process of regression and progression, and end in a beautiful,
but unmistakable, death wish; the desire to be swallowed up
overcomes the need for separateness. As the gently rocking
water recedes, birth and death imagery unite; the dark, womblike lake, which "We never enter/ Alone," is both beginning
and end of the journey.

"I Cry, Love! Love!" was originally the last poem in *Praise
to the End!* However, perhaps because of the negative ending,
with its implicit acceptance of the death wish, Roethke added
a poem to the sequence when it was reprinted in *The Waking*

[46] Cf. Elinor Wylie, "Nonsense Rhyme": "Reason's a rabbit in a
hutch."
[47] Cf. Roethke's dance with Blake in "Once More the Round." (*FF,*
95)

(1953). Much of "O, Thou Opening, O" is a recapitulation of old materials: birth and creation, the vision of the father face to face, aphorisms which express the conflict and Becoming of the world, the journey from the darkness of the womb and sexual guilt to spiritual light. But certain sections, particularly the "prose" of the second section, seem specifically to reject the "easy" kind of mysticism, "that pelludious Jesus-shimmer." (*WW*, 108) The problem of aloneness cannot be solved by giving up the self, the life of the spirit cannot be attained by denial of the flesh. "The dark has its own light," says the protagonist, "A son has many fathers." (*WW*, 108) Roethke embraces all of reality, he repudiates light that has no relation to the dark; his redeemer must come a dark way. (Cf. *WW*, 95) And Roethke denies the validity of "single vision"; the multiplicity of our "fathers," the dead who affect our lives, reflects the complexity of our own nature.[48] The "Yes" with which this section ends seems closely related to the "yes" that concludes Joyce's *Ulysses;* each is an affirmation of the value of the totality of our experience. And this union of flesh and spirit informs the poem's conclusion: "flesh has airy bones"; the "near" but still seeking poet asks his skin to be true to him. (*WW*, 110)

In this last poem, Roethke clearly rejects ascetic mysticism; even extrovertive mysticism is viewed ambivalently, since it so easily becomes a denial of this world, and grounds the source of meaning in another. "Going is knowing" (*WW*, 110) Roethke says, near the conclusion of his sequence.[49] Perhaps, he hints, there is no "knowing," no penetration of the world

[48] Cf. footnote 40.
[49] Cf. "I learn by going where I have to go," "The Waking." (*WW*, 124)

of appearances, apart from the "going," our limited, everyday perceptions of reality; perhaps there is a faith transcending mystic experience, born of despair, the true light in darkness. As Ingmar Bergman phrased it, in *The Magician*, "One walks step by step into the darkness. The motion itself is the only truth." [50] But the suggestion of a possibility is not equivalent to its acceptance; this marks the beginning rather than the end of one of the major areas of conflict in Roethke's thought.

Roethke's attempt to "trace the spiritual history of the protagonist (not 'I' personally but of all haunted and harried men," [51] is probably his most original achievement; for many readers, it will remain his best. No one had previously written anything quite like the poems of *Praise to the End!*, and it is hard to imagine anyone successfully imitating them in the future. Yet, it is difficult to define precisely what it is that Roethke has done that no one else had.

Kenneth Burke, starting a fruitful line of thought, wrote: "Though Roethke has dealt always with very concrete things, there is a sense in which these very concretions are abstractions." [52] Burke seems to be referring to the fact that through the repeated use of obsessive imagery to define particular states of mind, Roethke has created from this imagery a kind of new language, a new mode of abstraction from reality. Hilton Kramer combines this idea with his own recognition of a "new primitivism": "Primitivism and abstraction—once they seemed to us polar opposites; and we have indeed come full cycle

[50] *Four Screenplays of Ingmar Bergman*, trans. Malstrom and Kushner (New York, Simon and Schuster, 1960), p. 291.

[51] "An American Poet Introduces Himself and His Poems," *SP*, p. 10.

[52] Burke, p. 107.

when they meet in a single sensibility. . . . Both abstraction and primitivism suppress history, and thereby suppress the human image in which our values subsist." [53]

However, to call Roethke's concretions abstractions is to impose upon a symbolism, which in fact depends on its suggestiveness for the depth of its effect, an artificial rigidity; and any analysis of Roethke's language which calls it "the loose diction of a view which has not yet learned to recognize human moral history as anything separate from life as a primordial whole" [54] is surely overemphasizing psychological themes at the expense of the moral and spiritual processes they often represent. But these speculations do perhaps lead us after all to the unique nature of Roethke's achievement: rather than remaining within the limits of a prerational or prehistorical sense of life, Roethke uses that sense to define and illuminate rational and historical action; that is to say, he has evolved an effective moral symbolism from the self-centered (and therefore amoral) world of primary process thought. [55] It is a kind of ultimate correspondence between inner and outer (private and public) realities. By tracing myth, symbol, and even language, to their origins within the human mind, Roethke is able

[53] Kramer, pp. 145–46.

[54] *Ibid.*, p. 132.

[55] Primary process thought, characteristic of the child, the dream world, and the schizophrenic, may be described as follows: "First: the more 'primary' the thinking, the more it is organized and controlled by drives. Second: primary thinking can be recognized not only from its preoccupation with instinctual aims. It also has certain peculiar formal characteristics. These include autistic logic instead of straight thinking, loose and nonsensical types of association links, and distortion of reality in numerous ways." *Schizophrenia: A Review of the Syndrome,* ed. L. Bellak (New York, Logos, 1958), pp. 18–19.

to use them to convey with great psychological acuteness and emotional power a process of spiritual development most often described in terms of lifeless abstractions and conventional formulas that have lost their meaning. In short, he is recharging language with experience.

An intuitive feeling for evocative particulars, for words that stir images deep within the mind of the reader, is certainly crucial to Roethke's success. But not least important to his efforts to portray the reality of inner life are the rhythms with which he attempts "to catch the movements of the mind itself." [56] From the comparatively crude imitation of the crushing action of the machine—dropping the final foot of each stanza—in "The Adamant," Roethke's mastery of his verse's movement evolved to the complex imitations of expansion of consciousness of "The Lost Son" and "A Field of Light," the communication of sexual excitement in the rapid movement of nursery jingles, the use of diminishing rhythms to accompany, among other things, the fading death wish.

In a rather technical article, Charlotte Lee summarizes the ways in which Roethke achieves the building up and relaxation of tensions by means of rhythmic patterns: "The interplay of lines of approximate but not identical length, the number and placement of the stresses within those lines, and the treatment of terminal degrees of stress must therefore constitute a deliberate method, which the poet consciously employs to create tension and *emotional* imbalance." [57]

We can most appropriately end this chapter with Roethke's own judgment of *Praise to the End!:* "It is the longish pieces

[56] "An American Poet Introduces Himself and His Poems," *SP*, p. 20.
[57] Lee, p. 22.

that really break ground—if any ground is broken. And it is these that I hope the younger readers, in particular, will come to cherish. I think of myself as a poet of love, a poet of praise. And I wish to be read aloud." [58]

[58] "Theodore Roethke Writes . . ." *SP*, p. 60.

CHAPTER 5

The Ghostly Dance

1952 – 1953

The first three poems of the New Poems of *The Waking* (1953),[1] all originally published in 1950, share many of the characteristic qualities of tone and style of *Praise to the End!* "The Visitant" in particular echoes the content as well as the techniques of the earlier volume. A voice calls, "Stay by the slip-ooze." (WW, 113) The familiar regression to the slime has taken place; and the protagonist emerges from the mire, as he did in "Praise to the End!" "alert as a dog." The sense of communion with nature is again expressed in terms of "the stone's eternal pulseless longing" (WW, 100): "I felt the pulse of a stone." (WW, 113)

However, this poem is not all repetition; the particularly beautiful evocation of the female visitant strikes a new and

[1] *The Waking* has been reprinted intact as Part One of *Words for the Wind* (1958). It includes a selection of seventeen poems from *Open House*; all the greenhouse poems (with the addition of "Frau Bauman, Frau Schmidt, and Frau Schwartze") and most of parts II and III of *The Lost Son*; all of *Praise to the End!* (with the addition of "O, Thou Opening, O"); and a selection of New Poems (called Shorter Poems, 1951–1953 in *Words for the Wind*). It is this latter section, consisting of five short poems and Four for Sir John Davies with which this chapter will be concerned.

important note in Roethke's poetry. While in the earlier poems there were frequent hints of apparitions, and personifications of the spirit, they were not described in any detail, and certainly were not at the heart of any poem. And more significant than the mere personification of the spirit is the fact that it is embodied in the image of woman, an image which dominates the entire last part of *The Waking*.

"A Light Breather" is another delicate portrait of the spirit, this time in terms of plants, minnow, and snail; in spite of the poem's gentle rhythms, there seems to be no real connection between the female personification of the previous poem and "music in a hood," the figure of some "small thing,/ Singing." (*WW*, 115) And yet there may be more of a link between these images than is at first apparent. The only other use of "hood" in Roethke's poetry is in "Sensibility! O La!" a poem of the same period, in which the protagonist asks his mother to put on her dark hood. (*WW*, 76) In addition, the movement of the spirit in "The Visitant" and in "A Light Breather" is expressed in similar rhythms, and even in terms of a common analogy (fish). Although these indications are hardly decisive, "A Light Breather" need not be completely excluded from the pattern of woman-dominated poems.

The figure of woman is viewed in a soberer light in "Elegy for Jane, *My Student, Thrown by a Horse*," the first, and perhaps the finest, of Roethke's elegies. In a remarkable shift of tone, the now familiar vocabulary—birds, fish, plants, stones —is adapted to new purposes. The dead girl is established early in the poem as one of the small, loved creatures of the world; her death is a violation of the natural order, and, more important, a denial of the notion that life continues through those

who remain. The last words of this moving poem are a recognition not of any consoling powers, but of the finality of
nature's cycle: the contrast between the neckcurls like *damp*
tendrils, and the *damp* grave, is absolute.[2]

In "Old Lady's Winter Words," the antecedent to Meditations of an Old Woman, there is a sharp shift in style, marking
the end of the *Praise to the End!* period; the slow, flowing lines
of the earlier poems have given way to the tense, quick, and
tough rhythms of this soliloquy. However, the poems of the
section we have been considering are united not by style but
by the image of woman, in this case, the poet's mother. Since,
for the first time in Roethke's poetry, the experience of a poem
is recorded not in the mind of the poet (or a near double, as
in *Praise to the End!*), but by means of an apparently alien
persona, it is essential that we understand the nature of this
dominant image before going any further. And by now we
have gathered sufficient evidence to draw some conclusions.

She seems to be no particular woman—she appears as personification of the spirit, student, mother, and (in Four for Sir
John Davies) both the sensual partner and figure of Beatrice
—but rather an image of woman in general. She is often larger
than life, and, in "The Visitant" and the Davies poems, she
seems at least partially a projection of the poet's mind. All this,

---

[2] In "Some Remarks on Rhythm," *SP*, p. 82, Roethke describes the
methods of this poem: "enumeration, the favorite device of the more ir-
regular poem. . . . Then the last three lines in the [first] stanza lengthen
out. . . . A kind of continual triad. In the last two stanzas, exactly the
opposite occurs. . . . There is a successive shortening of line length, an
effect I have become inordinately fond of, I'm afraid. This little piece
indicates in a way some of the strategies for the poet writing without the
support of a formal pattern—he can vary his line length, modulate, he
can stretch out the line, he can shorten."

together with our knowledge of Roethke's interest in Jung, leads us to the idea of the anima, which Jung describes as follows:

> An inherited collective image of woman exists in a man's unconscious, with the help of which he apprehends the nature of woman. . . . So long as the anima is unconscious she is always projected, for everything unconscious is projected. The first bearer of the soul-image is always the mother; later it is borne by those women who arouse the man's feelings, whether in a positive or negative sense. . . . Just as the father acts as a protection against the dangers of the external world and thus serves his son as a model persona, so the mother protects him against dangers that threaten from the darkness of the psyche.[3]

If the poems of *Praise to the End!* represent the son's search for the father, the wish to be reconciled with him and, by finding his own self, to become the father, the New Poems of *The Waking* seem to be an invocation of the anima, an appeal for assistance in dealing with the still unconquered forces of the unconscious. And, for the poet, the anima seems to afford a convenient ground for the projection of the torments of his own soul. It is in the light of this concept that we must understand Roethke's taking on the persona of his mother in "Old Lady's Winter Words." The poem represents not only Roethke's intuition of his mother's thoughts and feelings (as drawn—according to Jung—from the anima), but also the projection of his own soul when confronted with the prospect of death, of nonbeing.

The "old lady" first longs for a glimpse of the world beyond

[3] *Two Essays on Analytical Psychology* (New York, Meridian, 1956), pp. 200–1, 207–8.

death, "for some minstrel of what's to be." (*WW*, 117) Unable
to see forward, her thoughts turn to the past, but this too
eludes her; her "good day has gone." And then the entire poem
is brought to a focus in a manner by now completely characteristic of Roethke; the sense of waiting for death—the old
lady's, the soul's—is given a correspondence in the outer world:
the old lady listens for the "thin sound" in the chimney, "The
fall of the last ash/ From the dying ember." (*WW*, 118) The
"self-delighting" days of the flesh are then successfully recalled
and contrasted, without passion, to her present, shrunken physical existence. The will to live is dying with the flesh, her "dust
longs for the invisible." And accompanying the final coming
of death is the increasing sense of aloneness, of separation from
the world of nature, of the end of life as negation rather than
an entrance into another world; it is perhaps the most pessimistic conclusion in all of Roethke's poetry. As the old lady draws
more and more into herself, her spirit hardens.

And yet these lines are not entirely without comfort. Not in
content, for the emptiness of the poem's vision holds no solace;
but rather in the verse's tough, unsentimental tone. The diction is even barer than in the supposedly stripped-down early
poems; and adjectives are used more sparingly than ever. But
it is the rhythms of the poem which do most to produce its
sense of direct confrontation of reality. The lines are shorter
than in previous poems, their flow is not allowed to continue
soothingly. The rhythm is that of speech tensely uttered between clenched teeth, restrained and strong. There is no ro-
manticizing of the "good day" of the past, there is no self-pity
at its having gone. Only once in the poem does rage at the human condition threaten to break through, and even here its

expression is controlled and conditional: "if I were a young man,/ I could roll in the dust of a fine rage." (*WW*, 118) This is strong-lined, classic verse in the same sense that the poetry of Yeats's maturity was strong-lined and classic. And from this point on, the influence of the Irish poet will be of the greatest significance to Roethke's own work.

Yeats is beyond question the most important of Roethke's "spiritual fathers." And this is hardly surprising when one considers the common characteristics these two poets share. Both protested strongly against a materialistic view of reality, and against the modes of social conduct based upon it; both were interested in the possibilities of knowing spiritual reality directly by means of mystic or theosophic systems; both were concerned with the tensions between body and spirit, between the temporal and the eternal; and both used their arts to confront the emptiness of death, to construct a vision that would endure. Four for Sir John Davies is, in one way or another, involved with each of these mutual concerns; and although no epigraph is given, Roethke's text for his exploration of the creation of the eternal from the temporal, the spiritual from the sensual, could be taken from Yeats's "Ego Dominus Tuus," where Dante, "mocked by Guido for his lecherous life," "found/ The most exalted lady loved by a man."

Four for Sir John Davies

"The Dance" of the first portion of the Davies poems is, in part, Yeats's dance from which the dancer cannot be distinguished; it is the symbol of the living of one's life, of the creation of art. However, as the title of the entire sequence indicates, the primary reference of "The Dance" is the six-tenth-century poem which outlined the metaphor of the universe as harmonious dance, "Orchestra." And although this is the poem in which Roethke wrote those ill-fated lines—"I take this cadence from a man named Yeats,/ I take it, and I give it back again" (*WW*, 120)—which caused critics from this point on to see Yeats's ghost wherever they turned, the cadences of this particular poem are probably less like Yeats's than, for example, those of "Old Lady's Winter Words."

Roethke commented: "Oddly enough the line 'I take this cadence, etc.' is, in a sense, a fib. I had been reading deeply in Ralegh, and Sir John Davies; and they rather than Willie are the true ghosts in that piece." [4] And although the stanzaic pattern of Roethke's poem is similar to many of Yeats's adaptations of traditional forms, it is also a close variation on the stanza used by Davies:

> Lo, this is Dancing's true nobility:
> Dancing, the child of Music and of Love;
> Dancing itself, both love and harmony,
> Where all agree and all in order move;
> Dancing, the art that all arts do approve;
>   The fair character of the world's consent,
>   The heav'n's true figure, and th' earth's
>   ornament.   (ll. 666–72)

Roethke's purposely unsophisticated use of end-stopped lines in an effort to produce something bare and powerful is far

---

[4] "How to Write Like Somebody Else," *SP*, p. 69. However, Roethke also insisted Yeats's spirit—one of the "helping dead"—was literally present in the room when the poem was written. See "On 'Identity,'" *SP*, 24.

closer to the techniques of Davies and Raleigh than of Yeats.[5] Yeats's ghost is certainly invoked in an effort to reestablish the "universal dance," and even has a modifying effect on the poem's rhythms, and its occasional slant rhymes ("moon"-"none," "song"-"tongue," "Yeats"-"beats"); but there is by no means any slavish imitation obscuring Roethke's own identity.

"The Dance" begins by acknowledging that the image of harmony is "slowing in the mind of man/ That made him think the universe could hum." (*WW*, 120) The orderly chain of existence has been broken, the circle shattered; material and spiritual aspects of reality are no longer in step. But the poet, who had promised to "sing and whistle romping with the bears," commits himself to the dance in spite of this. Alone, but "dancing-mad," the poet somehow exceeds "the joyless union of a stone." Not only does he sway with the bears in the rhythms of nature, he also surpasses his natural existence and, like Yeats, tries to fling his shadow at the moon.[6]

But a man alone can dance only so far; "The Partner" begins with the poet perplexed between "animal and human heat" (*WW*, 121), between the mindless motions of the bears and Yeats's higher dance. And so, like Yeats, like Dante, Roethke furthers his art, and his mystic perceptions of reality, through the figure of a woman; once again, the dominant image of the last part of *The Waking* makes her appearance.

Characterized as "the body of his fate," the partner of this ghostly dance is first placed in a Yeatsian context.[7] However,

---

[5] Roethke points this out in "How to Write Like Somebody Else," *SP*, p. 70.

[6] This may be a reference to Yeats's "Phases of the Moon."

[7] "Body of Fate," like "Phases of the Moon," is a phrase from *The Vi-*

kissing the poet, and then doing "something else," she is introduced as an unmistakably sensual woman rather than as a mystical symbol. And it is the sensual itself that provides the key with which to transcend the senses; inspired by the music of the "lively dead" (Davies, Raleigh, Yeats, Dante), this couple seem to find, in the intensity of physical experience, something beyond flesh. They shout to a horse (symbol of reason from "The Long Alley") that they live beyond their outer skin, that they are experiencing a joy which outleaps the animality of a dog. A "ghost" is awakened; once again it seems to be distinguished from the collective "dead," and represents the protagonist's father, or, as is more appropriate in this case, a projection of the protagonist's sexuality. The use of the word "ghost"—which can mean "spirit"—is particularly apt here, since it is the vehicle which unites, or seems to unite, the sundered worlds of flesh and spirit, which reestablishes the "universal dance"; both body and soul now play in the "dark world where gods have lost their way." (*WW*, 121)

This last line of "The Partner" has generally been understood to refer to the world of the passions, or, at any rate, to a world that is specifically human and not supernatural.[8] However, the context of the entire sequence suggests a more important meaning. The "dark world" is the result of the breakdown of the "universal dance"; it is a world without meaning, without order, without spiritual truth, unless its darkness can be transcended by love—it is the world of impermanence and death.

---

sion (New York, Macmillan, 1956), Yeats's mystical interpretation of reality.

[8] See, for example, Mills, *Theodore Roethke*, p. 33.

In this world, the gods, symbols of immortality, are indeed swallowed up.

This interpretation is supported by the first stanza of "The Wraith," which brings the entire sequence to a focus. The "pastures of the dead," where the couple continue their dance attended by both gaiety and dread, are not simply the dwelling places of the "lively dead"; for these pastures stretch "before" as well as "behind." They represent the world of nonbeing, the "dark world," that surrounds the poet and his partner during the brief "darkening day" of their life. (*WW*, 121–122) Only through love can the couple escape the harsh terms of their existence.

The dance now becomes a metaphor for sexual intercourse; but the language and imagery of the poem never let the reader forget the spiritual implications of this physical love. Certain lines recall John Donne's "The Extasie," with its similar vision of the union of body and soul in love. Each becomes the other, as the partner "laughed me out, and then she laughed me in;/ In the deep middle of ourselves we lay." (*WW*, 122) Here, the images of intercourse, and of two souls (or spheres) as one are united, as the couple take "arms against their own obscurity." And the poem ends with an explicit representation of the creation of the spiritual from the sensual: at the sensual cry, a shape leaps forward, a shape that "was and was not she." (*WW*, 122) Sexual climax becomes a complex symbol which draws together the meanings of the poem; it represents the creation of spiritual love from physical, of the work of art from "reality," of the eternal from the temporal, of meaningful existence from the emptiness of a "dark World." And not least important, this shape "Impaled on light" represents the projection of the soul, or anima, upon a living woman.

The development of the anima in the New Poems of *The Waking* roughly follows its development, according to Jung, within the individual mind; it has progressed from a projection of the unconscious as spirit (its state in primitive man), to a projection on the mother, to a projection on a sexual partner. And finally, in "The Vigil," it is identified with the classic instance of woman protecting man from the dark powers of psyche or soul and leading him to light and salvation: Dante's Beatrice.[9]

The first stanza recapitulates the creation of the spiritual from the physical, and defines the figure of Beatrice as a projection of Dante's mind upon a living woman, as a vision summoned and declared "pure." (*WW*, 123) However, projection of the poet's mind or not, the figure of Beatrice is shown to be an effective guide for transcending the physical universe. Echoing the mystic vision of "Unfold! Unfold!" (*WW*, 103), Roethke writes: "The visible obscures." All things, all manifestations of concrete reality, are seen as "shards" of the poet, suggesting the subjectivity of the relation between visible and invisible reality, and, by implication, of the figure of Beatrice. The entire action is shown against the background of a "dark night," a "black/ And shapeless night that made no answer back" (*WW*, 123), which, along with the "dark wood," emerges as Roethke's main symbol for the anxiety produced by the individual's confrontation of his own impermanence, of imminent

[9] Although it is tempting to identify Beatrice with the poet's wife, Mrs. Roethke has told me that the poem was written before she and Roethke were well acquainted.

nonbeing. However, the lovers defy the mocking darkness, and combine sexual ecstasy with the mystic vision of transcendent reality of the last cantos of *Paradiso*:

> Alive at noon, I perished in her form.
> Who rise from flesh to spirit know the fall:
> The word outleaps the world, and light is all.

(*WW*, 123)

In spite of this apparently unambiguous conclusion, no clear-cut philosophical position emerges from this poem; the central paradox—the vision that is both real and not real—is neither resolved nor completely assimilated as a final perception of reality. And a second look at the poem's last lines reveals that their meaning is not so clear as first appears. The merging of sexual union ("I perished in her form"), which is highly impermanent, with mystic union, which partakes of the eternal, is simply a renewal of the paradox. The victory over the powers of darkness and nonbeing of Four for Sir John Davies is at best tentative; and this sets the pattern for the bulk of Roethke's remaining poetry, which is characterized by a tormenting vacillation between hope and despair rather than by any consistent point of view.

It should be no surprise, then, to discover that "The Waking," which stands as a kind of epilogue to Four for Sir John Davies, makes no reference to the transcending of the natural world of the previous sequence, but rather marks a return to the stoical position of "Old Lady's Winter Words." "The Waking" takes the form of a villanelle. This serves to emphasize Roethke's return to traditional forms after the free verse and experimentation of the greenhouse poems and *Praise to the*

End![10] And the villanelle is perfectly suited to a poem dealing with man's involvement in the natural cycle.

"Going is knowing" (*WW*, 110) wrote Roethke at the end of *Praise to the End!*, denying the possibility of knowledge transcending the limits of man's temporal condition. "The Waking" applies a similar check to the mystic claims of Four for Sir John Davies; the protagonist learns only "by going where I have to go." (*WW*, 124) There is no denial of the finality of the natural cycle when applied to the individual; there is only the faith that this cycle is "right." [11] The epithet "stoic" can be applied in its strictest sense; the "rightness of the natural cycle seems based on a conception of a "Nature" very similar to the Stoic's *logos:* "Great nature has another thing to do/ To you and me." (*WW*, 124) Nature's last operation is, of course, death, the swallowing up of our individual existences into the impersonal natural order. We can only acquiesce; the poem's central image is that of a purgatory without paradise, of the ultimate equality of man with the worm who "climbs up the winding stair." The poem's slow, steady rhythms support its meaning; the end-stopped lines, miraculously avoiding monotony, convey the sense of step-by-step

[10] However, it should not be supposed that Roethke completely abandoned the use of freer rhythms; while the traditional lyric forms an important part of Roethke's poetry from this point on, it does not overshadow Meditations of an Old Woman or the North American Sequence, both of which develop the techniques of *Praise to the End!* Roethke scrupulously chooses the appropriate form for each particular poem. Four for Sir John Davies, for example, requires the regular rhythms and consistent framework of the dance.

[11] Cf. the key line in Roethke's last villanelle, "The Right Thing": "The right thing happens to the happy man." (*FF*, 94)

movement. "The Waking" is one of Roethke's most successful unions of form and content.

The New Poems of *The Waking* marks a crucial point in Roethke's poetry. In keeping with the indications of *Open House*, Roethke devotes his verse to the various modes of exploring the self; but now we encounter a shift in emphasis. Roethke's poetry has previously been concerned with the self from the point of view of its origins and development; to this end the growth metaphors of the greenhouse poems, and the regressive journeys in search of individual consciousness of *Praise to the End!* were employed. Threats to the self appeared primarily in terms of relapse. But from this point on the threat increasingly approaches from the future rather than the past. The death with which Roethke is now concerned is not metaphorical (as, for example, onanism, or psychological relapse), but the real death, the physical dissolution of the individual being.

Roethke's attitude toward these matters is not consistent: he moves from utter despair, to resignation, to mystic faith, to faith beyond mysticism, and back to despair. We shall not find in his poems the development of a systematic philosophy; there emerges rather the complex figure of a man directly confronting the limitations of his existence, with none of life's possibilities—not joy nor hopelessness nor indifference—excluded.

CHAPTER 6

Being and Nonbeing

1954 – 1958

In 1958, Theodore Roethke published his major collection of poetry, *Words for the Wind*.[1] The New Poems of this volume reflect several events in the poet's life: his marriage to Beatrice O'Connell in 1953, his readings in philosophy and religion, and a period of extreme anxiety and illness just before the publication of the book. His readings (consisting mainly of existentialist theologians such as Kierkegaard, Martin Buber, and Paul Tillich, and writers on various aspects of mystic experience)[2]

[1] *Words for the Wind* actually appeared first in London in 1957; it was the only book by Roethke published in England. It was issued in New York the next year, with the addition of the following poems: "The Pure Fury," "The Renewal," "Plaint," "The Swan," "The Exorcism," and "Her Becoming."

Part One of *Words for the Wind* is entitled The Waking and is an exact reprint of that earlier volume. Part Two, New Poems, consists of five unnumbered divisions: Lighter Pieces and Poems for Children (An Interlude); Love Poems; Voices and Creatures; The Dying Man (In Memoriam: W. B. Yeats); and Meditations of an Old Woman. This chapter will be concerned with the New Poems; however, no special attention will be given Lighter Pieces and Poems for Children, which forms, as Roethke indicated, an interlude, and is not essential to the development of his serious verse.

[2] The general drift of Roethke's readings was supplied by his widow, and by Stanley Kunitz, in conversation. However, more specific conclusions will be drawn from the poetry itself in the course of this study.

correspond to the fundamental themes of his new poetry: the nature of the self, and of its being-in-the-world. And his marriage and illness respectively correspond to the extremes of joy and despair which give this poetry its sense of conflict and tension. The remarkable fusion of these three concerns, the transformation of love and anxiety into modes of metaphysical exploration, makes Roethke's Love Poems one of the most effective sequences of its kind in contemporary poetry.

Love Poems

The poems which make up this division are not identical in subject or tone: some are concerned with love in its sometimes delightful, sometimes terrifying, purely physical aspects; the greatest number are, in varying degrees, centered on the figure of the beloved as the means of the poet's salvation; and a few, which scarcely seem to justify the label "love poem" at all, seem placed in this sequence to emphasize Roethke's belief that to be able to love, one must have a full understanding of aloneness, that in order to arrive at faith, one must first be immersed in despair.

The first of the purely sensual poems, "I Knew a Woman," seems, at first glance, completely innocent; but closer examination reveals that the poem's words, like its lady, move "more ways than one." (*WW*, 151) Double meanings dominate the poem: the lady teaches "Turn, and Counter-turn, and Stand"; the protagonist comes "behind her for her pretty sake"; and love, which likes a gander, "adores a goose." Even lines easily passed over have hidden sexual connotations: ". . . what prodigious mowing we did make." "To mow," in Scots dialect, means to have sexual intercourse. And should there be any doubt as to Roethke's knowledge of this meaning, the reader need only turn to "Reply to a Lady Editor" (*WW*, 133), the poet's tongue-in-cheek response to the editor of a woman's magazine who had clearly missed the poem's suggestiveness; Roethke there calls Dan Cupid a "braw laddie-buck," and advises the editor just to lean herself back if he should arrive.

This is the lighter side of sensuality; but it also has its terrors, reminding us that we are fastened to a dying animal. In "The Sensualists," the familiar ghost in the wall (symbol of father and of sexual guilt) stalks the halls clothed in "the tattered robe of death." (*WW*, 162) "All sensual love's but dancing on a grave" (*WW*, 188) wrote Roethke in The Dying Man; love may begin with the flesh, but, for Roethke, it must quickly move to higher levels if it is to save rather than destroy.

As in Four for Sir John Davies, this "rise from flesh to spirit" is accomplished with the aid of a Dantesque figure, who is this time closely related to the poet's own Beatrice. The connection between the beloved of Love Poems and the image of woman in earlier poems, such as "The Visitant" or the Davies sequence, is apparent from the first of the new poems, "The Dream," where a shape "encircled by its fire" floats toward the protagonist, as the bushes and stones dance on. (*WW*, 143) And the poems that follow celebrate two important characteristics of this bearer of the soul-image: the anima-like figure is both source of protection against the forces of darkness, and key to a vision of transcendental reality.

In "All the Earth, All the Air," the poet's joy at the sight of the beloved is very much like the comfort a mother affords her frightened child, who has been lurking until then in the "sullen dark." (*WW*, 146) The image of lover as child is carried through other poems, as, for example, "The Other," in which the adoring poet watches his beloved with the "absent gaze" of a child who "stares past a fire." (*WW*, 154) And some of the womb imagery of earlier poems is recalled by "She." Here, the poet's lady "lilts a low soft language" heard through "long sea-chambers of the inner ear." (*WW*, 153) "She moves as water moves"; the engulfing waves of the maternal sea become the symbol of the beloved. And in the lovely final poem of the sequence, "Memory," the image of the lover and his lady is dreamily imposed upon a memory of mother and child (doe and fawn), as if to define the childhood source of the poet's adult affection.

However, the beloved's powers are not confined to passive strength; she is the agent of a more active salvation. In "The Voice," she seems to open the door to a vision of supernatural reality, to what seems to be a realm of Platonic essences in which the one stands for, and is, the many; in her voice, the poet hears "More than a mortal should." (*WW*, 152) The lady's intimate relation to nature, to the very stuff of which the universe is composed, is reiterated in "Words for the Wind": root, rose, leaf, oyster, even the "incipient star," all are part of what she is. (*WW*, 150) The poet is able to "see and suffer myself/ In another being"; as in Martin Buber's conception of the "I-Thou" relationship, the individual's own full identity emerges in the recognition of the self in another, of the self in the world. The beloved enables the poet to perceive the essential unity of being and, paradoxically, his own distinctness.[3] She leads him, at times, beyond time and flesh. In "The Swan," Roethke describes this aspect of her powers with a conceit which shares the grotesque as well as the forceful qualities of seventeenth-century metaphor: searching for a "way out of that coursing blood," the poet is rescued by his darling, who "sighs me white, a Socrates of snow." (*WW*, 167) He escapes what Yeats called "the fury and the mire of human veins," the flood of temporality.

In spite of Roethke's praise for the almost mystical qualities of his beloved, in spite of his insistence on the lofty nature of his love, he never forgets, or seriously tries to forget, the physical basis of this love. Even the Socratic aspirations of "The Swan" are consumed in earthier vision: "I am my father's son, I am John Donne/ Whenever I see her with nothing on." (*WW*, 167) Love, insists Roethke, is a tension-filled yoking together of opposites rather than their complete resolution. Opposites, formerly lost, bend down, as the swan, symbol of art and love, of the eternal, floats upon a stream of temporality and flux. "The Depth calls to the Height" (*WW*, 107) Roethke wrote in "O, Thou Opening, O." And in "All the Earth, All the Air," he echoes this statement of mutual dependence: "The ground needs the abyss." (*WW*, 145).

This union of contraries is evident throughout the Love Poems. The poet's lady in "Words for the Wind" is no less a young animal than a symbol of mystical union with nature; as the poet kisses "her moving mouth" and "swart hilarious skin," the beloved "frolics like a beast." (*WW*, 150) In "The Sententious Man," Roethke tells us that "spirit knows the flesh it must consume"; his love changes him from "ice to fire, and fire

[3] See footnote 30, page 94, above.

to ice." (*WW*, 155) But the division's most striking image of the intertwining of opposites, referring not only to the union of body and soul, but also to the physical union of the lovers, is that of the vine circling the tree. "Words for the Wind" begins by comparing the beloved to a tree, while the poet is brother to the vine; and this figure is taken up again near the poem's close, as the "wind wreathes round a tree." (*WW*, 150) And in "Love's Progress," "long veins of a vine/ Journey around a tree." (*WW*, 163)

We have already examined those poems which describe the saving and protecting powers of the beloved, and those which are concerned with exclusively sensual love; there now remain to be considered the third group of poems, those dealing not primarily with love, but with aloneness and anxiety. Roethke's placing these poems in the sequence is still another illustration of his view of reality as a conflict of opposites; we cannot understand love without understanding man's essential aloneness. This aspect of human existence can be treated lightly, as in "The Surly One," where the poet, drunk to forget failure in love, keeps a dog, and barks himself. (*WW*, 165) Or it may resolve itself into a sad wish for the end of separateness, and reunion with the natural world, as in "Plaint." The poet "lived with deep roots once" (*WW*, 166) and will again; he longs for the embrace of subhuman reality, for the deep sleep of death. However, for Roethke, aloneness is most keenly felt in the context of human death; in fact, one might say that the aloneness is produced by death, the ultimate separation that love seems powerless to overcome.

"The Pure Fury" and "The Renewal," both of which were added to the American edition of *Words for the Wind* after a period of illness and extreme anxiety, are the clearest instances of Roethke's confrontation of nonbeing. They deserve our detailed consideration, not only because of their importance to the series of love poems, which is great, but also because they provide a kind of key to the understanding of much of Roethke's later poetry. We have already seen how certain obsessive images or ganglions of images—for example, the "ghost" associated with "wall," "stones" and "moon" with mystical experiences, "dancing" with the image of the beloved—gather meanings through successive uses, and sometimes can be understood only within the context of several poems. In the poems we are about to examine, the imagery of anxiety and its resolution is given the concrete forms that are used almost like leitmotivs in Roethke's final poems; and the confrontation of nonbeing will itself become these poems' dominant theme. In addition, "The Pure Fury" and "The Renewal" begin to yield the fruits of Roethke's readings in philosophy and theology, and so will help us establish the metaphysical framework which we will find increasingly relevant to Roethke's verse.

In "The Pure Fury," the poet, acknowledging the uselessness of "knowledge lacking inwardness" (WW, 158), begins with the image of "a fearful night." Roethke had already written of this "black/ And shapeless night that made no answer back" (WW, 123), and his equivalent of St. John of the Cross's "dark night of the soul" will appear more and more frequently from this point on, culminating in "In a Dark Time" and the Sequence, Sometimes Metaphysical. As Stanley Kunitz has pointed out,[4] the mystics' "dark night," their sense of the soul's

---

[4] In Ostroff, p. 208.

permanent alienation from God, is a far from obsolescent symbol; it is perfectly appropriate to modern man's estrangement from his God, world, and self, his anxiety in the face of imminent nonbeing.

That this particular anxiety is the precise cause of Roethke's "fearful night," of his conviction of the meaninglessness of things, is suggested by his list of philosophers who were of no use that night. Roethke presents Parmenides, Boehme, and Plato in terms of their concern with the nature of being and nonbeing, with the relation of negation to life. However, these philosophers are not the direct source of the poem. Paul Tillich is the unseen puppet-master, and the second stanza of "The Pure Fury" should be compared with the following passage from *The Courage To Be*:

> Nonbeing is one of the most difficult and most discussed concepts. Parmenides tried to remove it as a concept. But to do so he had to sacrifice life. . . . Plato used the concept of nonbeing because without it the contrast of existence with the pure essences is beyond understanding. It is implied in Aristotle's distinction between matter and form. . . . Jacob Boehme, the Protestant mystic and philosopher of life, made the classical statement that all things are rooted in a Yes and a No.[5]

If the finding of the names of the three philosophers in such close proximity, with Aristotle tossed in to account for the "golden mean," were not enough to establish this passage as the source of Roethke's stanza on nothingness, the phrase "Great Boehme rooted all in Yes and No" (WW, 158) would be conclusive; for Tillich is true to the spirit rather than the

[5] Paul Tillich, *The Courage To Be* (New Haven, Yale University Press, 1959), pp. 32–33.

letter of "Der Leser soll wissen, dass in Jah und Nein alle Dinge bestehen," [6] and I know of no other commentator who uses the word "rooted." This knowledge of the source throws further light on a sentence in the first stanza as well: "For every meaning had grown meaningless." (*WW*, 158) Meaninglessness, for Tillich, is particularly characteristic of modern man,[7] and Roethke's own despair would then seem to have specific reference to man's existential predicament, whatever its other connotations may be.

The main source of anxiety in this poem can be pinpointed with unusual certainty. The source of relief from the state of terror is also clear. Morning comes, and with it a feeling of rebirth, of resurrection. The stone's surface is the same as the poet's skin: touching is communion. We have already learned, however, that stones have a special significance in Roethke's work. They are frequently used to illustrate the Hermetic theory of correspondences, and almost always proclaim the unity of the seen and unseen, of the material and spiritual universe.[8] The poet counters the isolation of death with a sense of mystical union; the stones are alive, and he is one with them, and

[6] From Boehme's *Questiones Theosophicae*, III, 2.

[7] Tillich, p. 57: "We find that at the end of ancient civilization ontic anxiety is predominant, at the end of the Middle Ages moral anxiety, and at the end of the modern period spiritual anxiety. [Fear of death, condemnation, and meaninglessness respectively.] But in spite of the predominance of any one type the others are also present and effective."

[8] E.g., "Speak to the stones, and the stars answer" (*WW*, 103); "Was it the stones I heard? I stared at the fixed stars." (*WW*, 202) Cf. pages 98–99, 100–01, above. (Roethke may also have had in mind the Elizabethan use of "stones" as "testicles"; this would make "stones," filled with creative power, particularly appropriate as symbols of God's ubiquity.)

with the world. I shall have more to say about the nature of this experience later; it should be noted, however, that in this particular instance the sense of union does not seem to be very strong, the comfort it affords is not permanent.

The second stanza introduces the poet's beloved, as well as his contradictory philosophers. No longer an active, dominating force, she is here the manifestation of Roethke's conflict, the concrete representation of his uncertainty as to the nature of being. The beloved's dual nature, which has been carefully developed throughout the sequence of love poems can now be used for maximum effect: she is body, she is of the transient world of the senses, and so she refutes Parmenides' denial of nonbeing; but she is also spirit, capable of the Platonic "squeak" of undying essences. She is both aspects of the poet's reality; in her empty face he sees both salvation and extinction.

The third stanza is crucial, but it is also the most difficult. The tentative resolution of anxiety achieved at the close of the first stanza is clearly no longer functioning; nothingess will not stay in place. The awareness of his temporality has led the poet to envision man as a beast that in and by the process of time consumes himself. "How terrible the need for solitude" (*WW*, 158) deserves close attention; the word "need," implying either absolute necessity or moral necessity, is ambiguous. In the first sense, the phrase is a protest against the human condition itself, against the fact that man, because of his mortality, is doomed to isolation, against the fact that once torn out of nature, he can never again be returned to it. In the second sense, the phrase refers to the individual's need to confront his isolation in order to affirm his own existence. "Courage," says Tillich, "is the self-affirmation of being in spite of the fact of nonbeing." [9] And the need for this courage is indeed "terrible."

What, however, are we to make of "the thing he almost was," and what exactly is the "pure fury"? It would seem that the attack of anxiety which began the poems is being repeated or redescribed, but what do the terms of the description mean? There is no clear-cut answer to this, which is almost certainly what the author would have wished; the feeling of terror is largely communicated by its indefiniteness. But we can none-theless illuminate a great deal if, applying our knowledge of Roethke's use of obsessive imagery, we compare the close of this stanza with another of the poems added to the 1958 edi-tion of *Words for the Wind*, "The Exorcism":

> In a dark wood I saw—
> I saw my several selves . . .
> Lewd, tiny, careless lives
> That scuttled under stones. . . .
> I turned and turned again,
> A cold God-furious man
> Writhing until the last
> Forms of his secret life
> Lay with the dross of death.   (WW, 176)

This is clearly another instance of Roethke giving an inner, psychological state a correspondence in the outer world; but what concerns us most is that he does this with essentially the same imagery as we found in "The Pure Fury." The Dantesque "dark wood" corresponds to the trees coming "closer with a denser shade" (WW, 158); the "cold God-furious man" writh-ing his way to death and extinction is the man consumed by the

[9] Tillich, p. 155.

"pure fury": and this "fury" is further illuminated by reference
to a line in still another poem—"The fury of the slug beneath
the stone," (*WW*, 190) The Dying Man—where "fury" is identified with an equivalent of the selves which "scuttled under
stones."

Roethke glosses this condition as "the dissociation of personality that can occur in states of terror." [10] A man in this
psychological state must find "the thing he almost was" because his self has been fragmented into parts at once identical
and distinct. The "fury" is the attack of anxiety itself, with connotations of the frenzy resulting from a struggle with God, and
of the impotence the slug beneath the stone shares with a man
involved in that struggle. In short, the terrible need for solitude leads to the terror of St. John of the Cross's "dark night
of the soul" and Dante's "dark wood" in one. It leads to a sense
of alienation from the self which, according to Tillich, has become increasingly existential and less necessarily pathological
in our time.

We should note that the movement of "The Pure Fury" is
anything but consoling. It begins with night turning to morning, and the light—in every sense—mood is maintained in the
second stanza with words such as "pure," "golden," "squeaks,"
"flies loose." But with the third stanza comes the wood's "denser
shade," anticipating the "thick shade of the long night" (*WW*,
159) with which the poem ends. The poet, living near the
edge of the abyss of nonbeing, depends upon the "Dream of a
woman," the beloved, to give him back his breath, that is, his
spirit of life. But the "Dream of a woman" and the "dream of
death," described in the second and third stanzas respectively,

[10] Introduction to "The Exorcism" in *Poems in Folio*, I, no. 9, 1957.

threaten to merge into one destructive image. The word "pure" unites the stanzas; and the word "fury" applies to a violent woman, or a mythological, anima-like presence, as well as to the night of terror and death. The dream of the woman itself contains the dream of death. Yet, there is hope of some sort. The poet hopes to stay until his eyes have seen a "brighter sun." This image brings Plato back to mind, and with him the allegory of the cave, in which the "brighter sun" belongs to the real world of ideal forms rather than to the world of appearances. When the imagery of the first stanza is taken into account, the hope actually to see this sun suggests a development of the mystic potentialities in Platonism.

The very writing of "The Pure Fury" is, as Roethke said in his introduction to "The Exorcism," "a sign of spiritual health: a willingness to take at least a look—if not Hardy's 'full look' —at the worst." And this is perfectly in accord with Tillich's idea that the self-affirmation of a being is stronger in proportion to the amount of nonbeing it can take into itself. But the conclusion of "The Pure Fury" iterates a hope for something more certain than Tillich's faith born of absolute despair. And with this in mind, we can turn to "The Renewal."

Once again, the problem is that of the affirmation of being in the face of nothingness. The centaur and the "sybil" romp and sing within the poet's mind; they are archetypal figures in Jung's sense, and so, "Such affirmations are perpetual" (*WW*, 160), a permanent part of the history of the human race. (The sibyl should also be considered an image of mind or spirit, the centaur of body,[11] representing Roethke's tormenting dichot-

[11] Cf. "The Centaur" in *New Poems by American Poets, # 2*, ed. Rolfe Humphries (New York, Ballantine, 1957), p. 135.

omy. The anima, and physical man containing and creating her, is also suggested.) But in spite of the eternal elements within him, the poet, although he lengthens his sighs into songs—that is, works of art—in his bid for immortality, must, "like a tree, endure the shift of things." (*WW*, 160)

As before, reflections upon mutability lead to the image of the "dark night." As the "night wind rises," "Dark hangs upon the waters of the soul;/ My flesh is breathing slower than a wall." (*WW*, 160) For the slow breathing, we can refer to "The Pure Fury," where the light air took the poet's breath away. The attack of anxiety, in Roethke, is characterized by an inability to breathe; and "slower than a wall" indicates both the lifelessness and sense of confinement of the poet's condition.

But the imagery of this poem, unlike that of "The Pure Fury," contains within itself the seeds of creation, of renewal. The question "Does my father live?," in addition to preparing for the wall, invokes God as the Holy Spirit, the "raw ghost" of the following lines. The allusion to Genesis, the dark hanging "upon the waters of the soul," announces the re-creation of life. "Unblood my instinct, love" (*WW*, 160) cries the poet, asking love to help him transcend bodily limitations. And the waters of the soul ambiguously put his anxieties to sleep, offering what may be immortality, or death.

A "Sudden renewal of the self" takes place, but Roethke's reaction is ambivalent. Where does this renewal come from? Is it really in the best interests of the self? Its form, we know, is chilling: a raw ghost drinking the fluid in the poet's spine. A new spirit ("ghost") has indeed come to the breathless body, refreshing itself by a drink of the life fluid. But though there

is life once more, the self, which knows not where it is, has no
identity; it is lost. In fact, to the poet pawing the dark and
midnight air, the renewal seems hardly better than what preceded it. The wish to be gathered into the eternal implicit in
"Unblood my instinct" now threatens to result in annihilation,
and the poet finds himself on the brink of madness; he struggles to keep mind ("five *wits*") and body ("*five* wits"—or
senses) together in one being.

Then, something unexpected happens: although the self is
scattered, it remains the self; rather than isolated, the poet
feels united to all of existence. The last stanza should be examined in detail:

> Dry bones! Dry bones! I find my loving heart,
> Illumination brought to such a pitch
> I see the rubblestones begin to stretch
> As if reality had split apart
> And the whole motion of the soul lay bare:
> I find that love, and I am everywhere.   (WW, 160–61)

The dry bones, a traditional image of the Resurrection (e.g.,
Ezekiel), give us little difficulty in this poem of rebirth. But
what precisely is the nature of the experience being described,
of the expansion of consciousness? There have been expressions of sympathy with the mystic's point of view throughout
Roethke's poetry: from the early derivative poems in the tradition of Vaughan and Blake, to the light within light of "The
Lost Son," and the statement of the doctrine of correspondences characteristic of Boehme and other mystics in "Unfold!
Unfold!" [12] But those were all public approaches to mysticism,
which made use of traditions of poetic convention and meta-

---

[12] See my discussions of mysticism in Roethke's earlier verse.

physical symbolism. The mysticism of "The Renewal," if it is mysticism, is presented in terms of psychological experience rather than simply the broad philosophical significance of that experience. This approach makes it possible to document the relation of Roethke's own experience to accepted descriptions of mystical union.

First, we should set beside the stanza from "The Renewal" other examples—drawn from the Love Poems—which seem to describe the same experience most explicitly: ". . . I saw the world with second sight . . . I touched the stones, and they had my own skin" (*WW*, 158); "I know the motion of the deepest stone./ Each one's himself, yet each one's everyone." (*WW*, 156) (The association of stones—Roethke's favorite object for the presentation of the Hermetic unity of the seen and unseen worlds—with the sense of union persists.) Then, let us compare all three passages with the following selection from Plotinus:

> They see not in the process of becoming, but in being, and they see themselves in the other. Each being contains within itself the whole intelligible world. Therefore all is everywhere. Each is there all and all is each.[13]

and with this quotation from a modern mystic, R. M. Bucke:

> . . . There came upon me a sense of exultation, of immense joyousness accompanied or immediately followed by an intellectual illumination impossible to describe. . . . I saw that the universe is not composed of dead matter but is, on the contrary, a living Presence; I became conscious in myself of

[13] Quoted by Rudolph Otto in *Mysticism East and West* (New York, Collier, 1962), p. 60.

eternal life . . . the foundation principle of the world, of all the worlds, is what we call love.[14]

These are descriptions of extrovertive mystic experiences.[15] I think it is reasonable to assert that the experience described by Roethke is essentially of the same kind (although there is no reason at all to assume that his metaphysical interpretation of this experience would be the same as that of Plotinus, Bucke, or anyone else).[16]

Is this sense of mystic participation in reality, then, the answer to the threat of nonbeing? Does "The Renewal" mark the termination of a period of anxiety and doubt? Or is it simply a part of a recurrent cycle, identical to the feeling of rebirth described in the first stanza of "The Pure Fury" which gives way once more to terror? The association of stones with both the resurrection of "The Pure Fury" and the mystical illumination of "The Renewal" suggests that the experiences are identical (although, admittedly, the intensity of the expansion of consciousness seems far greater than the vague sense of rebirth involved in the touching of the stones in the first poem).

Once again, there is no certain solution to this problem. But perhaps Tillich, whose thought is so essential to the perspective of these poems, can shed some further light on it. Tillich does not really question the validity of mysticism as an important form of human experience, but it does not, he says, go

[14] Bucke, author of *Cosmic Consciousness* (Philadelphia, 1901), is quoted by William James in *The Varieties of Religious Experience* (New York, New American Library, 1958), pp. 306–7.

[15] Extrovertive and introvertive mystic experiences are defined in footnote 29, page 90, above.

[16] Roethke has stated that he experienced the mystical loss of self in the oneness of the universe "so many times, in so many varying circumstances, that I cannot suspect its validity" "On 'Identity,'" *SP*, p. 26.

far enough in confronting the complex problems of encroaching nonbeing:

> The God above God is the object of all mystical longing, but
> mysticism must be transcended in order to reach him. Mys-
> ticism does not take seriously the concrete. It plunges directly
> into the ground of being and meaning, and leaves the concrete,
> the world of finite values and meanings, behind. Therefore, it
> does not solve the problem of meaninglessness.[17]

Tillich then goes on to embrace a Kierkegaardian solution: the
individual *as individual*—not in the paradoxical sense in which
individuality is maintained in a mystical experience, but in the
sense of *complete* individuality—must, through the courage
born of total despair, stand in an absolute relation to the absolute.[18] "God for me," wrote Roethke, rejecting the finality of
mystical knowing, "still remains someone to be confronted, to
be dueled with." [19] For a man who asks Tillich's questions
about the nature of reality, as Roethke clearly did, there are
three essential positions: mysticism, despair, and the faith born
of despair. From a certain point of view, the three are so
closely related that to slip from one to another is not only easy
but almost inevitable; it is even possible to hold all three positions at once. Despair, in the Kierkegaardian tradition, is actually part of faith; and as Tillich has shown, and Roethke ech-
oed, mysticism does not necessarily remove existential despair
or supersede existential faith.

It may be objected that these metaphysical speculations,
which are evidently crucial to Roethke's last poems (from

[17] Tillich, p. 186.
[18] See Kierkegaard's *Fear and Trembling* (New York, Doubleday,
1954), especially p. 91. Cf. Tillich, pp. 155–90.
[19] "On 'Identity,'" *SP*, p. 26.

about 1956 on), have comparatively little to do with the Love
Poems, which, for the most part, belong to an earlier, more
optimistic period. While it is true, however, that there is an
unquestionable shift in tone, owing, perhaps, to a period of
severe illness, it is hardly as clear that there is any change in
Roethke's overall view of reality. The negative, or threatening, visions of the "anxiety poems" provide the context essential to a full understanding of the role of the beloved in the
poet's life; giving precise meaning to this Beatrice's saving
powers, these poems define the "dark world where gods have
lost their way" which forms the backdrop for the "rise from
flesh to spirit." And Roethke's refusal to reject the concrete
and take refuge in mysticism parallels his refusal to reject
flesh and devote himself to completely spiritual or "Platonic"
love. In each case, Roethke insists on an acceptance of the full
range of human possibilities.

When we turn to an examination of some of the methods of
the Love Poems, this intimate relation between the poet's
philosophical and amorous activities must have our attention
first; feelings toward the beloved function as a kind of metaphor for his attitude toward reality. At times, this woman
seems an essential principle of being. "I find her everyplace,"
the poet cries, "She happens." (*WW*, 154) She is an integral
part of the natural world, and shares its magical powers; more
than mortal knowledge is arrived at by means of "Bird, girl,
and ghostly tree." (*WW*, 152) Always associated with motion,
the beloved at times seems to *be* motion, the reestablisher of
the universal dance.

By the development of these relationships, Roethke endows
the protective and saving powers of the beloved—which we

have abstractly attributed to her function as anima (or type of Beatrice)—with a poetically felt reality. We should note that while Roethke occasionally makes use of metaphysical conceit (as in "The Swan," *WW*, 167) in obtaining this effect, he more often tries to convey a sense of animistic vitality in the natural world by means of the highly charged imagery of *Praise to the End!*; the intensity of the child's perception of reality is retained as it is applied to the adult's world. When Roethke writes "My brother the vine is glad" (*WW*, 147), he shares the vision of child or saint, and the tired symbol of true love—the vine circling the tree—is given new freshness.

However, Roethke's effects in these poems are not exclusively the results of the nature and sources of their imagery; the poet's manipulation of formal lyrical patterns is fully as important. "Words for the Wind" is probably the outstanding example of Roethke's virtuosity in the Love Poems. The dance-like flow of the beloved's "motion" is partially conveyed by the development of the imagery of the first stanza: the vine around the tree, the interplay of even and odd, the movement of flowers in the wind. The images form and dissolve in various configurations: "All's even with the odd" (*WW*, 147), for example, disappears until the third section, where it recurs in "I'm odd and full of love" (*WW*, 149); the wind weaves in and out until it wreathes itself around a tree; lily becomes rose, which finally unfolds in the increasing light; and so on. But this development of imagery is exactly paralleled by the poem's technical elements. The rhyme scheme of the first section is ottava rima, *abababcc*, with heavy use of the slant rhymes characteristic of all sections. But this highly traditional pattern loses a line and becomes, in the second section, *abcbdbc*; in the third, *abcdacb*.

And, in the fourth, regaining the lost line, it forms the more regular *abcdabcd*. This is, in short, the forming, dissolving, and reforming of the poem's structure, accompanying the movement of the imagery. All of this takes place to the rhythm of quickly flowing trimeters (sometimes based on a count of strong accents alone, sometimes regularly iambic), completing the union of form and content.

This use of trimeters for a serious purpose brings Yeats to mind (e.g., "The Fisherman," the last section of "The Tower"); and indeed Yeats's influence is strongly felt throughout the sequence. The transformation of traditionally light rhyme schemes, such as ottava rima, into a vehicle for the most serious of verse by the use of slant rhymes is certainly characteristic of Yeats (e.g., "Among School Children" and "Sailing to Byzantium"). And so is the rhetorical question, used extensively by Roethke: "What's hell but a cold heart?" (*WW*, 146); "Are flower and seed the same?" (*WW*, 147); etc. And most characteristic of Yeats in all the sequence is the philosophical poem itself; the listing of philosophers in "The Pure Fury" is reminiscent of Yeats's "Among School Children." [20]

However, Roethke's differences from Yeats are at least as evident as his similarities, and should not be ignored. The end-stopped line is still prominent, as opposed to Yeats's more continuous flow, in an effort to achieve the bare, powerful statement. But it has developed considerably since the last time we saw it in Four for Sir John Davies and "The Waking."

[20] Auden shares many of these characteristics; but he too was greatly influenced by Yeats. See also Yeats's discussion of the idea as symbol, "The Symbolism of Poetry," *Essays and Introductions* (New York, Macmillan, 1961), pp. 160–63.

The single line, in Roethke's verse, must bear an enormous burden of meaning; and it is learning how to do it. The proverbs that appear toward the close of *Praise to the End!* have culminated in a richly aphoristic poetry: "The ground needs the abyss,/ Say the stones, say the fish" (*WW*, 145); "Those who embrace, believe" (*WW*, 149); "The pure admire the pure, and live alone." (*WW*, 158) The line itself is beginning to break down; it is no longer the fundamental unit:

> We did not fly the flesh. Who does when young?
> A fire leaps on itself: I know that flame.
> Some rages save us. Did I rage too long?
> The spirit knows the flesh it must consume.   (*WW*, 155)

The movement toward increased concentration will be one of the most important tendencies of Roethke's last poems.

Voices and Creatures

Voices and Creatures forms a kind of interval between the Love Poems and the two final divisions of *Words for the Wind*. Its gap-stopping character, however, comes from the composition of the sequence rather than any failure in quality of the poems themselves. The Voices poems are so different in content, tone, and method from the Creatures poems (although they can all ultimately be shown to relate to the same state of mind), that the sequence lacks cohesion. This has resulted in the comparative neglect of some of Roethke's finest poems of this period—for example, "The Exorcism," and "A Walk in Late Summer."

The Voices poems essentially concern a series of encounters of the poet with persons and events, or even conditions, outside himself, which reveal his own inner torments, and which seem to owe their very existence to these same torments. " 'The Shimmer of Evil' *Louise Bogan*" is perhaps the clearest instance of the pathetic fallacy in the section. The weather weeps and the trees bend down; the peculiarly individual quality of each item of the landscape (each vision "purely was its own," *WW*, 171) is an outer analogue of the inner sense of separation from the natural world: "And I was only I." In this poem, where "there is no light at all," illumination, and the mystic communion with the rest of creation it represents, are lacking; the feeling of isolation leads not to reaffirmation of the self but to despair. To use Tillich's categories, the poet is experiencing the moral aspect of threatening nonbeing: the sense of condemnation or guilt. And this is to be the keynote for the Voices poems that follow.

Guilt is precisely the theme of "Elegy." The occasion of this poem is the death of another person—Roethke ultimately assigned it to Dylan Thomas, although the Welsh poet was not its original inspiration—but it immediately becomes an examination of "the Motion of Man's Fate" (*WW*, 172), the human condition as defined by death, in its application to the poet's own existence. The thought of death reminds him that he himself bears "an inner weight of woe" that Christ could scarcely bear; and this woe somehow comes under the heading of "essential sin." "I am here to fear," says the poet, hinting that God is sympathetic to this fear because he shares it. Indeed, the universe as man knows it is defined by the passage of the seasons, the "crumbling skin," "Heat,/ Scars, Tempests, Floods," in short, by the passing out of existence of all life. Once this dissolution has occurred, man can no longer atone for his guilt; his "essential sin," his condemnation, is fact forever.

"The Beast" is another view of the poet's separation from nature, from the "lush and green" world of the unicorn, which here represents not only the world of childhood, but of myth and racial memory. Expelled from this prelapsarian existence, the poet weeps; the poem's last word, "alone," is its most important. (*WW*, 173) And in "The Song," "the small voice of a child" (*WW*, 175) joins with the poet's, after the latter has been frightened by the vision of a ragged man, his own self as subject to time. Singing into "a fissure of ground," a "watery hole" (*WW*, 174), the adult finds his world of time meeting the child's sense of eternity; singing, for Roethke, is the creation of art, the symbol of the temporary permanence of a poem. We should note that the anxiety that led to the creation of this poem is characterized by difficulty in breathing, and the image of the wall. And this leads into the final "guilt" poem, "The Exorcism."

We have already discussed the presentation of anxiety in the second section of the poem; but it is essential that we consider the context provided by the first section. Seeing a shape in a cloud (cf. *WW*, 69, 98), Roethke's symbol for the father, and for God, the protagonist runs in terror. Lacking the courage to face himself, the "God-furious man" is also running from God, from his sense of guilt.[21] However, this "guilt" sequence is oddly inconclusive; the rising waves of terror do not seem to be assimilated into the poet's being, nor do they reduce him to the complete madness which threatens but does not prevail.

[21] Cf. "Running from God's the longest race of all." (*FF*, 88)

The next two poems concern the "small" of the world as the medium through which the poet confronts himself.[22] "Things throw light on things" (*WW*, 178) says Roethke in "The Small," announcing that the visible no longer obscures, "All the stones have wings." In the "fearful small," and in the dead who "will not lie still," the poet finds both the sense of his own identity, and of his oneness with all that is or has been.[23]

However, in "A Walk in Late Summer," the value of this communion as a source of comfort against the various threats of nonbeing is not reaffirmed without serious reservations. The small, "singing in the soft summer air" (*WW*, 179), are again present; but the kind of continuous existence they promise— that is, being part of a collective, impersonal nature—both does and does not transcend time:

> God's in that stone, or I am not a man! [24]
> Body and soul transcend appearances
> Before the caving-in of all that is;
> I'm dying piecemeal, fervent in decay;
> My moments linger—that's eternity.   (*WW*, 179)

Roethke appeals once more to the stones to establish a transcendent reality; but although there is a kind of transcending of appearances, eternity is not distinguished from decay—it *is* the decay from a different point of view. The poem's ambiguity is never resolved. The central image of the final stanza is a tree, "Thinned by the wind" (*WW*, 180), seen in the light of the dying day.[25] But this is followed by two wood thrushes

---

[22] Cf. "The Minimal," *WW*, 59.

[23] See Roethke's "On 'Identity,' " *SP*, pp. 24–26.

[24] See footnote 7.

[25] Cf. "The Renewal," in which the poet, "like a tree, endures the shift of things." (*WW*, 160)

singing as one, expressing creation's delight both "in being and in time." Time and eternity are once more brought together, as the evening wraps the poet "steady as a flame." This is light, but it is light that consumes.

And so we must be careful to distinguish the paradox, the vision of two-in-one with which the poem ends, from traditional mystic paradoxes. It is true that for the mystic the transient world and the world of the eternal are aspects of the same transcendent reality, but that reality essentially *is* the eternal, while change and decay are seen as illusion. Roethke is here following Tillich rather than mystic tradition. He accepts Tillich's concept of God as absolute being (which delights both in being—that is, the absolute, the eternal—and in time); and his idea of eternity seems best glossed by Tillich's "eternal now":

> The world, by its very nature, is that which comes to an end.
> . . . There is no time *after* time, but there is eternity *above* time. . . . Every moment of time reaches into the eternal.
> . . . It is the eternal "now" which provides for us a temporal "now." Sometimes it [the eternal now] breaks into our consciousness and gives us the certainty of the eternal, of a dimension of time which cuts into our time and gives us our time.[26]

It is this sense of existential "presence," rather than the mystic's sense of union with the "one," which informs "A Walk in Late Summer." Although time partakes of the eternal, the individual's time is limited; Roethke, celebrating the former, laments the latter. He does not give up his commitment to the concrete reality he must leave behind in death.

[26] *The Eternal Now* (New York, Scribner, 1963), pp. 125, 131.

The Creatures poems of this division mark a change in method as well as content. While the Voices poems display the same characteristics as Love Poems, these are far less concentrated in language, and depend much more upon the manipulation of the rhythms of everyday speech for their effects. The verse is Roethke's most "imagistic" since the greenhouse poems; all energies seem directed toward the vivid, visual impression. However, the poet's presence is always felt, and in his relation to the scene he has painted lies the ultimate meaning of each poem.

In "Snake," the poet admires that "pure, sensuous form" (*WW*, 181) as this clearly Freudian symbol becomes the focus for hints of transmigration of souls, the metempsychosis so often associated with mystical doctrine. And another of Roethke's favorite symbolic creatures, the "Slug," which is frequently found wandering about the poet's representations of the unconscious, is treated in a naturalistic manner. This "loose toe from the old life" refuses to "die decently," as the poet mows his lawn and sets his inner landscape in order. (*WW*, 182) Wondering whether Blake would have called this "odious" creature holy, the poet makes the closely described death of the slug an image of the ugly and disgusting of the world, the reality that apparently cannot be transcended. And finally, in "The Siskins," Roethke reestablishes a sense of communion with nature, identifying himself with the "sunlit leaping" of the small birds. (*WW*, 183)

Coming after the concentrated intensity of the Love Poems and Voices poems, the comparative discursiveness of this verse may seem anticlimactic; Roethke has not taken care to provide these poems with a context that shows them to their best advantage. But this smoothly flowing, anecdotal poetry is the first expression of a method that becomes of increasing importance in Roethke's last volume of poetry, and which provides some of the more significant elements of Meditations of an Old Woman.

Man's confrontation of nonbeing—of death, meaninglessness, and condemnation—functions as a kind of backdrop for the Love Poems; but in the final two divisions of *Words for the Wind,* this encounter has the center of the stage. The Dying Man and Meditations of an Old Woman are the poet's evaluation of life in the face of death, using the personae of father and mother as means of coming to grips with reality.

The Dying Man

In the first of these divisions, the death of this father forces the poet to see himself as a "dying man." The "father" here is both Roethke's own father, and his spiritual father, W. B. Yeats. The five poems are lyrics in the manner of middle and late Yeats, in tribute to the great Irish poet; but Roethke unmistakably retains his own identity throughout, which is not the least remarkable achievement of these poems. For if the mode of expression is Yeats's, the universe being expressed is Roethke's, related to that of the "spiritual father" to be sure, but firmly rooted in the "son"'s imagery, diction, and metaphorical peculiarities. A careful reading shows that there is almost no image or symbol that has not been specifically anticipated in Roethke's earlier work; it is almost as if all of the poet's energies had been drawn together and focused on this one concentrated vision of reality.

The Dying Man's words open the poem, "His Words." The soul, "a fresh salted skin" being "hung out to dry" (*WW*, 187), recalls the poet lying in his "own dead salt" at the conclusion of "The Exorcism." (*WW*, 177) The sweat of anxiety and terror becomes the active agent in this vision of life as a "curing" process. But although the Dying Man does not expect to use his soul again, he immediately affirms that "What's done is yet to come" (*WW*, 187); although the flesh decays, "a kiss widens the rose." It is hardly necessary to elaborate the highly charged significance of the rose, symbol of beauty and transcendent reality through the ages, from Dante to Blake to Yeats. And in Roethke's own work, the coming of "Papa" in "The Lost Son" is signaled by the appearance of "the big roses" (*WW*, 84), the beloved announced by "the unfolding rose" (*WW*, 150) in "Words for the Wind."

"Eternity is Now" (*WW*, 187) is the message of the rose. This is the mystic's perception of the eternal in the temporal; and it is also Yeats's vision of the moment beyond time being perpetually relived, as in *Purgatory*. But we must not forget that this is knowledge known "as the dying know"; and in the case of Tillich's "eternal now," this eternity is *above* time rather than a continuation of time *after* time, and there is no qualification—at least not at this point—of the finality of death. The Dying Man defines himself as "that final thing,/ A man learning to sing." Implicit in this remark is the recognition of death as the transformation of a being conscious of his own existence into a nescient "thing," an impersonal part of nature. But by "learning to sing" the Dying Man hopes to transcend his mortal state, to create something that will endure. (Roethke too tried to teach his "sighs to lengthen into songs" [*WW*, 160] to defeat time.)[27]

"What Now?" is indeed a questioning poem. "Caught in that dying light" (as Yeats's creatures are "Caught in that sensual music"), the poet must examine himself. Atavistic hooves and the weight of racial memory attend this "rebirth," this probing of the self. "Reborn," of course, also looks forward to the ghost moaning to be reborn in "The Wall." For the poet has, in a sense, taken on at least a part of the identity of the Dying Man by becoming, or seeing himself as, another dying man.

The mire of the regressive journey appears; and now the poet finds that the dead in the dark wood remind him to stay alive.[28] Burning his flesh away, the poet too is becoming a "final thing." "The casement blurs," anticipating, to be sure, the "sill" of the next poem; but it also seems to refer to Yeats's "The Ghost of Roger Casement," another disturbed (and disturbing) spirit attempting to enter a closed house. This examination by the poet of his own self, this confrontation of his death, lead once more to the anxiety of the "dark night," to "the worst night of my will." (*WW*, 188)

In "The Wall," as in "The Renewal," a horrifying ghost "out of the unconscious mind" (*WW*, 188) appears at the moment of crisis. Ghosts, for Roethke, have been associated with walls since he found "the ghost of some great howl/ Dead in a

[27] See "Sailing to Byzantium," by Yeats, in which the soul's singing is an image of immortality. See also Yeats's letter to Lady Elizabeth Pelham: "When I try to put it all into a phrase I say, 'Man can embody truth but he cannot know it.' I must embody it in the completion of my life." *The Letters of W. B. Yeats*, ed. Allan Wade (New York, Macmillan, 1955), p. 922.

[28] Cf. the helping dead in "Unfold! Unfold!" (*WW*, 103) and the old lady reminded to stay alive in "Old Lady's Winter Words." (*WW*, 118)

wall" (*WW*, 73) in "Give Way, Ye Gates." [29] They have also been associated with the father, whom the poet now finds as he does his work. Moaning to be reborn in the son, this paternal spirit offers renewal; by regressively searching the world of the dead within himself, the poet breathes with new life. And yet, this ghost and this search invoke a new vision of darkness in which the poet is lost. The father's ghost, as we have already learned, may be an objectification of the son's sexuality, which in turn is connected with mortality; and so, "All sensual love's but dancing on a grave." (*WW*, 188) As both the Dying Man and the poet already have insisted, "flesh deserts the bone" and is "burned away." Unless body and spirit can both partake of human love and action, unless what Yeats called "unity of being" can be achieved, a man's life is meaningless. But between body and spirit there seems to be an impenetrable wall, the "madman staring at perpetual night," "raging at the visible." The poet and ghost stand at opposite ends of existence, and cannot meet.

The terrible night passes, finally it is dawn; but even now there is a "dazzling dark behind the sun." (*WW*, 189) Daylight does not effectively dispel the night that stretches without limit at both ends of man's existence. The term "dazzling dark" deserves further notice. It is taken directly from the tradition of negative theology begun by Dionysius the Areopagite, who used it to describe the God of Mystic Union as impersonal and without attributes, as undifferentiated being.[30]

---

[29] "What Now?" ended with "Who's beating at the gates?" (*WW*, 188) Cf. Roger Casement's ghost "beating at the door" in Yeats's poem.

[30] "The simple, absolute, and unchangeable mysteries of heavenly truth lie hidden in the dazzling obscurity of the secret Silence, outshining all brilliance with the intensity of their darkness." *Dionysius the Areopagite*

In using this metaphor, Roethke alludes to that aspect of mystic experience which, as Tillich pointed out, gives no importance or meaning to the concrete or differentiated qualities of being, and therefore tends to deny the possibility of "unity of being."

"The Exulting" begins with a cry for something more than the mere material existence to which we seem limited. The poet wants "more than the world," more than the "after-image of the inner eye." (*WW*, 189) He delights in the search for Platonic essence in the natural world. All exultation is dangerous, but the father provides the proper example by his behavior. "Shrinking in his skin," like the soul of "His Words," this birdlike figure walks the "edge" yet still dares "to fix his vision anywhere." [31] The figure of the father, of Yeats (whose presence is appropriately symbolized by the bird), successfully confronts the darkness.

"We never enter/ Alone," (*WW*, 106) Roethke wrote in "I Cry, Love! Love!" And now he echoes this: "I die into this life, alone yet not alone." (*WW*, 189) The poet calls upon the image of the bird for assistance; although the father's ghost has not provided the clear-cut path to the eternal the poet sought, it does supply a source of courage by which a kind of "unity of being" can be achieved in any case. Roethke sums up what he has learned: "By daily dying, I have come to be." (*WW*, 189) The possibilities of this cryptic remark are practically endless. But two meanings in particular seem more pertinent than the rest: the "daily dying" refers to the con-

---

on the Divine Names and the Mystical Theology, trans. C. E. Rolt (New York, Macmillan, 1957), p. 191. See also Eckhart's Godhead above God, and Boehme's Unground.

[31] Cf. "I live near the abyss" in "The Pure Fury" (*WW*, 159); and "The Edge is what I have" in "In a Dark Time." (*FF*, 79)

tinuous process of rebirth by which the individual's identity is formed, and also to the continual encounter with nonbeing, with the prospect of death and meaninglessness that each new day brings. Each day our self is different from what it was the previous day. We are defined by these successive "deaths"; but it is only through an awareness of the necessity of nonbeing for a definition of being that we realize the nature of our existence and begin to *be* in a significant sense. Roethke emphasizes this point by expressing all of life in terms of death: for birth, he writes "I die into this life"; life itself he calls a "daily dying"; and death therefore is the end to these deaths— "I shall undo all dying by my death." (*WW*, 189)

In "They Sing, They Sing," the final poem of The Dying Man, Roethke turns once more to love as a means of uniting body and spirit. The opening stanza, at first puzzling, becomes clear when we read it in the context of its origins in Four for Sir John Davies. The cry of the beast which takes the poet back to where he was born is a descendant of the "sensual cry" of the earlier poem. The stanza here describes the sexual act, and the projection of the soul-image originally borne by the mother upon the beloved; as in the Love Poems, the poet looks toward the image of woman for salvation. The language echoes Yeats's "dolphin-torn," "gong-tormented sea" of time and flux, from which Roethke is trying to escape.

The crucial questions are asked: Is "love but a motion in the mind?" a completely materialistic phenomenon? Is the poet himself "but nothing leaning toward a thing?" a meaningless existence heading toward extinction? The poet can either sigh in terror, or sing; joined by the birds of previous poems, he chooses the latter. With the Dying Man, he has learned to sing, to know the Eternity that is Now. But this final vision is filled with horror: eternity is defined as "The fury of the slug beneath the stone." (*WW*, 190)

We have already examined the relationship of this "fury" to "The Pure Fury"; but an even more revealing gloss is provided by the last lines of an uncollected poem, "The Advice": "What you brought back from the Abyss,/ The slug was taught beneath his stone." [32] Eternity, then, produces in man an equivalent of the impotent rage of the "odious" slug beneath his stone; eternity is the abyss, the dazzling dark, the undifferentiated being of the absolute, which, from the point of view of the individual, or differentiated being, amounts to annihilation, to nonbeing. This vision of the slug, which moves without changing, becomes Roethke's comfortless symbol of the eternal in the temporal.

All of the hope and despair of the previous lines of this poem, perhaps of all of Roethke's work, is brought to bear on the great final stanza. This verse is Yeatsian, but only in the sense that it, like Yeats's best poetry, is both cold and passionate, the classic, public expression of a deeply felt conception of reality:

> The edges of the summit still appal
> When we brood on the dead or the beloved;
> Nor can imagination do it all
> In this last place of light: he dares to live
> Who stops being a bird, yet beats his wings
> Against the immense immeasurable emp-
> tiness of things.   (*WW*, 190)

[32] *New Statesman*, LXV (Aug. 9, 1963), 176.

We cannot put the abyss of nonbeing out of our lives, not even with the help of the "dead" or the beloved (Roethke's chief sources of renewal). Even the creation of art seems feeble when contemplated in the "dying light" of a man's last moments. Only the man who confesses he cannot transcend the human condition, but continues to live as if he can, the man who accepts despair and in it finds faith—only he can dare to live.

The brilliantly expanded last line, following a series of regular pentameters, is the result of Roethke's most striking textual change. The line originally appeared in the *New Yorker* as: "Against the wide abyss, the gray waste nothingness of things." [33] The elimination of "wide abyss" and "gray waste," which gave definite, multiple, and commonplace attributes to this supposedly indescribable void, and the stringing together of ponderous "m" sounds, raised this ordinary line to greatness. Even before this change, however, Roethke had hit upon the effective device of contrasting the songlike rhythms of the end-stopped lines with the prosaic directness of the last three or four.

The trimeters of the first two poems, the use of slant rhymes in typically Yeatsian arrangements in the last three, and the intentional echoes of Yeats's verse throughout, are some of the ways in which Roethke pays tribute to Yeats as a "poetic" as well as "spiritual" father. But in this case, at least, there is as little point in claiming that Roethke is imitating Yeats as in criticizing Auden's elegy for the same reason. And in the intensity of its confrontation of nonbeing, an intensity brought about by a system of imagery developed in the course of a

[33] *New Yorker*, XXXII (Aug. 18, 1956), 22.

lifetime, The Dying Man stands as one of Roethke's most personal achievements.

Meditations of an Old Woman

The five poems of Meditations of an Old Woman were originally published in the period of two and one-half years between the last quarter of 1955 and the first quarter of 1958. Although they are not as exclusively concerned with death as The Dying Man, these meditations begin with the protagonist's vision of death, which provides a kind of frame of reference for the consideration of life, and which, often reappearing overtly, is never far from the poem's surface. The overwhelming dominance of this theme during this anxiety-filled time in Roethke's life is well illustrated by the fact that The Dying Man, and all of the poems dealing with the darker side of love, were first published during the same period.

Constructed according to principles of association and musical alternation of themes, with the archetypal journey as their central, unifying motif, the Meditations bear many superficial resemblances to the poems of *Praise to the End!* But the differences are even more crucial than the similarities. Perhaps most important, the protagonist is no longer the child-hero struggling toward consciousness, but an old woman, modeled in part on the poet's mother, facing permanent loss of consciousness in imminent death. From this basic change proceed the main alterations of technique. No longer concerned with reproducing the primary process thought of the child's world, approaching myth through the medium of the conscious mind rather than searching out its unconscious origins, Roethke's verse is less highly concentrated and more discursive than in *Praise to the End!;* as in the last poems of Voices and Creatures, the visual imagination has increased importance, and the coherent image rather than its component parts tends to be the vehicle of the poet's symbolism.

The "First Meditation" begins with the description of a landscape representing the Old Woman's inner state of mind: "stones loosen," "a tree tilts from its roots," the "obscure hillside" abounds with intimations of death. (*WW,* 193) "The spirit moves," but its direction is uncertain; the "strange piece of flesh" rebels, "the rind, often, hates the life within." This new and terrible condition requires a new perspective. "I need an old crone's knowing," says the Old Woman, stressing her sense of herself as a different, alien creature; she is approaching the vision of "death's possibilities" of the Dying Man, who knew as the dying know.

The second section introduces specifically the idea of the journey suggested by the movement of the spirit in the first section. The archetypal nature of the journey is acknowledged in the Old Woman's awareness that "All journeys . . . are the same." (*WW,* 194) The particular bus trip that comes to mind becomes the pattern of all excursions: the wavelike movement is up and down, over hill and ridge, forward and then backward. And then comes the journey within a journey, the movement back in time. The Old Woman suddenly envisions the greenhouse of her childhood, and of Roethke's. Two sparrows, one inside the greenhouse, one without, sing at each other, establishing an important relationship between inner and outer worlds. However, the sense of joy and vitality evoked by the image of the greenhouse is quickly dissipated in the thoughts of the Old Woman's journey away from this childhood world. A series of frustrated journeys follow in quick succession: the mislaid ticket, the shut gate, the boat pulling out. And the section closes with the image of the tangled reins of a sleigh, and the horses lurching and lunging down the hillside; the horses' black skins shudder in this strangely evocative vision of the fall.

The Old Woman's thoughts again search for a way of understanding or expressing the arduous journey of the spirit since its fall from childhood happiness, from a world in which inner and outer, spirit and flesh, seemed to live in perfect harmony. The third section presents two powerful similes for the spirit's movement: the grotesque struggle of the crab against the drifting silt of the muddy pond water; and the exhausted salmon slipping into a back eddy, then renewing his upstream swim. In each case, the struggle is almost unendurably discouraging, in each case the forward motion is accompanied by continual backsliding.

In the fourth section, the Old Woman returns to the feeling of desolation with which the poem opened. She has visited "waste lonely places/ Behind the eye," "lost acres at the edge of smoky cities." (*WW*, 195) This appears to be the location of the first section of "The Long Alley," where the sulphurous waters descend from the smoky factory on the plateau; and here, as there, this image of destructive waste corresponds to the inner state of mind of the protagonist, whose soul is stifled by a view of reality that, completely materialistic, denies the possibilities of the spirit. There follows a vision of musty decay, represented by "motes of dust," "falling hair," "lint," "vines graying to a fine powder." (*WW*, 195) Against this en-croaching lifelessness, the spirit indeed has a formidable strug-gle. And yet, there are still times when the Old Woman feels a sense of communion with living nature; she hears the calls of the cerulean, the phoebe, the whippoorwill—and in such times, reliving her greenhouse past, she is still happy.

In the second meditation, appropriately entitled "I'm Here," the Old Woman reaffirms her still continuing existence; how-ever, as the first line asks, "Is it enough?" (*WW*, 197) Is this life as a crone or hag in her shrunken skin worth enduring? The sound of the bickering sparrows (as opposed to the harmoniously singing sparrows of the "First Meditation"), the "April cheeping" of rebirth, the child's prattle—all these signs of life seem to have become unbearable. Needles and corners, the small details of life, perplex. But this section's last line an-ticipates the poem's ultimate affirmation of life: "Some fates are worse" (*WW*, 197), she says.

The second section turns abruptly from the December open-ing to a recollection of the summery past, when the protagonist, for a short time, was "queen of the vale." Her thighs would brush against the flower-crowns, she could make a sapling quiver with her body. But the young girl is ironically impatient to grow old. "So much of adolescence is an ill-defined dying,/ An intolerable waiting." (*WW*, 198) The idea of the process of individuation being a kind of dying is not new in Roethke,[34] and is particularly appropriate to the adolescent's continual becoming.

In the third section, the young girl, probably somewhat older now, immerses herself even further in the sensual world:

[34] Cf. The Dying Man, *WW*, 189.

she finds herself tangled in the thorns of a rose bush, nearly "smothered" by the "scent of the half-opened buds." (*WW,* 198) The natural world in particular is experienced intensely. Then, the Old Woman recalls the time she had a fever, and imagined she saw tree-shrews and rats dancing around a fire.[35] This magical childhood world is associated immediately with the bird the girl's grandmother insisted was always singing in her inner eye.

But all these memories ultimately serve only to intensify the contrast between the sensual happiness of the past and the "strange piece of flesh" of the present. The fourth section begins with another outer image of an inner state: "My geranium is dying . . ." (*WW,* 199)[36] But she now seems to hint at the new way of knowing that has come with age: she can wear roses by looking away, she can satisfy herself with the "after-image," the memory, as well as with the thing itself. The sensual commotion of the second and third sections has been surpassed by a longing for rest. The hemlock branch and the "last of the sun" (*WW,* 200) keep death before the Old Woman's eyes, but she meets it calmly now, preferring "the still joy": "A snail's music." This image, taken from "A Light Breather" (where spirit is "like a snail," "music in a hood," *WW,* 115), asserts once more the Old Woman's faith in the ultimate supremacy of the spirit, in a life beyond the sensual. And in the fifth section, "Birds are around." (*WW,* 200) The singing of childhood, the music of eternity, accompany the Old

[35] Cf. "Are the rats dancing?" in "Give Way, Ye Gates." (*WW,* 72) This, and the many other links with *Praise to the End!,* too numerous to list, indicate that whether or not Roethke had his mother in mind as protagonist, the world he describes is his own.

[36] Cf. "The Geranium," *FF,* 63.

Woman. "It's not my first dying," she says, recalling the ill-defined dying of adolescence. And finally she reaches toward the eternal by intensely experiencing the present: "I'm here!" she cries, "Here."

In "Her Becoming," the spirit reaches the high point of its journey. The poem begins with the Old Woman sitting quietly, meditating. She thinks of light, of a field, of rolling water, anticipating later sections of the poem. The shape "lighted with love" foreshadows the mystical illumination which will dominate the poem. Still trying to understand her existence, still "becoming" something new each moment, the Old Woman turns from statements to questions; and the questions culminate in: "Who knows/ The way out of a rose?" (*WW*, 201) What is the relation between temporal and eternal, body and spirit; how can one link the two worlds?

In the second section, the Old Woman explores the possibility that our only contact with the eternal is through the impersonality of death, "The sleep of the changeless." (*WW*, 202) The question "Is it the sea we wish?" picks up the wave imagery of the previous section, and implies the central metaphor of Virginia Woolf's *The Waves*, viewing life as the process of individuation from the undifferentiated flux of the sea to which we ultimately return. From this point of view, man seems cut off from knowledge of the eternal, from "a jauntier principle of order." "We start from the dark," and our lives teach us little. "Is there a wisdom in objects?" the Old Woman finally asks. Does the physical universe carry news of the spiritual?

The third section answers these last questions affirmatively: "There are times when reality comes closer:/ In a field, in the actual air . . ." The reader of Roethke's earlier poetry is already familiar with this moment of direct apprehension of reality; as before, the field is its necessary locus.[37] The entire scene that follows seems to be identical to the mystic illumination of "Unfold! Unfold!," to which it should be carefully compared:

> Was it the stones I heard? I stared at the fixed stars.
> The moon, a pure Islamic shape, looked down.
> The light air showed: It was not night or day.
> All natural shapes became symbolical.   (WW, 203)

There is, then, wisdom in objects, in stones, for example, since there is a correspondence between the seen and unseen worlds; and, caught up in this vision of eternity, the Old Woman is filled with love.

The poem's final section maintains this joyful note. The shifting shadows of the second section's death wish is altered to an image of permanence opposed to flux; the protagonist's "shadow steadies in a shifting stream."

From the evanescent sense of union of "Her Becoming," the "Fourth Meditation" turns again to the feeling of aloneness, always a condition of human existence, but more keenly felt than ever by the Old Woman approaching death. At first, aloneness is seen in its positive aspect; the Old Woman "was always one for being alone,/ Seeking . . . eternal purpose." (WW, 205) But this waiting for the pure moment at the edge of a field soon gathers somber implications; the Old Woman thinks of the "songs we hide, singing only to ourselves." The result is a soul "lonely in its choice." Diminishing rhythms an-

[37] Cf. "The Lost Son" (WW, 85), "A Field of Light" (WW, 91), and "Unfold! Unfold!" (WW, 103)

nounce a world without revelation; although a lark rises from
a stone, there is no song. The "life of the mouth," the sensuous
self-indulgence of the body, is no longer sufficient.

In the second section, the Old Woman repudiates the view
of woman as simply a "mouth," a "vessel," something "contained"; this is life as seen by the "self-involved," "ritualists of
the mirror," "lonely drinkers," "Women who become their
possessions." (*WW*, 206) These self-centered "cat-like" figures
become symbols of the egoistic self cutting itself off from
reality, dooming itself to emptiness. They do not need simply
a "roaring boy," the animal vitality of sex; they rather lack
"captains of intuition," that flash of insight that links the isolated individual to all of creation. The Old Woman prays that
these women may "flame into being," that they may experience
their existential presence. And the last portion of this section
contains the protagonist's view of an Eden-like "greeny garden," through which walk the as yet unborn souls that have
come to full consciousness, and therefore love, of reality; they
are the culmination of the evolutionary process, they are freed
from the terrors of "the subliminal depths." (*WW*, 207) These
are the women, unfortunately imaginary, who have flamed
into being.

In the third section, the Old Woman turns from these
reveries to the symbolic landscape around her. Here, using a
metaphor from the "First Meditation," she sees an image of
the spirit jouneying from those "subliminal depths" toward
a vision of the eternal, toward a vision of the unity of all being: "the fish keep heading into the current." In spite of the
obstacles, the frightening isolation of human life, the spirit

never stops struggling. Seeing the lake breathing like a rose, another of the Old Woman's symbols of the path to the eternal, encouraged by the "dead" and by mystical stones, the protagonist arrives once more at a union of body and soul. And, transcending both of these, she feels life even in the dead matter of the universe.

Following the archetype of the journey of the spirit established in the "First Meditation," we have seen the exploration of the past in "I'm Here," the temporary sense of mystic union in "Her Becoming," and the growing awareness of aloneness in the face of death in the "Fourth Meditation." Although, as in life, the spirit travels successively forward and backward, its general movement has been toward an increasing feeling of isolation. As death approaches, the soul's certainty about the nature of existence, and, in particular, about what will happen to it itself, decreases. And this is precisely the lament of the first section of "What Can I Tell My Bones?" The soul, a "perpetual beginner," "knows not what to believe." (*WW*, 209) It lives in a "fearful ignorance," "Longing for absolutes that never come." The image of "shadows crawling down a sunny wall" seems to be a variation of Plato's allegory of the cave; the true reality is not perceived. We hear that "A bird sings out in solitariness/ A thin harsh song." This should be compared to the two sparrows of the "First Meditation," which symbolized the unity of inner and outer reality; now, the spirit, enclosed in a dying body, is cut off from the rest of creation, and, fearful of annihilation, has a "swan's dread of the darkening shore."

The third section finds the Old Woman's spirit cast down to the deepest depths of the Meditations. "What can I tell my bones?" asks the Old Woman. The crucial question, unanswerable, becomes: "Do these bones live?" Is there time after time, life after life? Faced with these questions, the Old Woman comes dangerously close to absolute despair; yet, she continues to hope, to yearn "to be delivered from the rational into the realm of pure song." (*WW*, 211) She still seeks and cares. Although man cannot become God, although his self may not exist eternally, man can still be like God, can enter into an important relationship with the absolute; in fact, if he is to exist in the full sense of the word, he *must* enter into an important relationship with the absolute. The Old Woman thinks, "God has need of me." This phrase is glossed by—if not actually taken from—some lines from Evelyn Underhill's *Mysticism:* "The homewards journey of man's spirit, then, may be thought of as due to the push of a divine life within answering to the pull of a divine life without. . . . 'God *needs* man,' says Eckhart. It is love calling to love." [38] "The dead love the unborn," says the Old Woman; the eternal cries out to the temporal.

From the depths, the Old Woman's spirit has once more climbed toward the heights. There is again "speech of light among the stones." Living in the extremes of this light, the Old Woman stretches "in all directions." At times, she thinks she is "several." (*WW*, 212) Her "spirit rises with the rising wind," she loves everything alive, as what was once vague

[38] New York, Meridian, 1955, pp. 132–33. We can assume that Roethke had some knowledge of Underhill's book, since the obscure epigraph to "Song," *Poetry*, CIII (Oct.–Nov. 1963), 87, was quoted from page 331. Stanley Kunitz also has suggested (in conversation) that Roethke got much of his material on mysticism from this source.

becomes, at least temporarily, certainty. And this certainty comes, or seems to come, as much from the outer world as from her own being; her knowledge is "Unprayed-for,/ And final."

Whether this mode of knowing is mystic in the full sense of the word, as it was for Meister Eckhart and Jacob Boehme, or is quasi-mystical, as for Buber and his "I-Thou" relationship between the individual and the external world, and for Tillich with his "eternal now," is not crucial.[39] These may after all be simply different aspects of the same kind of experience, or different interpretations of the same experience; perhaps Roethke himself was not completely certain as to how the relation to reality he describes should be classified.[40] What is important is that his protagonist has found a significant way of relating to the absolute, of experiencing the meaningfulness of her existence. However, even though this occurs repeatedly in Roethke's poetry, it never occurs finally. The poet must again and again turn to confront the threat of nonbeing, of death, meaninglessness, and condemnation.

Nonetheless, these experiences leave their mark on the poet's life and give him courage to find faith in the midst of despair. Buber's description of the evanescence of the eternal moment,

---

[39] There is evidence that Roethke was familiar with each of these figures. He quotes Eckhart in "Straw for the Fire," p. 116; Boehme appears in "The Pure Fury"; Mrs. Roethke has told me he read Buber, and there is an unmistakable paraphrase of the "I-Thou" relationship in "On 'Identity,'" *SP*, p. 25; and the importance of Tillich to Roethke's thought has been demonstrated throughout this chapter.

[40] Actually, Roethke seems to have distinguished between different aspects of mystic experience. See "On 'Identity,'" *SP*, pp. 25–26. This will be discussed in greater detail at the beginning of chapter 7.

and its relation to human life, applies to Roethke's approach to reality, whatever its specific classification:

> There are moments of silent depth in which you look on the world-order fully present. Then in its very flight the note will be heard; but the ordered world is its indistinguishable score. *These moments are immortal, and most transitory of all;* no content may be secured from them, but their power invades creation and the knowledge of man, beams of their power stream into the ordered world and dissolve it again and again. This happens in the history both of the individual and of the race.[41]

It also happens throughout Roethke's poetry. But it is not without significance that the final words of the Meditations, as well as of most of his other poetry, are affirmations of life.

When we consider *Words for the Wind,* which won the National Book Award, as a unit, we discover an organization that makes it one of the most remarkable volumes in contemporary poetry. (My only reservations, concerning the Voices and Creatures division, have been made above.) Part One, The Waking, shows the organic development of style and theme, from the metaphysical intellectuality of the early lyrics, to the more sensuous greenhouse poems, to the archetypal journey from the slime of *Praise to the End!* This part concludes with the emergence of the self; and Part Two, New Poems, turns from the concern with growth to the threat to the self of approaching nonbeing. The struggle for life is followed by the struggle for meaning. The full range of human possibilities is described in terms of the individual's movement toward aware-

---

[41] *I and Thou* (New York, Scribner, 1958), p. 31. (My italics.)

ness, and of the terrible responsibilities that awareness implies. *Words for the Wind,* read from cover to cover, is the spiritual autobiography of a man whose excessive sensitivity to his experience magnifies rather than distorts man's universal condition.

CHAPTER 7

The Dark Time
1959 – 1963

The Far Field, published posthumously in 1964, is the first of Roethke's volumes since *Open House* not to confront the reader with major developments in both style and content. Having spent a lifetime continually expanding his techniques, the poet here pauses to bring them to perfection for a final, powerful statement. That Roethke sensed it would be his final book is clear throughout.[1] The last ten years of his poetic activity were increasingly centered on the prospect of his approaching death, and *The Far Field* marks the culmination of this preoccupation.

[1] *The Far Field* was put together by Roethke shortly before his death. Its actual publication was supervised by Mrs. Roethke, who closely followed her husband's plan of composition. The first and final parts, North American Sequence and Sequence, Sometimes Metaphysical, appear exactly as Roethke edited them. There are, however, slight alterations in the middle two parts, including some deletions. Also, several of the poems which now appear in the Mixed Sequence—"The Manifestation," "The Tranced," and "The Moment," for example—presented special problems. They seem to belong with the poems of Sequence, Sometimes Metaphysical. However, partly because it would have been impossible to know where Roethke would have placed these poems had he decided to include them, they were finally relegated to their present position.

In connection with Roethke's awareness of the finality of this book, it should be noted that he told Ralph Mills, "a year before his death, that this might well be his final book." *Poetry,* CV (Nov. 1964), 124.

The first and last parts of *The Far Field* (as well as many poems of the middle parts) are concerned with Roethke's sense of mystic participation in reality. However, while the opening North American Sequence treats mystical experience as the main source of joy in a gloomy world, Sequence, Sometimes Metaphysical seems to view it with terror. Actually, this ambivalence has been present throughout Roethke's poetry. The death of the self in poems such as "The Pure Fury," "The Renewal," and "The Exorcism" is experienced with fright and loathing. Mystical union in these poems brings news of man's relation to the universe which must be met with courage; selflessness, the mystic's goal, is not, for Roethke, a source of comfort, but rather an ultimate horror. And yet, the mystical visions of spiritual correspondences to the visible world of poems such as "Unfold! Unfold!" and "Her Becoming" are unmistakably cause for exultation; union with nature is a source of strength. Paradoxically, the same kind of "steady storm of correspondences" which produced joy in "Unfold! Unfold!" and "Her Becoming," is precisely the origin of terror in "In a Dark Time." It would appear that Roethke is distinguishing between different aspects of the same experience. And this is, in fact, the case.

In his essay "On 'Identity,'" Roethke talks both of a "heightened consciousness" in which all of nature comes to life, and helps to define the individual identity, *and* of "the sense that all is one and one is all . . . accompanied by a loss of the 'I,' the purely human ego, to another center, a sense of the absurdity of death, a return to a state of innocency." Roethke adds that these feelings may or may not come together. The "heightened consciousness," produced by the sharp sense of a being other than the self, is a "break from self-involvement, from I to Otherwise, or maybe even to Thee." This is clearly borrowed from Buber's "I-Thou" relationship. The second part of the feeling, the sense of oneness in all the universe and the loss of the self in that oneness, is in the more traditional class of mystic experience (as described in Eckhart, St. John of the Cross, et al.) And the statement that even after mystical union there is no finality, that "God . . . still remains someone to be confronted, to be dueled with,"[2] places Roethke in the Kierkegaardian tradition which culminates in Tillich.

While the construction of a logically consistent philosophical system would demand some kind of synthesis or choice when confronted with these positions, poetry, more intimately related to experience itself than to its intellectualization, is far less rigid. Both the North American Sequence and the Sequence, Sometimes Metaphysical are concerned with transcending the sensual; the former approaches this goal by means of a heightened consciousness of the natural world, the latter by means of a direct leap into the ground of being, but both arrive at the same point.

North American Sequence

The North American Sequence, then, which begins *The Far Field*, is a series of six poems devoted to the problems of transcending the sensual. However, owing to the lack of a consistent philosophical base for Roethke's verse, it is not surprising that the implications of this purpose have been dis-

[2] *SP*, pp. 25–26.

puted. In his careful study of the sequence, Hugh Staples begins by assuming that Roethke is a mystic, and finds in the
poems the mystic's search for form in flux.[3] But Louis Martz
reaches a completely opposite interpretation of Roethke's
search for order. After reading several oblique references to
T. S. Eliot as repudiations of the mystic's withdrawal from the
flow of physical life, Martz goes on to say, "For Roethke, as
for Wallace Stevens, whom he also echoes in a few expressions,
the wonder of human apprehension, the wonder of creative
imagination is enough." [4]

Actually, the problem is not crucial. If we modify Staples
by saying that Roethke was a mystic, but not merely a mystic
who rejects the world of the senses, and alter Martz by saying
that the wonder of creative imagination was extremely important to Roethke, but not "enough," we shall find that both
interpretations, and others besides, are poetically valid. Explication must illuminate the poem without limiting its meaning.

From many points of view, North American Sequence is
very much in the manner of Meditations of an Old Woman:
the verse is generally discursive (with, however, more frequent
excursions into concentrated lyricism than the earlier poems),
the visual image dominates, with accompanying effects produced by the manipulation of the rhythms of everyday speech.
This time, however, the protagonist is for all practical purposes the poet himself; and the symbolic landscape is not
limited to the narrow confines of a backyard but is drawn
from the vastness of the North American continent. The se-

[3] Staples, p. 191.
[4] Martz, p. 297.

quence is again an archetypal journey; its wide spatial range, its cataloguing of flora and fauna in the manner of Whitman, its use of Homeric simile, its celebration of a nobler past, its plunging *in medias res,* beginning in middle age and returning to childhood before coming back to the present, its Vergilian descent to the Underworld of "Journey to the Interior"—all give the sequence what Staples has called "a dimension curiously suggestive of the epic." [5]

Now we have encountered this archetypal journey often in Roethke's earlier poetry; the continual regression in order to progress provides the basic movements not only of the Meditations, but of *Praise to the End!* as well. The descent to the Underworld is perhaps less specifically Vergilian than an instance of Jung's immersion in the slime in the search for renewal, the night journey under the sea. "I have left the body of the whale," says Roethke in "The Longing," alluding to Jonah's voyage, the prototype of night journeys, "but the mouth of the night is still wide . . ." (*FF,* 14) As in previous sequences, there is a correspondence between the protagonist's descent to the slime, and the probing of the depths of his psyche. And also as in previous sequences, there is a correspondence between the poem's outer landscape and the landscape of the protagonist's inner mind; Roethke, in a very important sense, *is* the North American continent, and his explorations of it in time and space continue his search for the self by retrieving the past and analyzing the present. And so the "kingdom of stinks and sighs" (*FF,* 13) with which the first section of "The Longing" begins, should be understood not only as a condemnation of the materialistic stagnation of contemporary Ameri-

[5] Staples, p. 189.

can life, but also as a representation of the protagonist's inner despair, his loss of hope.

The main question of the entire sequence is clearly stated in this opening section: "How to transcend this sensual emptiness?" Just as our society is caught in a dead end of its own creation, in its rejection of spiritual values, so the individual bound exclusively to the life of the senses is trapped by his own animal decay when "the spirit fails to move forward." For the spirit has become that odious creature, "a slug, a loose worm," unable to see.

In the second section, the free verse and discursive language of the first part have appropriately become more nearly regular in rhythmic structure, more concentrated in imagery, and have the additional formal element of a shadowy rhyme scheme, as the poet for the first time renews his hope of transcending this "dark dream." He seeks unity of flesh and spirit, "body with the motion of a soul!" (*FF*, 14) And, as for the boy in "The Lost Son" and the Old Woman of the *Meditations,* the way to bring these two worlds together is by means of the rose, which "exceeds us all."

A Whitmanesque concentration on the first person wish begins the poem's final section. The poet, his "eye quiet on the growing rose," longs for the motion of the struggling salmon, the mad lemmings, children dancing, a winding stream, in order to dispel the stagnation; for, by means of this motion, he would attain "the imperishable quiet at the heart of form," the spiritual reality behind the physical. The allusion to Jonah tells us that although the poet has previously traveled in the body of the whale, the night remains with him. He must make still another journey. The dying buffalo prefigure his own

bodily death; his soul, like the Indian, must explore the coun-
tryside in search of something beyond. "Old men ought to be
explorers," Eliot said in "East Coker." Roethke agrees; but his
explorations will be made over a terrain far more concrete than
Eliot's:

> Old men should be explorers?
> I'll be an Indian.
> Iroquois.   (*FF*, 15)

"Meditation at Oyster River" begins and ends with water.
As Staples has pointed out, the middle four poems of the sequence are alternately dominated by water and earth imagery,
even in their titles, as the main themes introduced in "The
Longing" are thoroughly analyzed before being reunited with
new significance in "The Rose." [6] However, these elements
are not assigned allegorical meanings; they are rather part of
a far more complex symbolism. Water, for example, appears
as stagnant pond, flowing stream, and rocking, engulfing sea,
with different implications associated with each aspect; most
important, water is neither exclusively beginning nor end, but
both, since it travels in a continuous cycle, at various stages of
which it appears to change its nature while really retaining it.
This is Roethke's most frequently used symbol of permanence
in apparent change. And earth also varies in its connotations,

---

[6] "The sequence, then, can be regarded as a tone poem consisting of
an overture ('The Longing'), in which the major themes appear, followed by four movements in which the tensions and oppositions of the
whole sequence are summarized and move towards a resolution." Staples,
p. 193. But Staples, ignoring complexity, limits his reading to simple
opposition between water (goals, flux, life) and earth (origins, stability,
death).

from the death-laden landscape of "Journey to the Interior" to the revelation at "The Far Field."

The complexity of the water imagery is nowhere better illustrated than in "Meditation at Oyster River." In the first section, the moody poet sees in the river suggestions of death: "dead clam shells," "a dead tree in the rivermouth," "a last glint of the reflected sunlight" (*FF*, 16); the very foam of the barely moving water is "brackish." But even here, the "child-whimpering" of the gulls anticipates the birth imagery to follow. The second section pictures the self as "a dying star,/ In sleep, afraid." (*FF*, 17) The self wishes an end to isolation; it wishes to be gathered up in the arms of nature, to be at one with the animals who have no consciousness of their separation, to merge with the sensuously creeping waters. The self, afraid of death, ironically wills its death to escape fear.

However, as we have seen time and time again in Roethke's work, this immersion in origins, this descent into stagnant water, leads to a renewal, to the imagery of birth and rebirth. The newborn child or the reborn man gains strength from his temporary identity with the natural world, from "this first heaven of knowing." (*FF*, 17) The poet on his rock, for the moment beyond the movements of time, thinks first of the birth of a Michigan brook in April, then of the rebirth of the Tittebawasee as the winter ice melts, and finally longs for his own rebirth, his debris-loosening blast of dynamite within.

In the fourth section, the poet's thoughts return to the opening scene of waning light; he rocks "In the cradle of all that is" (*FF*, 18), his spirit ambiguously united with the small waves. But the poem ends optimistically, with "A shining"; the "shimmer" of light, apparently lost in "The Longing," has been restored.

If "Meditation at Oyster River" brings a certain amount of hope, "Journey to the Interior" reminds both poet and reader that hope is not the fulfillment of hope, that an arduous struggle filled with dead ends and false starts still remains: "In the long journey out of the self," in the attempt to transcend this sensual existence, "There are many detours." (*FF*, 19) Particularly uneven rhythms announce the dangerous washed-out road, the winding path across a "swamp alive with quicksand," which will provide the principal journey metaphors of this poem.

The second section describes in detail one of the detours mentioned at the poem's beginning, an automobile trip along a dusty road; but Roethke reminds the reader that both the movement of the car *and* the barren highway are part of the protagonist's psyche: ". . . The road was part of me, and its ditches . . ." This difficult up-and-down journey is reminiscent of the bus trip in the Old Woman's "First Meditation"; and although it is a detour, a movement away from the sea, and therefore a regression, this trip too leads the poet out of his self-created waste land. (Here again, the parched, lifeless terrain brings to mind an Eliot poem.) Passing sluggish water under an old bridge, a cemetery, "dead snakes and muskrats," "turtles gasping in the rubble," the poet suddenly feels that all is flowing by, that he himself is motionless (*FF*, 20); heat-lightning flashes, a false promise of rain. But suddenly, a vision of the eternal sea imposes itself upon the dusty imagery: the poet rises and falls "in the slow sea of a grassy plain," caught up again in that rocking motion. "I rise and fall, and time folds/ Into a long moment . . ." Hearing the lichen speak, the ivy advance on the road, the poet has again returned to timeless origins; the dusty road shimmers, the self is absorbed. This detour has now taken on far more significance than we first imagined. The journey began at the side of the sea, in eternity, and moved toward the interior in the course of life; and here, in the midst of the dusty journey, comes a vision of eternity, the endless sea.

The third section returns us to the present after this excursion into the poet's younger years; the road through the "parched land" fades into a quiet meditation at the shore of "the flower of all water," the soul is at a "still-stand." This eternity is annihilation of the individual; the "still-stand" is "The stand at the stretch in the face of death." (*FF*, 21) Roethke here rejects neither the temporal nor the eternal; he rather laments the lack of connection between them. He has come to "a place leading nowhere." And instead of transcending the self, escaping its limitations, he is in danger of losing it completely. But if the poet has come to a blind alley, if, like the "eyeless starer" of "The Longing," his soul cannot see spiritual reality, yet his faith remains; he knows, "As a blind man, lifting a curtain, knows it is morning." (*FF*, 21) This journey into the past, into the world of lichen and ivy, has not been without its compensations, even if it does represent a false start; for "the dead begin from their dark to sing in my sleep," the helping dead will lead the poet to salvation.

"I reject the world of the dog" (*FF*, 22), says the poet at the start of "The Long Waters." [7] Roethke is again rejecting

---

[7] Cf. "Happiness left to dogs and children—/ (Matters only a saint mentions!)" ("The Longing," *FF*, 13), which in turn recalls "I've

the appeal of annihilation of self-consciousness, the death wish; he seeks a solution that allows man to stand outside his subjective self without destroying that self, without denying the knowledge of concrete reality that defines it. Acknowledging his "foolishness with God," his desire for peaks, black ravines, "fields where no lungs breathe" (*FF*, 22)—in short, turning his back on the path of isolation—the poet finds himself once more at that most important of places, "Where the fresh and salt waters meet," the point of intersection between the temporal (flowing streams) and the eternal (sea into which they flow). Here, the sea winds blow with renewed life; but here too, on these charred shores, the self is threatened. Having rejected his childhood death wish, the poet cannot so easily reject death. He must come to terms with it.

The second section of "The Long Waters" begins with an invocation of "Mnetha, mother of Har," [8] whose name suggests wisdom based on memory, and whose function in Blake's *Tiriel* is as a nurse in close touch with nature. [9] Roethke appeals to her to protect him from the flux, "The dubious sea-change, the heaving sands," which threaten his dying self; he is calling upon memory, personal and racial—"tentacled sea-cousins" are in his mind—to ascertain his identity, he is calling upon nature to teach him to accept the natural processes, and he is calling upon intuition to deliver him from the purely

crawled from the mire, alert as a saint or a dog . . ." ("Praise to the End!" *WW*, 100).

[8] Cf. Dylan Thomas' "Before I Knocked."

[9] The Valley of Har (which means mountain in Hebrew) is, for Blake, a peak ironically leveled to a valley, rather than the traditional biblical valley raised to a peak. With the peaks and black ravines appearing in the first section of "The Long Waters," Roethke may have been making use of the same pun.

rational.[10] The self, formerly a dying star, now a "star winking beyond itself" (*FF*, 23), will not give up its sensual identity: pleasure dies slowly.

Beginning again at the shore of the bay, the poet makes another attempt to fuse temporal and eternal in the third section: staring at the shimmering water, he sees flowers in the waves. We have already seen "the flower of all water" (*FF*, 20), and this image, developing into the rose of the final poem, will become increasingly important as a symbol of the relation between time and eternity.

In the fourth section, a stone breaks the eddying current; representing the poet's escape from the flux of time, it is appropriately described as a "vulnerable place." (*FF*, 24) And in the poem's concluding section, contact, although of a tenuous sort, is finally made with the eternal. The image of the bat, another of the "blind" creatures that pervade the sequence, sets the tone for man's groping search for the world beyond. The sea wind, the breath of the eternal, seems to bring a renewal of life, an awakening of desire. A vision takes form in the poet's dreaming mind; the weeping figure is "The eternal one, the child . . . The numinous ring around the opening flower." (*FF*, 24)[11] This Blakean image of childhood innocence recalls the time when the poet responded to all the natural world as a living presence, as—in Buber's terminology —a "Thou." The trip to the depths, cited in the last stanza, has resulted in a glimpse of the eternal. And the opening flower is combined with the long waters, as the poet's "eyes

[10] Cf. "Mother, mother of us all, tell me where I am!/ O to be delivered from the rational into the realm of song." (*WW*, 211)

[11] Cf. "a kiss widens the rose." The Dying Man. (*WW*, 187)

end beyond the farthest bloom of the waves." Losing and finding himself in these waters, as he had in his descent to the slime, he embraces the world. The near merging of the poet's shimmering form with the waters has many elements of the mystic consciousness; but complete union is not experienced, for here the self is found rather than lost.

"I dream of journeys repeatedly" (*FF*, 25) says Roethke at the start of "The Far Field," for life, as well as the North American Sequence, is composed of a continual succession of journeys of the soul. The bat, flying "deep into a narrowing tunnel," is again a type of the spirit, as is the car, with churning wheels, stalled in a snowdrift. The difficulties and terrors of this journey are expressed more directly in the second section: the place of revelation is the far field, near the garbage dump, where one learns of the eternal "in the shrunken face of a dead rat, eaten by rain and ground-beetles," and in the dead tomcat with "Its entrails strewn over the half-grown flowers." We have encountered this kind of image before, in "A Walk in Late Summer": "I'm dying piecemeal, fervent in decay;/ My moments linger—that's eternity." (*WW*, 179) Eternity does not deny decay; it is decay. This is the eternity of impersonal particles which remain forever, while organisms compose and decompose.

And yet this facing of a horrible truth does not, for the poet, repudiate all human possibilities; although he grieves, and justly so, for birds and young rabbits caught in the mower—an image which may have been taken from Marvell's "Appleton House" —he is still able to say that "to come upon warblers in early May/ Was to forget time and death." (*FF*, 26) The entrails of the tomcat are—in a carefully chosen word—"strewn" over the half-grown flowers, suggesting some kind of fertility rite, the cycle of death and rebirth. Perhaps, thinks the poet lying in the shifting sand beside the flowing river, the self is preserved even in nature's flux; perhaps he will return as a snake, a bird, or, "with luck," a lion. Echoing the first section of "Unfold! Unfold!" (*WW*, 101), another poem of revelation in the field, Roethke recites the field's lesson: he has "learned not to fear infinity," "the windy cliffs of forever," "The dying of time . . . ," "on-coming water." (*FF*, 26) Turning on himself, entering himself, the poet reaches that principle of being which he shares with the entire universe; he finds a "still, but not a deep center,/ A point outside the glittering current." (*FF*, 27)

The implications of this possible reference to Eliot's "still point of the turning world" are not entirely clear. It may indeed be, as it was for Eliot, the point of intersection of the eternal and the temporal in mystic experience. Or, if we accept Martz's "esthetic" interpretation of Roethke's point of view, we may conclude that "from this standpoint, the still center lies in the sensitive, observant, imaginative mind, responding affectionately to the flow of physical life." [12] And finally, this point outside the glittering current, the flux of life, may represent existential ec-stasis, man's standing-out from himself, his full realization of his being.

The question of which of these possibilities is most important to Roethke's own philosophy is not easily decided; but we should not be surprised to discover that within the context of the sequence each of these themes seems appropriate to the poems' interpretation. Not only are esthetic, existential, and religious approaches to reality not mutually exclusive, they

[12] Martz, p. 296.

are precisely the themes Roethke considered to be of greatest concern to the contemporary poet.[13] Beauty, being, and God are the most important subjects not only of the North American Sequence, but of the entire last volume.

In the fifth section, the self, characterized throughout the poem as eternal but changing, is symbolized by the "seashape," Proteus, and by Prospero ("in garments of adieu"), the self bidding farewell to its present form. This Proteus-Prospero is specifically Roethke himself, "A man faced with his own immensity" (*FF*, 28); but he is also within his deepest depths an archetypal, universal figure, "He is the end of things, the final man." (*FF*, 28) This line, which calls to mind *Notes toward a Supreme Fiction,* is possibly one of the echoes of Stevens to which Martz refers. But it also recalls "that final thing,/ A man learning to sing" (*WW*, 187) of The Dying Man; the Proteus figure, the vision of reality as a single being undergoing continual metamorphosis, is the key to the Dying Man's assertion that "Eternity is Now." Or, as Roethke now puts it, echoing Blake and the entire tradition of mystic poets, "All finite things reveal infinitude." (*FF*, 28) Nonetheless, the conclusion of this poem is not unambiguously joyful. To have seen eternity in decaying flesh is not to love it, necessarily; and although the

[13] Roethke actually listed four principal themes: "(1) The multiplicity, the chaos of modern life; (2) The way, the means of establishing a personal identity, a self in the face of that chaos; (3) The nature of creation, that faculty for producing order in the arts, particularly in poetry; and (4) The nature of God himself." "On 'Identity,'" *SP*, p. 19. The first theme is the basic perception of reality to which the others are reactions: (2) philosopical or psychological, (3) esthetic, (4) religious. Earlier in Roethke's work, (2) was mainly psychological; but in this last phase, the emphasis is existential: "The human problem is to find out what one really *is:* whether one exists, whether existence is possible." *SP*, p. 20.

universal self may persist, the individual is lost. A particular man's memory is just a ripple from a single stone which winds around the waters of the world.

"There are those to whom place is unimportant," begins "The Rose," in what may be a reference to Eliot ("Ash Wednesday" and "East Coker"), "But this place, where sea and fresh water meet,/ Is important—" (*FF*, 29) Here, Roethke is reaffirming the importance of the point at which the temporal and eternal intersect; but unlike Eliot, or the introspective mystic tradition (which does *not include* such poets as Blake, Vaughan, or Whitman), he emphasizes the specific "place" in space and time, rather than the unchanging eternal. It is only through the finite that the infinite is revealed. But also, this place is the final place; here, the river of the individual is lost forever in the universal sea. The middle lines of this section are filled with images of death: morning birds are gone, the sun is setting, the last geese fly across, the moon retreats behind a cloud, the owl cries, an old log subsides with the waves. Only the flash of the kingfisher, a possible symbol of Christ, betokens life. However, in this vision of finality is born a corresponding vision of creation. Standing outside himself, the poet sees the light heighten; "in a mist out of nowhere," the first rain gathers, water is drawn up from the sea to be rained down again and fill the rivers. The very moment of death is the moment of birth as well.

Finally breaking through the barrier between the temporal and the eternal, the poet, in the second section, unites his contending worlds. Neither completely bound by his senses, nor having left behind the concrete in mystical ecstasy, he finds his unity of being in the rose in the sea wind. All is in motion, all but the rose, a single rose emerging from the slime, the mire, the *dreck*. This vision of the rose, embodiment of unity of being for Dante and Yeats, is followed by a flashback to childhood paradise, the Eden of the greenhouses, with the poet's "father standing astride the cement benches." (*FF*, 30) And, just as the rose in the sea wind beckons the adult, the greenhouse roses beckon the child out of himself. We are reminded that it is through the exploration of childhood, and of the racial past, that we have come to this perception of the eternal while still within time: "What need for heaven, then,/ With that man, and those roses?" Roethke sees no promise of afterlife; his eternity is above time, and it is reached through time. It is Now.

The third section, a tribute to Whitman, catalogues the American continent. In all that he hears, the poet hears the voice of the eternal. "Beautiful my desire, and the place of my desire" (*FF*, 31), writes Roethke, in the most Whitmanesque line of all. It is through place that one exceeds place. And in the final section, the poet once again visits the "sea slime," the origin of the rose; beyond the process of "becoming and perishing," he stands outside himself. (*FF*, 32) He finally *is*, he finally experiences his existence fully, by perceiving it in the rose, with which he sways yet remains still. The sequence ends not with mystic union, the selflessness that threatened earlier, but rather with a heightened awareness of one's own self obtained by a special relationship with the external world; it ends with "a break from self-involvement, from I to Otherwise, or maybe even to Thee." [14] The nature of being has been

[14] "On 'Identity,' " *SP*, p. 25.

revealed by this rose, "Rooted in stone, keeping the whole of light."

The difficulties in the interpretation of the North American Sequence have required that the emphasis of this discussion be placed on the content rather than the form of these poems; and indeed, in technique they are similar to the Meditations of an Old Woman. But we ought to note one particular aspect of Roethke's technique which has been so greatly developed as almost to constitute an entirely new method: the use of leitmotiv as symbol. The image, or cluster of images, has always borne a crucial part of the meaning of Roethke's verse; but here, the significance of many sections is communicated almost exclusively by recurrent or obsessive imagery. There is no room in this study for a detailed analysis of this imagery, but one example should suffice to illustrate Roethke's method.

The tree, one of his favorite symbols of the self, plays an important part in the North American Sequence. In the first section of "The Longing," "great trees no longer shimmer" (*FF*, 13), for the poet is bound by sensual emptiness. "A sunken log" (*FF*, 16) is among the dead objects at the start of "Meditation at Oyster River," appearing again as "a dead tree in the rivermouth"; the self is at a "still-stand," ready to be loosed in the explosion of rebirth which sets free the branches and logs in the third section. In "the long journey out of the self" of "Journey to the Interior," the detour is caused "by a fallen fir-tree." (*FF*, 19) The waste land of the self in that poem is characterized by "two scrubby trees" (*FF*, 20), the stagnant soul is "a tree idling in air." (*FF*, 21) In this last image, the tree, exposed to the breath of the wind, is subject to renewed

.e, which the poet himself is about to receive. And the rebirth imagery at the start of "The Long Waters" is signaled by
the "sea-winds [which] move through the pine trees." (*FF*,
22) "Fallen fir trees" (*FF*, 23) again appear after the poet's
relapse into terror, and the vision of eternity in decay in "The
Far Field" is accompanied by a "dead tree in the chicken-
yard." (*FF*, 26) Another "wet log" symbolizes the lost self in
the same section. And when the poet draws into his "deep
center" for a glimpse of the universal, "The tree retreats into
its own shadow." (*FF*, 27) The ripple of memory with which
this poem ends disturbs the quiet water "above a sunken tree."
(*FF*, 28) A fir tree is one of the important landmarks of the
"place" with which "The Rose" opens, and the imagery of the
poet's approaching death, which follows in that first section,
includes an old log. The pine and the oak overlook the vision
of the rose in the second section, and "the wind tries the shape
of a tree" (*FF*, 31) in the calm that precedes the final infusion
of spirit. And the rose of the final section grows from "among
the half-dead trees." (*FF*, 32)

The movement of the entire sequence can be traced in terms
of these trees; sometimes a particular portion of the poem can
be understood only by reference to tree imagery. Water, flowers, birds, and stones are among the other similarly crucial
leitmotivs. And while the leitmotiv is hardly peculiar to
Roethke alone, his use of it is characteristic. His images do
not simply appear or disappear; they are constantly undergoing metamorphosis, like the Protean self they help define.

Love Poems

In considering the middle two parts of *The Far Field*, we must remember that their organization is not entirely Roethke's own; they lack the cohesion that most sequences of his previous volumes possess. However, the first six of the new Love Poems do form a kind of abbreviated version of Yeats's "A Woman Young and Old," and so provide a center of gravity for the sequence they appear in. Although Roethke's new lyrics are very much concerned with the tensions between body and soul, they are less closely related to the Love Poems of *Words for the Wind* than are the poems of Sequence, Sometimes Metaphysical. For, strongly influenced by the Elizabethan lyric, and by a year of drinking and singing in Irish pubs (during a trip the Roethkes took in 1960), they replace intellectual complexity with the simple, powerful outcry, and multiplicity of imagery with the single, dominant image. Their songlike quality is the only real development of something new in Roethke's verse in the volume.

The persona of the sequence, to whom this more lyrical mode of expression is perfectly suited, is introduced in the title of the very first poem: "The Young Girl." This young girl approaches the contradictions of body and soul from a point of view opposite to that of the old poet,[15] but although she starts from flesh and he from spirit, they converge on the same

[15] Some of the later poems of this part indicate that Roethke was contemplating balancing the young girl's poems with a sequence in his own voice; but although the poet ultimately appears in his own right, the poems concerning flesh and spirit which would have been most appropriate to this conception are scattered through other parts of the book.

paradoxes. "We are one, and yet we are more" (*FF*, 35), says the young girl, referring both to the union of lovers and of flesh and spirit; the old man and the young girl themselves represent opposing aspects of reality. The evocation of bird—symbol of soul in Roethke—and blood—symbol of body—gives this attempt at unity concrete form. The strict scheme of rhymes and slant rhymes, and lines that scan—like songs—by quantity rather than accent, provide the appropriate framework for this delicate lyric.

The next poem, "Her Words," records the first ecstasy of love, in which all the world is transformed into an image of the young girl's passion; raging all about is "the storm of a kiss." (*FF*, 36) In this world, the girl's words control, they act as magic counters. However, the harmony of inner and outer worlds, of words and action, soul and body, is soon shattered. In "The Apparition," the girl is alone; her lover has taken her soul, "and it like to die." (*FF*, 37) Even though the lover's spirit walks by, she remains apart, body deserted by soul. This song, with its Irish turn of phrase and simple quatrains, is perhaps the best illustration of the new infusion of lyricism.

Hurt by the impossibility of full unity, the young girl wishes for less involvement of both body and soul in "Her Reticence": she would send him only a "sleeve with my hand in it,/ Disembodied, unbloody." (*FF*, 38) But this is no longer possible. Formerly, she "lived serene as a fish" (*FF*, 39), she tells us in "Her Longing"; but now the sea itself cannot contain her. She has become wild and violent, like the predatory seabirds; but she is also the phoenix, symbol of rebirth. She protects the sea cliffs, her wings "beating against the black clouds of the storm." (*FF*, 39) In these lines, reminiscent of the conclusion of The

Dying Man, the girl pits her love against the sea of eternity; she attempts, through love, to give meaning to her time, her portion of the eternal. And indeed, the sequence comes to an end in an ambiguous poem entitled "Her Time." Abandoning the songlike forms of the previous poems, and returning to Roethke's usual lengthening and shortening of rhythms, these two last poems also supply the essential link between the young girl's thoughts of life, and the older poet's preoccupation with death. "Her Time" in particular, with its image of the motionless sea, seems to emphasize an acquiescence to death rather than the conquest of it. In a sudden realization, in which she breaks through to share the Dying Man's point of view, the girl fully aware that her desires too are subject to time.

"Song" ("My wrath, where's the edge") returns to the old poet. He lacks the wrath and rage of the young girl, but also, by implication, her vitality. The appeal to those who hear "The slow tick of time" in their "sea-buried ear" (*FF*, 41) unites this lyric to the girl's final thoughts of sea and death. "What's to come?" is the poem's crucial question, and, sharing the ambiguity of "Her Time," it remains unanswered.

"Light Listened" returns briefly to the methods of *Words for the Wind*. The poet's beloved is clearly the object of physical love: "Who'd look when he could feel?/ She'd more sides than a seal." (*FF*, 42) Yet, she is also his salvation, his means of transcending the physical: she sings a "final song," and light itself listens when she sings. As fine as this poem is, however, its tone seems thoroughly out of keeping with the wistful lyrics which have preceded it, and its content seems almost naive when compared with the young girl's sad acceptance of love's limitations. And the light song, "The Happy Three," about a domestic quarrel and a goose—Marianne (Moore)—destroys what is left of the atmosphere of the opening poems. "His Foreboding," which in title as well as content seems to have originally been planned to stand in direct relation to the young girl's poems, is thus left standing without a context. It is nonetheless one of the best poems in the section.

The poem begins with an image of the sea; the poet is still filled with the "incommensurate dread/ Of being." (*FF*, 45) He fears death as separation from life, which is here embodied in "one comely head." In the second stanza, he recognizes that far from providing a solution to difficulties, thought may actually be a burden to the soul; and even speaking to the stones, once a symbol of direct communication with the natural world, is no longer sufficient. In the third stanza, the fear of nothingness becomes explicitly associated with the poet's sense of separation: the loneliest thing he knows is his "own mind at play." The beloved appears as the last ray of light in the final stanza, as the poet sniffs the darkening air. The poem ends where it began, at the side of the sea; but now a storm is rising. Death threatens to cut him off from his beloved, from life, forever. The rhythm, based on something approximating a three-beat line, follows the at once even and uneven rocking of the sea; the complex rhyme scheme, which links the stanzas together, threatens to dissolve completely before reforming more regularly than ever at the end: *abbab, baacd, efcga, hdhdh.* The uneasy play of the poet's mind is well reflected by this undercurrent of forming and resolved tensions. Also particularly effective are the contrasts of "incommensurate dread" with the largely one- or two-syllable words of the poem, and the abstraction "nothingness" with the poet "sniffing" the dark.

"The Shy Man," a song straight from the Irish pubs,[16] cele-brates the poet's love for "the O'Connell's daughter" (*FF*, 46), his wife (the former Beatrice Heath O'Connell). And "Her Wrath" laments the resemblance this Beatrice's wrath holds to that of Dante's in Purgatory. But these poems represent a lapse from the universal to the particular, and allow the Love Poems to trail off in anticlimax. "Wish for a Young Wife" is the dying poet's prayer for the best of possible lives for his wife "When I am undone,/ When I am no one." (*FF*, 48) Here, Roethke succeeds in making the personal universal once more, but even this fine poem cannot draw the section together into a coherent sequence.

Mixed Sequence

If the movement of the Love Poems tends to dissipate the coherent structure with which the section began, Mixed Se-quence fails to come even that close to a sense of order. This lack poses serious problems for a group of poems which for the most part reexamine old concerns without contributing anything new in technique or perspective; there is no definite context to enrich the meanings of these poems, no system of interrelationship by which individual limitations might be transcended. Nonetheless, Roethke is by this time a consider-able poet, and his established powers are enough to give many

[16] This poem originally did appear as one of the two "Pub Songs" in *Poetry*, XCVIII (Aug. 1961), 283. The other was "Gob Music," to ap-pear in the new collected edition of Roethke's verse.

of his poems great force and beauty, especially for the reader
not familiar with his earlier work.

"The Abyss" is a redefinition of the "immense immeasurable
emptiness of things" that dominates Roethke's last poems. "I
live near the abyss" (*WW,* 159), he had written several years
before (1958); but now, the abyss is "right where you are."
(*FF,* 51) The first section places the elusive purgatorial stair
(cf. "The Waking") in direct opposition to this gaping nothingness; the road to salvation is a blind alley, a road going
nowhere, and the abyss, unavoidable, waits. The sense of terror implicit in this view of approaching death is supported by
quatrains of two-beat lines, a verse pattern similar to the ones
used to obtain effects of frenzied excitement in *Praise to the
End!*

In the second section, the pace is slowed, the poet reflects
upon the implications of his sudden insight into the nature of
things. He is seized by the fear that he has not truly lived, that
he has not in any meaningful sense experienced his being; his
existence has often been vague, arid, neither in nor out of life.
He then hears "the noise of a wall" (*FF,* 52), an image we
have long since learned to identify with the "dead," with the
"spiritual fathers," in Roethke's verse; and sure enough, we
soon find the poet invoking Whitman, "maker of catalogues,"
to assist him in testing the reality of the world, to help him
satisfy "the terrible hunger for objects," for the concrete. The
caterpillar is specifically named as symbol of the protagonist;
he moves toward death, the condition of pure spirit, as the
caterpillar moves toward being a butterfly. But this crawling
creature has further connotations, for Roethke soon takes the
form of a "mole winding through earth,/ A night-fishing

otter." [17] Here again is the "night journey under the sea"; the abyss is not only the darkness of the future, but also that familiar "slime" of the past in which the poet must immerse himself in order to achieve salvation.

Confronting reality, the threat of nonbeing, is for Roethke, as for Tillich, the only way of affirming one's being. And yet, this confrontation seems to be more than man can endure: "Too much reality can be a dazzle, a surfeit:/ Too close immediacy an exhaustion." (*FF*, 52)[18]

If we can somehow survive "the fearful instant" (*FF*, 53), if we can wait beyond it, then the agonizing fires of the abyss may yet be quenched by water's all-encompassing peace. But in the fourth section, the sea itself becomes a threat, still another image of the abyss. The terror of the past, of the knowledge of one's identity (as symbolized in the previous section by the scene from childhood, the smells of the florist's storeroom), gives way to the even greater terror of the future, the lack of individual existence, "the final sea." "Do we move toward God, or merely another condition?" is the poet's tortured question; is the future nothingness, the present meaningless? The two abysses, that of past and that of future, merge as Roethke continues his journey, rocking "between dark and dark." His dead selves, his past, sing to him, the ancestral dead add their voices, and the poet moves once more toward acceptance. The mechanics of this process are the same as those of *Praise to the End!*, Meditations of an Old Woman, and North American Sequence: regression in order to progress, immersion

[17] Cf. the mole of "The Lost Son," (*WW*, 81) and the otter of that poem, and of "O Lull Me, Lull Me." (*WW*, 78)
[18] Cf. T. S. Eliot's "human kind/ Cannot bear very much reality," in "Burnt Norton."

in slime and darkness to find light, the arrival at faith by way of despair.

In the poem's concluding section, the poet uses familiar imagery to announce the establishment of a new "I-Thou" relationship with the natural world, symbolizing also the acceptance of his self and of his fate: he hears "the flowers drinking in their light," he takes "counsel of the crab and the sea-urchin." (*FF,* 54) God's existence, and therefore the meaningfulness of the poet's life, is reaffirmed. Once more, the union of spirit and matter is achieved, as the poet merges, "like the bird, with the bright air." (*FF,* 54) The poem ends with a line the significance of which is heightened by its being isolated from the rest of the text to form a stanza in itself: "Being, not doing, is my first joy." This is again an affirmation of the importance of the existential experiencing of one's being, in a world in which activity for its own sake is becoming an increasingly universal standard. But it may also be praise of the mystic's direct participation in reality, of Boehme's union with the Abyss, of Eckhart's union with the abysmal Godhead. "Being, not Doing, is the first aim of the mystic," writes Underhill, characterizing the mystic consciousness.[19] The existentialist fear of nonbeing is precisely paralleled by still another familiar motif, the mystic's "dark night of the soul."

The "abyss" itself is the image of this "dark night," which, according to St. John of the Cross, has two aspects: 1) the contemplation of the Divine as a ray of darkness "for the natural strength of the intellect is transcended and overwhelmed

---

[19] *Mysticism* (New York, Meridian, 1955), p. 380. For evidence of Roethke's familiarity with this book, see footnote 38, p. 168, above.

by its great supernatural light," [20] or, as Roethke puts it, "Too much reality can be a dazzle, a surfeit"; 2) by "the profound immersion of its spirit in the knowledge and realization of its evils and miseries," the soul, coming to feel its unworthiness, "believes that God has cast it away," [21] a fear reflected in Roethke's question, "Do I move toward God, or merely another condition?"

This vision of the "dark night" is not in the least incompatible with the Jungian connotations of the "abyss" as the depths of the "night journey." Indeed, the "dark night," in which the soul moves away from God in order to approach him more closely, has many of the characteristics of Jung's regression and progression. "Immersion" in darkness is a crucial concept for St. John of the Cross as well, and it is no accident that he uses the image of Jonah's "night journey" to express the woeful state of the soul: "The soul feels itself to be perishing and melting away, in the presence and sight of its miseries, in a cruel spiritual death, even as if it had been swallowed by a beast and felt itself devoured in the darkness of its belly, suffering such anguish as was endured by Jonas in the belly of that beast of the sea. For in this sepulchre of dark death it must needs abide until the spiritual resurrection which it hopes for." [22]

Although the conflation of the religious and psychological implications of the "abyss" is not new to Roethke's verse, the skill with which these two systems of metaphor are interwoven

[20] *Dark Night of the Soul,* trans. E. Allison Peers (New York, Doubleday, 1959), p. 101.
[21] *Ibid.,* p. 102.
[22] *Ibid.,* p. 104.

in this particular poem, and the extent of the mutual enrich-
ment of themes, make "The Abyss" well able to stand on its
own, without definite context. If it does not really add to
Roethke's poetic world, it is nonetheless one of that world's
most powerful summaries.

"The Abyss" is followed by three poems which describe
friends and family rather than the poet's self directly. The
"Elegy" to Aunt Tilly presents Roethke's opposite, a woman
who never knew the war between flesh and spirit. She faced
the worst without blinking, she "fed and tended the infirm,
the mad, the epileptic." (*FF*, 55) She was unafraid. Ironically,
however, she too is a source of terror for the poet, since "she
died in agony,/ Her tongue, at the last, black as an ox's."

For the close description and accumulation of effects of this
poem, Roethke makes use of free verse, varying the patterns
of everyday speech. But appropriately more formal in manner
is the poem dedicated to the poet's Prussian father, "Otto." A
series of couplets followed by a triplet forms the stanzaic pattern for this evocation of the poet's "lost world." As usual in
Roethke's rhymed works, assonance, consonance, and disso-
nance are freely used; the combination of slant rhyme with
the insistent repetition of "world" at the poem's conclusion
produces a particularly powerful sense of unresolved tensions,
while alliteration (of "w") maintains an undercurrent of smooth
flow:

> I'd stand upon my bed, a sleepless child
> Watching the waking of my father's world.—
> O world so far away! O my lost world!   (*FF*, 57)

As usual, the father is seen as both tender and violent. An act
of God-like creativity (the building of the greenhouse) is

given motives rooted in vague guilt. In describing his father, Roethke has clearly outlined the prototype of his own personality, and the origins of his ambivalence toward self and God.

The trio of excursions into the past is concluded by "The Chums," a reminder that although his boyhood friends play no part in his life, and have almost certainly not even read his books, they, and all of a man's past, are part of his present experience, and help to define his self.

"The Lizard" begins a series of poems which, although they are not grouped together in Mixed Sequence, can all be treated as close relatives of the Creatures poems of *Words for the Wind*. They describe with prosaic simplicity living parts of the external world which in some way shed telling light on the poet's own existence. Roethke in fact appears directly in each of the poems, and, as in the Creatures poems, meaning lies in the relation between the poet and his world.

In "The Lizard," the poet has sat down upon a rock to smoke, when he notices a lizard sharing his "world." In the course of close observation of the reptile, the poet realizes the smallness of his own self, of man in general, and of human civilization; the span of the lizard, "Older than I, or the cockroach" (*FF*, 59), exceeds them all. The anecdote of "The Meadow Mouse" is one of Roethke's most effective parables. The poet finds a small mouse in the field, takes it home, and gives it food and shelter; after a time, he even comes to believe that the mouse is no longer afraid of him. But at the first opportunity, the mouse has gone to live "under the hawk's wing." (*FF*, 60) The mouse has "chosen" to face the terror of its existence; and, in the mind of the poet, the facing of this terror is expanded into a universal principle: he thinks of the small bird fallen from its nest, the turtle choking on a dusty road (cf. "Journey to the Interior"), the paralytic drowning in his tub—"All things innocent, hapless, forsaken." (*FF,* 61)

"The Geranium" illustrates the "I-Thou" nature of the poet's relation to the inanimate world, for in this poem he treats the flower as if it were another creature. He will not throw out this dying plant, which he himself seems to have placed in its sad condition by neglect, smoke, and alcohol fumes. The maid disposes of it, and the poet sacks the "presumptuous hag" to avenge his loneliness.

In "The Thing," Roethke describes with horror the destruction of some small flying object by a flock of larger birds. The poem's ironic point is made as the poet and his fellow picnickers turn to a meal of "veal soaked in marsala and little larks." (*FF,* 67) The "thing," we may note, was also "small as a lark."

The last of these poems, "The Pike," finds the poet staring into a pond, his "eye always beyond the surface reflection." (*FF,* 68) The sudden strike of the pike, "from out of a dark cove," gives a frightening touch to this symbolic representation of introspection; the terror of the dark recesses of the mind makes us forget for an instant that the poet has actually caught no more than he was seeking.

Closely related to these "Creatures" poems is "All Morning," with its "delirium of birds." (*FF,* 70) Whitmanesque catalogues are again brought into play, as the particular becomes the general, and the present includes both past and future. "It is neither spring nor summer: it is Always." A sense of eternity is achieved by sheer weight of numbers, and by still another reminder that the past, the extinct, is always part of the present.

The influence of the Elizabethan lyric, noted in connection with Love Poems, is also present in the Mixed Sequence. "Song" ("From whence cometh song?") finds the origin of song in pain, of love in the lowest forms of life, of death in hell. The archaic diction, and the bold alterations of rhythm —e.g., the stark "Whence death?" as the first line of the last stanza—are typical of Roethke's late ventures in song.

"On the Quay," which evokes a brief vision of sea and storm, is set next to a longer poem, "The Storm," for an interesting contrast of concentrated lyric and nearly discursive free verse. The former poem works by means of economical reference to the "sea's banter," and by the mystery of the unexplained final lines: "There's two more to drown/ The week after." (*FF*, 64) The latter works by accumulation of detail, and achieves its sense of awesome mystery not by failure to explain exceedingly terse lines, but by the direct presentation of a "paradoxical" natural phenomenon: ". . . The hurricane drives the dead straw in the living pine-tree." (*FF*, 64)

"Heard in a Violent Ward" stands alone in this part, an allusion to Roethke's idea that his genius and his illness were intimately related. He places himself in the company of Blake, Christopher Smart, and "That sweet man, John Clare" (*FF*, 62), poets who turned their so-called madness into great art. The poem moves by expansion: from the surname alone, to use of both names, to both names plus adjective. It moves also from madness to a condition of joy.

The three poems of this part we have yet to consider seem

displaced from the Sequence, Sometimes Metaphysical. "The Manifestation" first states the multiplicity of even the single human existence, the continual becoming of the self; the Protean poet is represented by tree, bird, seed, mole, and that "intrepid scholar of the soil," the worm. (*FF*, 71) Asking whether "these analogies perplex," Roethke follows them with four images of motion in stillness, symbols of intuitive penetration into the nature of reality, of essential oneness in apparent diversity. The final insight of the North American Sequence is recalled by the "sea-wind pausing in a summer tree." These speculations end in a kind of faith in sheer being: "What does what it should do needs nothing more." Whatever takes its place in the natural order fulfills its being. This is the conclusion of a poem which fuses the stoicism of "The Waking" with the mystical overtones of Roethke's later work. In its formal aspects, "The Manifestation" belongs with Roethke's free verse, although there is the unmistakable ghost of blank verse throughout, and the poem is drawn together by a network of imperfect rhymes (bough-ground-clouds, itself-soil, play-tree-why, more-desire).

"The Tranced," related both to the Love Poems of *Words for the Wind,* and to Sequence, Sometimes Metaphysical, begins with still further images of the many in one, motion in stillness: "several flames in one small fire," "we abide yet go." (*FF*, 73) In this moment of union, the poet asks, "Where was the Questioner?—" How can the knower be separated from the known, the lover from the beloved? But we learn in the second stanza that this knowledge of the nature of being is anything but comforting: the edge of heaven is "sharper than a sword;/ Divinity itself malign, absurd." Feeling his loneliness once more, the poet turns to his beloved. Together they struggle out of sensuality, going yet staying, rising from flesh to spirit in the manner of Four for Sir John Davies. The stones ring as Roethke returns to his favorite symbol for union of temporal and eternal, and the fourth stanza presents the very union of subject and object, seen and unseen, the poem has been leading up to. The final stanza links the concept of salvation by means of the beloved with the existential terror of the confrontation of death: through being, poet and beloved become part of eternity, what dies in them is "the will to die." (*FF*, 74)

Sexual involvement has again been invoked as a defense against nothingness. The echoes of Four for Sir John Davies are particularly strong (e.g., "it's the nature of all love to rise," the use of the seventeenth-century pun on "die"); indeed, the poem's main weakness is its failure appreciably to develop the content or means of symbolic expression of the earlier poems. The stanzaic form is different ($aa^5bb^6a^5$), the use of slant rhymes more liberal. But this hardly makes "The Tranced" an entirely original creation; it has the uncomfortable feel of a well-learned lesson repeated.

"The Moment," however, while it too deals with the familiar struggle of love against death, manages to reexamine this ground with freshness. The crux of this new encounter with the abyss is the struggle of space against time, the attempt to pit successfully one's physical existence against time's continual flux; the means is again love: "without, within,/ Body met body . . ." (*FF*, 75) The act of love is seen as a positive, creative assertion of being in the face of nonbeing. This theme is not in the least a new one for Roethke, but the tight compression of its lines, the dominance of a single stark image (the kiss at the edge of a dark ravine), give this poem the sense of a distinct and powerfully felt experience, instead of the left-over feeling of an old experience reworked.

The form of this lyric decidedly contributes to its effect. The movement to concentration on one all-encompassing but infinitely small point of being, the point at which the temporal and eternal intersect, the point of joy, of love, is reflected in the diminishing stanzas, and, at the poem's conclusion, the diminishing lines. The interlacing of lovers, and of time and space, is conveyed by the stanza-linking rhyme scheme, so that the poem, diagramed, looks like this: $aabcc^3$, $adda^3$, abb^3, ee^2. (The rhymes are most dissonant in the second stanza, which deals with the struggle of time and space.) It would probably be correct to call this poem a sonnet, though of a special sort, and one in which form has been molded to content rather than content to form.

Sequence, Sometimes Metaphysical

The final part of *The Far Field* is the Sequence, Sometimes Metaphysical, which consists of the description of a mystical experience ("In a Dark Time"), and eleven poems which form a kind of commentary on that experience. Much of the success of a sequence of this sort depends on the first poem; it must deserve the commentary which follows, or else the entire structure becomes artificial or meaningless. In this case, "In a Dark Time" bears its burden with distinction.

Thanks to the "Symposium" edited by Anthony Ostroff, "In a Dark Time" has received more detailed attention than any other of Roethke's lyrics.[23] However, it will be worth our while to go over the interpretation of this poem still another time, paying special attention to Roethke's use of imagery drawn from previous poems, particularly the "mystical" lyrics, "The Pure Fury" and "The Renewal."

Once again, we begin with the image of the dark night-dark wood, symbol both of religious despair and the attack of anxiety which, for Roethke, inevitably accompanies it. It is precisely in this dark time that the eye begins to see since, for Jung and St. John of the Cross (as well as for Roethke) one must immerse oneself in the depths to attain the heights. Meeting his shadow in the deepening "shade" (the pun suggesting a ghost is intentional), the poet encounters the specter of his own death; this vision, in addition to the echo in the wood, suggests the scattering of the self resulting from dissociation of personality, as described in "The Pure Fury" and "The Exorcism." The poet ironically calls himself "A lord of nature"; he weeps for the agonies of the human condition, which he has not yet transcended. He calls upon the magical powers of the natural world to aid him, to help him move beyond himself; he is also calling upon the prehuman within, lurking in the depths of his unconscious.

What is most important, however, is that the poet has hit the depths, "the purity of pure despair." (*FF*, 79)[24] He feels himself mad, but asks, "What's madness but nobility of soul/ At odds with circumstance?"[25] This line, consciously Yeatsian,

[23] Ostroff includes essays by John Crowe Ransom, Babette Deutsch, Stanley Kunitz, and Roethke himself.

[24] Cf. the "pure fury" eating away at the poet from within. (*WW*, 157)

[25] Roethke comments: " 'Madness' is a sociological term, a good deal

brings to mind the struggles for sanity of "The Pure Fury" and "The Renewal," particularly the image of the poet walking to keep his five wits warm. The "shadow pinned against a sweating wall" (*FF*, 79) is related to the "flesh . . . breathing slower than a wall" (*WW*, 160) in "The Renewal," as well as to the more spectacular image of the wall in The Dying Man. The cave or path among the rocks suggests Eliot's *Waste Land*, although Roethke denies this vehemently.[26] In any case, cave is both womblike, and, with "shadow," a possible reference to Plato's allegory, previously alluded to in "The Pure Fury." The path is still another symbol of the arduous journey of the spirit. "The edge is what I have" (*FF*, 79), the poet concludes, calling to the mind's eye the abyss, which first appeared in "The Pure Fury," and has been prominent throughout *The Far Field*. It is the vision of the universe as undifferentiated being, in which the individual self is inexorably swallowed up.

We have already met the "steady storm of correspondences" of the third stanza. Natural shapes blaze with unnatural light, as the Hermetic unity of the seen and unseen worlds allows the poet to transcend his self and perceive the unity of all being. "Death of the self" announces the moment of illumination and of union, as it did in "The Renewal." And once again, the loss of identity essential to this union is described in horrifying terms: "My soul, like some heat-maddened summer fly,/ Keeps buzzing at the sill. Which I is I?" (*FF*, 79)[27] Approach-

---

of the time: what is madness in the Northwest is normal conduct in Italy, and a hero's privilege in western Ireland." Ostroff, p. 216.

[26] Ostroff, p. 217. It also suggests the second section of "Journey to the Interior," and "I Waited." (*FF*, 91)

[27] The heat-maddened fly was, for Roethke, "more intolerable . . . than a rat." *Ibid.* The horror of this image is crucial to an understanding

ing complete union, the poet is filled with terror and disgust. Paraphrasing St. John of the Cross, he writes, "Dark, dark my light, and darker my desire." [28]

We must pay careful attention to what follows, because, even with Roethke's own commentary in hand, it is easy to be mistaken about the course of events. "A fallen man, I climb out of my fear" does not mean that the poet has fallen from his mystical union back to the world of the senses, but rather that having passed the moment of fear *before* union, union is now complete, and fear, in the normal sense of the word, is momentarily gone. As Roethke writes in "The Abyss," this is what happens "if we wait, unafraid, beyond the fearful instant." (*FF*, 53)

But this is not the end of our difficulties in this dense last stanza. For Roethke, mystic experience is *not* an end in itself; mystic union undeniably brings news of God and the universe, but this news does not in itself provide meaning for our lives, or put an end to our fears; "The mind enters itself, and God the mind,/ And one is One, free in the tearing wind." (*FF*, 79) The first line is a direct quotation from Richard of St. Victor.[29]

---

of the poem. Cf. the raw ghost drinking fluid from the spine in "The Pure Fury."

[28] The "light" is dark because it exceeds the intellect; "desire" is dark because the soul feels unworthy and impure. These are the two senses of St. John's "dark night of the soul."

[29] Quoted by Underhill in *Mysticism*, p. 315. The probability of Roethke's knowledge of this book has already been indicated. Also of interest are some of the other phrases in the paragraph in which Miss Underhill quotes Richard. She describes the soul, "still faintly conscious of the buzz of the external world. . . . It ceases to be a picture, and becomes a window through which the mystic peers out into the spiritual universe, and apprehends to some extent—though how, he knows not— the veritable presence of God." It is possible that these lines suggested

It describes the sensation of union with God.[30] But the last line indicates that mystical union is the beginning of the struggle with God.

Roethke's gloss is instructive:

> In the Platonic sense, the one becomes the many, in this moment. But also—and this is what terrified me—the one not merely makes his peace with God . . . he—if we read One as the Godhead theologically placed above God—transcends God: he becomes the Godhead itself, not only the veritable creator of the universe but the creator of the revealed God. This is no jump for the timid, no flick from the occult, no moment in the rose garden. Instead it is a cry from the mire, and maybe the devil's own.[31]

As the words "free in the tearing wind" indicate, the mystical experience, for Roethke, brings not a sense of security, but rather the terrible burden of freedom; the responsibility of giving meaning to one's life remains with the individual. As in the case of the earlier poems, it is an existentialist writer such as Tillich, rather than the mystic theologians, who provide the ultimate text for "In a Dark Time": "Absolute faith, or the state of being grasped by the God beyond God [cf. Godhead above God], is not a state which appears beside other states of mind. It is the situation on the boundary of man's possibilities. It *is* this boundary. Therefore it is both the courage of despair and the courage in and above every courage." [32]

---

the fly and sill imagery to Roethke. "Sill," of course, was prominent in The Dying Man.

[30] Cf. "The river turns on itself,/ The tree retreats into its own shadow," "The Far Field." (*FF,* 27)

[31] Ostroff, p. 218.

[32] *The Courage to Be* (New Haven, Yale University Press, 1952), pp. 188–89.

Though this mystic experience has provided the basis of faith in being in the most abstract sense, it does not provide any comfort for the individual self, soon to be lost in the abysmal emptiness of the Godhead. And so the rest of the sequence is not simply a reiteration of the lessons learned in "In a Dark Time," but rather a vital, sometimes desperate examination of the implications of the experience described in that poem.

Before going on to the rest of the sequence, we ought to pause briefly to note the technique of "In a Dark Time." There are no new developments, but many of the methods with which Roethke worked and experimented during the course of his career are here brought to perfection. The try for the bare, powerful, even terrible statement is nowhere more successful. End-stopped lines (often with two sentences within one such line) and reliance on a simple, largely monosyllabic vocabulary result in an unsophisticated and direct expression of feeling; the one line that does flow past its boundaries ("What's madness . . ."), and the few Latinate words, stand out all the more prominently, providing a sense of texture even on this bare surface. The tendency toward aphorism has led to what Stanley Kunitz has called "a style of oracular abstraction." And Kunitz accurately sums up the poem's formal pattern, and its function: "the pentameters are strictly measured and often balanced; the stanzaic units, with their formalized combination of true and off-rhyme, adhere to a tight pattern. If these fiercely won controls were to break down at any point, the whole poem would collapse in a cry, a tremendous outpouring of wordless agitation." [33]

"In Evening Air" picks up the "dark themes" of the first

[33] Ostroff, p. 207.

poem. Calling once more upon the "littles," as he called upon the beasts and birds previously, the poet asks God to make him "a last, a simple thing/ Time cannot overwhelm." [34] (*FF*, 80) He remembers his transcending of time, as bud turned into rose; but now darkness is falling and he beholds the dark side of a tree, his death. In the final stanza, he watches light shift on the wall, another image from Plato's cave, suggesting the illusory nature of this life, the flux of things; he sees "How slowly dark comes down on what we do." (*FF*, 81) The poet has clearly fallen back into his fear; he once transcended time, but now he is subject to time again, subject to final dissolution. Roethke is completely successful in turning a songlike formal structure (the stanza is $a^3b^5c^3c^3a^3b^5$) to solemn purposes by strictly avoiding lilting rhythm. The poem's last line ("How slowly . . .") is an instance of Roethke's ability to slow down the pace for a final, somber statement.

Doubts as to the positive value of the mystic experience become even stronger in "The Sequel." Feeling "too glib about eternal things," the poet asks, "who can be/ Both moth and flame?" (*FF*, 82) Since the self dies in mystic experience, of what use is that experience to the self, the consumed moth? Turning again to the natural world, and to his beloved, Roethke attempts to connect temporal and eternal, to know God and yet keep his self. Familiar imagery of motion, dancing in particular, is invoked to that end. This time, however, nature is not "kind." A tree again tells the poet what he is: a dying creature. The denial of desire, that is, of the physical self, is ironically recalled as the poet feels life ebbing from that self. Using the imagery of "The Pure Fury" and "The Renewal," he de-

[34] Cf. "that final thing,/ A man learning to sing." (*WW*, 187)

scribes himself as a man "Pacing a room . . . with dead-white walls." (*FF*, 82) He is trapped, and his vision of eternity has not offered an effective escape.

Rejecting his denial of desire, Roethke returns to the world of the senses with renewed vigor in "The Motion." Only lust keeps the mind alive; physical love is again the path to higher love, to the very basis of existence. In the act of love, "all creatures share, and thereby live." (*FF*, 84) The poem ends with hope, but not, ultimately, certitude: "our chance is still to be!" (*FF*, 85)

The three poems following "In a Dark Time," skillful as they are, draw much of their power from the abundance of that opening poem. This is perhaps as it should be; for these works, fulfilling their purpose within the context of the sequence, provide a necessary relaxation of climactic tension. But "Infirmity," although it too fills a definite place in relation to the other poems, could easily stand on its own. It begins with the image of Narcissus,[35] the desire to preserve the individual self, the fear of nonbeing: the poet prays "to be something else, yet still to be." (*FF*, 86) This echo of the final line of "The Motion" has turned an expression of hope into a desperate cry. Although it fills him with guilt and a sense of his own foolishness, the poet cannot escape this love of self. He calls upon Christ as a fellow victim of torture. Filled with drugs, his own fluid drained from him, he conforms to this "divinity": he dies "inward, like an aging tree." (*FF*, 86) The present passes even as it approaches, "The instant ages." And the poet's flesh, subject to time, decays. "I'm son and father of my only death," he cries. In a sense, this indicates that Roethke himself has now

[35] Cf. "The Long Alley." (*WW*, 87)

become the Dying Man, his father and his self, all of humanity. It also suggests that he is both active and acted upon in these final moments. But the strictly religious connotations of this statement, anticipated by the call to "Sweet Christ," should not be overlooked. Roethke again confronts the paradox of his existence. He partakes in being, and therefore possesses divinity, eternity; but at the same time, he is subject to decay and dissolution. This is precisely the mystery of the incarnation: the mortal son and immortal father are one and the same person. And so, Roethke himself can be thought of as both father and son.

"Infirmity" deals not only with the fear of death, as it at first seems to do exclusively, but also examines specifically the mystic experience with which the sequence began: what, Roethke here asks, does that flash of intuition tell us about the nature of death? The concern with mysticism, hidden until this point, becomes explicit in the fourth stanza: the poet's "deep eye sees the shimmer on the stone;/ The eternal seeks, and finds, the temporal." (*FF*, 86) As in "What Can I Tell My Bones?" (*WW*, 211), it is God, the eternal, who needs and seeks man. The self is afraid of being swallowed up in the impersonality of the Godhead; it is afraid to confront its imminent nonbeing. However, the voices of the natural world, symbolized, as usual, by the song of a bird, pull the poet back from the edge of despair: he still has his soul, he is still the Son. But the struggle is not by any means over. It is only with great difficulty that the poet wins the courage to face eternity and annihilation, and thereby affirm the meaning of his own existence. The mystic experience—when opposites fall into place, when eyes hear and ears see—is now used as a means of understanding the final death of the self, the last merging of one with One; the poet is taught "How body from spirit slowly does unwind/ Until we are pure spirit at the end." (*FF*, 87)[36]

"Infirmity," like the poems that immediately precede it, offers nothing unusual in the way of technique; it is contained within the same kind of form, with the same concentrated diction, as most of Roethke's philosophical lyrics. However, we can note still another consequence of Roethke's fondness for aphorism. Roethke was, as a matter of fact, a "line-writer." That is, he was in the habit of writing down lines as they occurred to him, putting them aside, and coming back to them years later, building poems around the nucleus they would provide. As he grew more skillful, he tried more and more frequently for the "great line." And "Infirmity" stands out because of the high concentration of these lines, which flash brilliantly from the text. This is, perhaps, a dangerous method, but in this instance at least, Roethke has employed it with distinction.

"The Decision," a kind of summary of "Infirmity," is also an epitome of the entire sequence, at whose midpoint it stands. It marks the turn from fear to commitment; from denial of reality to affirmation of being by absorption of nonbeing. "Running from God's the longest race of all" (*FF*, 88), cries the poet, who has been fleeing the eternal. The voice of the bird, that complex symbol of childhood paradise, the natural world,

[36] Cf. Yeats's "Hades' bobbin bound in mummy-cloth" which "May unwind the winding path" in "Byzantium."

and the soul, again marks the turning point. Still moving blindly, but with renewed determination, the poet turns to go, "As a man turns to face on-coming snow."

"The Marrow," along with "In a Dark Time" and "Infirmity" one of the three finest poems in the sequence, tempers all optimism. While it does not reverse the decision made in the previous poem, nor lapse into complete despair, it is decidedly an expression of suffering, and an indicator of the arduous nature of the path the poet has chosen. Apparently some time has elapsed since the mystic experience, and the routine of everyday life dominates once more: the sea wind brings nothing new. Pensive mistress and yelping wife form a kind of domestic hell; the will to die, conquered in "The Tranced," is making itself felt. Lifting himself from the quotidian, the poet forces himself back to contemplation of reality; he has learned the lesson that only by direct confrontation can the abyss be overcome. "Brooding on God," says Roethke, "I may become a man." (*FF*, 89) Calling on the "Godhead above my God," [37] the poet realizes the horror of his situation, the implications of his journey out of the self. "From me to Thee's a long and terrible way," he laments. Gathering together his waning powers, he envisions himself as a tree struck by lightning, by all the love and suffering involved in human existence. His illness has threatened to slay his will, but still he lives. He reaches now for his last reserve of strength in an attempt to be reconciled

[37] In Meister Eckhart's theology, the term "Godhead" came to mean the impersonal, quality-less, static aspects of God, while "God" was used to refer to personal, dynamic qualities. However, the term is common among conventional theologians as well as mystics. A phrase of Eckhart's does indeed appear in "Straw for the Fire," p. 116, but it is a misquotation which may have come by way of Erich Fromm, *The Art of Loving* (New York, Harper, 1956), p. 77.

with God, with the terms of human existence: "I bleed my bones, their marrow to bestow/ Upon that God who knows what I would know." (*FF*, 90)

The crisis having been overcome, Roethke returns to the problems of living in "I Waited." The movement of this poem is from dryness and dust and burning sun to the renewing breezes of the sea. The sea is reached by means of a steep path between stone walls.[38] The style of the poem (which was originally published in 1956) belongs to an earlier period, although its concern with renewal justifies its present position in the sequence. The free verse is discursive rather than aphoristic; the familiar imagery of the middle 1950s and earlier— e.g., the poet "dazzled in the dazzle of a stone" (*FF*, 91)— carries much of the poem's meaning. There is, however, enough continuity in the shimmering water, the sea wind, the heatweary animal, to place "I Waited" in close, organic relationship to the rest of the sequence.

In *Words for the Wind,* Roethke describes his special relation to the natural world in terms of "Bird, girl, and ghostly tree." (*WW*, 152) He returns to the first and last of these symbols in "The Tree, the Bird." The "girl" has helped him to come as far as he has; but in these last moments, strength must come from within. The poet begins by remembering his walks in the stony fields of revelation, where he experienced an "I-Thou" relationship with every existing thing, and the more frightening standing outside himself of mystic union. He sees himself as part of that scene, a leaf of "a tree still dark, still, deathly still." (*FF*, 92) There is a bird on the tree; the total image is one of body and soul, represented by aging tree and the endur-

[38] Cf. "In a Dark Time" and "Journey to the Interior."

ing song of the bird. The wings beat, the soul is liberated in mystic union, with a "lonely buzz behind my midnight eyes;—" Beating his wings against the immense immeasurable emptiness of things, the poet endures "this last stretch of joy,/ The dire dimension of a final thing." [39] The experience itself is terrifying; but in its acceptance is joy.

Acceptance is not final. In "The Restored," we find the poet's soul "like to die" whenever he thinks; it is only when reason fails, and intuition takes its place, that the soul grows back her wing, and dances on stone "In the still point of light/ Of my last midnight." (*FF*, 93) This song is written in trimeter quatrains, with the diminishing of the soul represented by the clipping of a syllable, or even an entire foot, from the appropriate lines.

Whether or not the poet will fluctuate again from his willingness to assume his place in the natural order is not certain, nor can it be. But it is clear that this acquiescence has reached its final form. In "The Right Thing," Roethke leaves the probing of "the mystery" to others; having brooded on God, he has become a man. "*Shall* and *will*" no longer plague him, for "The right thing happens to the happy man." (*FF*, 94) The bird, symbol of the soul, flies out, and then flies back again. "God bless the roots!" the poet cries, "Body and soul are one!" Finally, unity of being has been achieved; no longer seeking, Roethke abandons himself to the eternity that is seeking him. This poem, like Roethke's previous acceptance of the natural order, "The Waking," is a villanelle. The strict formal requirements, the slow repetition and cyclical movement, seem par-

---

[39] Cf. The Dying Man.

ticularly suited to this view of an eternal purpose behind the apparent flux of reality.

The same cycle of existence provides the context for "Once More, the Round." Here, the movement from despair, to struggle, to acceptance, comes to its conclusion. "Pebble"—symbol of the poet's self—and "pond"—symbol of eternal water— are united, the unknown can be known. The assistance of the natural world, of bird, leaf, fish and snail, and, above all, the Eye, the poet's own vision, are given credit, as Roethke dances with William Blake "for love's sake": "And everything comes to One,/ As we dance on, dance on, dance on." (*FF*, 95) As Roethke prophesied, he ends in joy.

The Far Field contains the most uneven poetry of any of Roethke's volumes, but it also contains some of his greatest work. In spite of the various merits of Love Poems and Mixed Sequence, all claims for this book, which received the National Book Award, Roethke's second, in 1965, must ultimately rest upon the two parallel sequences with which it opens and closes. These sequences approach reality from opposite perspectives; North American Sequence is epic, and starts from saturation in the world of the senses, while the lyric Sequence, Sometimes Metaphysical starts with annihilation of the world of the senses. But ultimately both arrive at Roethke's goal, a union of these conflicting aspects of reality, of temporal and eternal, flesh and spirit, body and soul.

CHAPTER 8

A Man Learning to Sing

The poetry of Theodore Roethke constitutes a kind of spiritual autobiography. Partly because of the nature of the poet's illness, the main concerns of this autobiography are the struggles, first to form the self, then, to preserve it from the threat of imminent nonbeing. Following the manic-depressive pattern of his own behavior, the poems alternate between extreme joy at the miracle of his existence, and unendurable anxiety at the thought of its tenuousness. However, using the depths and the heights of his emotional states creatively, he was able to make them an intensification rather than a distortion of the human condition: the agony of his finest works is existential rather than pathological.

Roethke turned to psychology, philosophy, and theology for support and justification for his view of reality; Jung provided the framework for the process of individuation of the self, religious existentialists and mystics were called upon as the self approached death. But these systems and beliefs tended to be fragments shored against ruins rather than the basis of a consistent philosophy. The careful reader may wind a path through the apparent contradictions of Roethke's thought, but he may often wonder whether Roethke did himself. His poems accurately describe the flux of human experience; they are direct and real expressions of his involvement in reality. But they are not particularly successful or subtle rationalizations of that experience, nor is it fair to judge them as such. Whatever pretensions Roethke may have had, it will be as a poet rather than as a thinker that he will survive.

As a poet, Roethke was involved in still another quest: for the best means of presenting that direct expression of human experience. Beginning with the intellectuality of the metaphysical school, with discourse and analysis, he moved inexorably toward the sensuous, the symbolic, the organic metaphor. Extending the doctrine of correspondences, he did not merely speculate about, but, in the greenhouse poems, actually entered the world of the subhuman and the prerational; and he used the techniques developed there for brilliant explorations of the growth of the psyche in *Praise to the End!* From the private world of psychology, Roethke's concern with death, and the meaning of life, brought him to the more public realms of philosophy and religion, and therefore to an appropriately more formal lyric. But even here, Roethke attempted to be less sophisticated, and more direct, than the poetic tradition he had assimilated. And the new sequences of meditations, more discursive versions of the "primary process" patterns of *Praise to the End!*, derive much of their power from a system of evocative correspondences between inner and outer, primitive and adult, worlds.

Roethke's achievement has been to perceive reality in terms of the tensions between subjective and objective, inner and outer, spirit and flesh, and to find a meaningful system of metaphor with which to communicate this perception. The confusion as to the boundaries of the self which must have plagued Roethke throughout his personal life provided him with the stuff of poetry. And his related ability to translate the rhythms of experience into the rhythms of speech and poetry, to give new meaning to the renaissance metaphor for the workings of the universe as cosmic dance, enabled him to give charged and vital form to his raw materials. He wrote some great lyrics —"Words for the Wind," "The Pure Fury," "The Renewal," "In a Dark Time," "The Marrow," "Infirmity"—and many more on the threshold of greatness. His contemplative sequences—The Dying Man, Meditations of an Old Woman, North American Sequence—show him at his very best, and are perhaps unrivaled in contemporary American poetry except by Eliot and Stevens. *Praise to the End!* remains unique. What is it, then, that stands between Roethke and unqualified acceptance as one of our great poets?

One of the most frequent criticisms leveled against Roethke's work is the reference to its derivative qualities. If a list of only the most important of the influences on his poetry were compiled, it would have to include Walter Raleigh, John Davies, John Donne, Henry Vaughan, Thomas Traherne, Christopher Smart, William Blake, William Wordsworth, John Clare, Emily Dickinson, Walt Whitman, W. B. Yeats, W. H. Auden, Louise Bogan, Léonie Adams, Elinor Wylie, T. S. Eliot, Dylan Thomas, Wallace Stevens, and Stanley Kunitz. Very few important poets would have so long a list of *significant* indebtedness. Although, as Roethke was the first to point out, imitation is an important way of learning how to write, his particular use of other poets seemed to go beyond this; while "learning his trade" might account for some of the derivative qualities of his earlier works, it is not a satisfactory explanation of the strong presence of other voices in even his very last works. Nor are we concerned with something like Eliot's wholesale "stealing" of lines and fragments; this is a question of Roethke's technique, his tone, his personality.

Roethke's uncertainty as to his own identity, his weak sense of self, seems to have made him especially impressionable, easily influenced by whatever he came in contact with. The lack of a distinct voice, particularly evident in his early work, is one of the signposts of all his less successful poetry. However, the remarkable fact is that Roethke did after all create one of the most original and distinctive voices in contemporary poetry, and that when he was at his best he could use anybody or anything and make them peculiarly his own. Louis Martz sums up the case for Roethke:

> In his case we must remove all pejorative implications from that word "imitation"; Roethke imitates as Pope and Ben Jonson imitated Horace, as Vaughan imitated George Herbert, as Keats imitated Spenser, as Yeats himself imitated Blake, as Pound imitated Propertius. This is creative imitation, in which the heart of the older poet is absorbed and then transformed into an expression of the poet's own self.[1]

Although neither as evident nor as well publicized, other defects in Roethke's poetry may in fact be more serious than the charge of imitation. Often, especially in his later poems, there seems a lack of organic wholeness; the reader is frequently called upon to decide whether a particular line is governed by its relation to the poem as a unit or by its effectiveness as an epigram. (E.g., "all that slow fire/ Denied in me who has denied desire." [*FF*, 83] This "denial" does not seem prepared for by the body of "The Sequel.") There is still another danger into which the search for the "great line" led Roethke. The aphorism often threatens to become an oversimplification

[1] Martz, p. 294.

which evades rather than confronts reality. (E.g., "What does what it should do needs nothing more" [*FF*, 71]; "The right thing happens to the happy man." [*FF*, 94] If these lines avoid platitude, they do so by only the slenderest of margins.)

However, the above criticisms do no more than underline the *kind* of weaknesses we might expect in Roethke's less successful work; occasional lapses do not alter the fact that for the most part his poems are successful, and are not marred by imitation, inconsistency, or triteness. But there remains still another possible accusation which, once again, questions not Roethke's competence, but his greatness: is Roethke's range too limited, his perspective too narrow, for him to be a truly great poet? This, I believe, is the point on which future evaluations of Roethke will ultimately center.

One aspect of this problem is contained in the fact that Roethke wrote almost exclusively about himself and his own personal concerns. However, he wrote about himself as universal man, not only in the sense that he contained within him the history of his race, but also that as a man of his age he was tormented by its characteristic anxieties, its existential anguish, its apparently unbridgeable gulf between the material and spiritual. Another aspect of the question of Roethke's limitations concerns the relative lack of development of new techniques and perspectives after the publication of *The Waking*. Few poets, including great ones, are responsible for nearly as many innovations as Roethke. Dealing almost exclusively with the growth of the self, and with its confrontation of nonbeing, Roethke had to shift his point of view continually in order to avoid simply repeating what he had said before. He may have been concerned with universal man, but since he drew only from within his own self for materials, he lacked the wealth of detail rich and varied in its own right which other poets possess. His ability to give fresh expression to essentially the same states of alternate joy and terror, which became associated with characteristic clusters of imagery, was incredible; it was possibly the most remarkable of his achievements.

However, especially toward the end of his career, his inventiveness diminished. The "night journey under the sea" of *Praise to the End!* also forms the backbone of Meditations of and Old Woman and North American Sequence. The Sequence, Sometimes Metaphysical adds little but polish to the Love Poems and The Dying Man of *Words for the Wind*. And even the Love Poems are in many respects a working out of the ideas of Four for Sir John Davies. Nonetheless, these poems are often superb; frequently, their reworking of old materials does in fact lead to new, if less comprehensive, insights. In addition, by the time of the publication of *The Waking,* Roethke had already reached a range of technique and depth of perspective achieved by few poets; and it is to be seriously questioned whether any of Roethke's volumes, except possibly *The Far Field,* really suffers from a sense of redundancy. The development of a theme is not inevitably repetitious.

The final evaluation of Roethke's work will be accomplished neither quickly nor easily. It is already clear that while he has not the truly great stature of, say, Yeats, he is an important poet, perhaps a major one. For a long time lost in critics' reluctance to recognize anything in the post-Eliot generation as really important, Roethke is now no longer an underdog. His reputation is unquestionably on the rise, although where it will ultimately settle is by no means certain. However he is judged, he will remain a rewarding poet to read, a human poet in an age that threatens to turn man into an object.

Bibliography

Works by Roethke

VERSE

Open House. New York, Knopf, 1941.
The Lost Son and Other Poems. New York, Doubleday, 1948.
Praise to the End! New York, Doubleday, 1951.
The Waking: Poems 1933–1953. New York, Doubleday, 1953.
Words for the Wind: The Collected Verse of Theodore Roethke.
    London, Secker and Warburg, 1957; New York, Doubleday,
    1958; Bloomington, Indiana University Press, 1961.
I Am! Says the Lamb. New York, Doubleday, 1961.
Party at the Zoo. New York, Crowell-Collier, 1963.
The Far Field. New York, Doubleday, 1964.
Sequence, Sometimes Metaphysical. Iowa City, Stonewall Press,
    1964.
Roethke: Collected Poems. New York, Doubleday, 1966.

ARTICLES

On the Poet and His Craft: Selected Prose of Theodore Roethke.
    Ralph Mills, Jr., ed. Seattle, University of Washington Press,
    1965.
New Republic, LXXXVII (July 15, 1936), 305.
New Republic, LXXXVII (July 22, 1936), 33 (initialed).

New Republic, LXXXVIII (August 26, 1936), 83–84 (initialed).

New Republic, XCIII (December 29, 1937), 234.

"The Poet and His Critics: A Symposium," edited by Anthony Ostroff, *New World Writing,* XIX (1961), 214–19.

"Straw for the Fire: From His Notebooks," arranged by David Wagoner, *Poetry,* CV (November 1964), 113–18.

Works about Roethke

Alvarez, A. The Shaping Spirit: Studies in Modern English and American Poets. London, Chatto and Windus, 1958.

Arnett, Carroll. "Minimal to Maximal: Theodore Roethke's Dialectic," *College English,* XVIII (May 1957), 414–16.

Arrowsmith, William. "Five Poets," *Hudson Review,* IV (Winter 1952), 619–20.

Auden, W. H. *Saturday Review,* XXIII (April 5, 1941), 30.

Baldanza, Stephen. *Commonweal,* XXXIV (June 13, 1941), 188.

Belitt, Ben. "Six Poets," *Virginia Quarterly Review,* XVII (Summer 1941), 462–63.

Bennett, Joseph. "Recent Verse," *Hudson Review* (Summer 1954), 305.

Berryman, John. "From the Middle and Senior Generations," *American Scholar,* XXVIII (Summer 1959), 384.

Bogan, Louise. "Stitched on Bone," in Trial Balances. Ann Winslow, ed. New York, Macmillan, 1935.

—— *New Yorker,* XXIV (May 15, 1948), 118.

—— *New Yorker,* XXVII (February 16, 1952), 107–8.

—— *New Yorker,* XXXV (October 24, 1959), 196.

—— *New Yorker,* XL (November 7, 1964), 243.

Bonner, Amy. "The Poems of Theodore Roethke," *New York Times Book Review,* October 5, 1941, pp. 9, 12.

Brantley, Frederick. "Poets and Their Worlds," *Yale Review,* XLI (Spring 1952), 476–77.

Breit, Harvey. "Pulitzer Poet," *New York Times Book Review*, May 16, 1954, p. 8.

Burke, Kenneth. "The Vegetal Radicalism of Theodore Roethke," *Sewanee Review*, LVIII (Winter 1950), 68–108.

Callahan, Margaret B. "Seattle's Surrealist Poet," *Seattle Times Magazine*, March 16, 1952, p. 7.

Carruth, Hayden. "The Idiom is Personal," *New York Times Book Review*, September 13, 1953, p. 14.

—— "Requiem for God's Gardener," *Nation*, CIC (September 28, 1964), 168–69.

Chang, Diana. "The Modern Idiom," *Voices*, No. 148 (May–August 1952), 42–43.

Ciardi, John. "Poets of the Inner Landscape," *Nation*, CLXXVII (November 14, 1953), 410.

—— "My Papa's Waltz," in How Does a Poem Mean? Boston, Houghton-Mifflin, 1959.

—— "Theodore Roethke: A Passion and a Maker," *Saturday Review*, XLVI (August 31, 1963), 13.

Ciardi, John, ed. Mid-Century American Poets. New York, Twayne, 1950.

Cole, Thomas. "The Poetry of Theodore Roethke," *Voices*, No. 155 (Sept.–Dec. 1954), 37–40.

Conquest, Robert. "The Language of Men," *Spectator*, CC (February 14, 1958), 210.

Cott, Jonathan. "Two Dream Poets," in On Contemporary Literature. New York, Avon, 1964.

Davidson, Eugene. "Poet's Shelf," *Yale Review*, XXXVII (Summer 1948), 747.

Davison, Peter. "Madness in the New Poetry," *Atlantic*, CCXV (January 1965), 93.

Deutsch, Babette. "Three Generations in Poetry," *Decision*, II (August 1941), 60–61.

—— "Fusing Word with Image," *New York Herald Tribune Book Review*, XXIV (July 25, 1948), 4.

—— "Roethke's Clear Signature," *New York Herald Tribune Book Review*, XXXIV (December 7, 1958), 3.

—— (Essay on "In a Dark Time.") "The Poet and His Critics: A Symposium," edited by Anthony Ostroff, *New World Writing*, XIX (1961), 201–6.

—— Poetry in Our Time. New York, Doubleday, 1963.

Dickey, James. "Correspondences and Essences," *Virginia Quarterly Review*, XXXVII (Autumn 1961), 635–40.

—— "Theodore Roethke," *Poetry*, CV (November 1964), 120–24.

Dickey, William. "Poetic Language," *Hudson Review*, XVII (Winter 1964–5), 596.

Drew, Elizabeth. *Atlantic*, CLXVIII (August 1941), 140.

Eberhart, Richard. "Deep Lyrical Feelings," *New York Times Book Review*, December 16, 1951, p. 4.

—— "Creative Splendor," *New York Times Book Review*, November 9, 1958, p. 34.

Ferril, Thomas. *San Francisco Chronicle Magazine*, June 13, 1948, p. 18.

Fitzgerald, Robert. "Patter, Distraction, and Poetry," *New Republic*, CXXI (August 8, 1949), 17.

Flint, F. Cudworth. "Seeing, Thinking, Saying, Singing," *Virginia Quarterly Review*, XXXV (Spring 1959), 313.

Flint, R. W. "Ten Poets," *Kenyon Review*, XII (Autumn 1950), 707–8.

Forster, Louis, Jr. "A Lyric Realist," *Poetry*, LVIII (July 1941), 222–25.

Fuller, John G. "Trade Winds," *Saturday Review*, XLVIII (March 27, 1965), 10–11.

Garrigue, Jean. "A Mountain on the Landscape," *New Leader*, XLVII (December 7, 1964), 33–34.

Gibb, Hugh. "Symbols of Spiritual Growth," *New York Times Book Review*, August 1 ,1948, p. 14.

Griffin, Howard. "Exciting Low Voices," *Saturday Review*, XXXI (July 10, 1948), 26.

Gunn, Thomas. "Poets English and American," *Yale Review*, XLVIII (June 1959), 623–25.

Hall, Donald. "American Poets Since the War," *World Review*, n.s. XLVII (January 1953), 48–49.

—— "The New Poetry: Notes on the Past Fifteen Years in America," *New World Writing*, VII (April 1955), 236–37.

Hall, James. "Between Two Worlds," *Voices*, No. 134 (Summer 1948), 57–58.

Hamilton, Ian. "Theodore Roethke," *Agenda*, III (April 1964), 5–10.

Heilman, Robert. "Theodore Roethke: Personal Notes," *Shenandoah*, XVI (Autumn 1964), 55–64.

Holmes, John. *American Poetry Journal*, XVII (November 1934), 2.

—— "Poems and Things," Boston *Evening Transcript* (March 24, 1941), p. 9.

Humphries, Rolfe. "Inside Story," *New Republic*, CV (July 14, 1941), 62.

—— "Verse Chronicle," *Nation*, CLXXIV (March 22, 1952), 284.

Husband, John Dillon. "Some Readings in Recent Poetry," *New Mexico Quarterly*, XXIV (Winter 1954), 446–47.

Keil, H. Charles. "Among the Happy Poets," *Cadence*, XII (Winter 1958), 7–9.

Kennedy, X. J. "Joys, Griefs and 'All Things Innocent, Hapless, Forsaken,'" *New York Times Book Review*, August 5, 1964, p. 5.

Kizer, Carolyn. "Poetry: School of the Pacific Northwest," *New Republic*, CXXXV (July 16, 1956), 18–19.

Kramer, Hilton. "The Poetry of Theodore Roethke," *Western Review*, XVIII (Winter 1954), 131–54.

Kunitz, Stanley. "News of the Root," *Poetry*, LXXIII (January 1949), 222–25.

—— (Essay on "In a Dark Time.") "The Poet and His Critics: A Symposium," edited by Anthony Ostroff, *New World Writing*, XIX (1961), 206–14.

—— "Theodore Roethke," *New York Review of Books*, I (October 17, 1963), 22.

—— "Roethke: Poet of Transformations," *New Republic*, CLII (January 23, 1965), 23–29.

—— "Roethke Remembered," *Show*, V (May 1965), 10.

Kunitz, Stanley, ed. Twentieth Century Authors: First Supplement. New York, Wilson, 1955.

Lee, Charlotte I. "The Line as a Rhythmic Unit in the Poetry of Theodore Roethke," *Speech Monographs*, XXX (March 1963), 15–22.

Levi, Peter. "Theodore Roethke," *Agenda*, III (April 1964), 11–14.

Lieberman, Laurence. "Poetry Chronicle: Last Poems, Fragments, and Wholes," *Antioch Review*, XXIV (Winter 1964–65), 537.

Malkoff, Karl. "Cleansing the Doors of Perception," *Minnesota Review*, V (October–December 1965), 342–48.

—— *New Mexico Quarterly*, XXXV (Winter 1956–66), 379–80.

Martz, Louis. "Recent Poetry: The Elegiac Mode," *Yale Review*, LIV (Winter 1965), 294–97.

Matheson, John William. Theodore Roethke: A Bibliography. University of Washington, masters thesis, 1958.

Maxwell, Emily. "The Smallest Giant in the World, and the Tallest Midget," *New Yorker*, XXXVII (November 18, 1961), 237.

Meliado, Mariolina. "Theodore Roethke," *Studi Americani*, IX (1963), 425–54.

Meredith, William. "A Steady Storm of Correspondences: Theodore Roethke's Long Journey Out of the Self," *Shenandoah*, XVI (Autumn 1964), 41–54.

—— "Cogitating with His Finger Tips," *Book Week* (July 18, 1965), pp. 4, 15.

Meyer, Gerald Previn. "Logic of the North," *Saturday Review*, XXXVII (January 16, 1954), 18–19.

Mills, Ralph J., Jr. "Keeping the Spirit Spare," *Chicago Review*, XIII (Winter 1959), 114–22.

—— "Theodore Roethke: The Lyric of the Self," in Poets in Progress. Edward Hungerford, ed. Evanston, Ill., Northwestern University Press, 1962.

—— "Roethke's Garden," *Poetry*, C (April 1962), 54–59.

—— Theodore Roethke. Minneapolis, University of Minnesota Press, 1963.

—— "Roethke's Last Poems," *Poetry*, CV (November 1964), 122–24.

Mills, Ralph J. Jr., ed. On the Poet and His Craft: Selected Prose of Theodore Roethke. Seattle, University of Washington Press, 1965.

Morgan, Frederick. "Recent Verse," *Hudson Review*, I (Summer 1948), 261–62.

Mowrer, Deane. "Reviews of Some Current Poetry," *New Mexico Quarterly*, XVIII (Summer 1948), 225–26.

Muir, Edwin. "New Verse," *New Statesman*, LV (January 18, 1958), 76–77.

Murphy, Richard. "Three Modern Poets," *Listener*, LIV (September 8, 1955), 373–5.

Napier, John. "Poetry in the Vernacular and Otherwise," *Voices*, No. 176 (September–December 1961), 54.

Nemerov, Howard. "On Shapiro, Roethke, Winters," *Kenyon Review*, XV (Winter 1954). Reprinted in Poetry and Fiction. New Brunswick, N.J., Rutgers University Press, 1963.

Ostroff, Anthony, editor. "The Poet and His Critics: A Symposium," *New World Writing*, XIX (1961), 189–219. Reprinted in The Contemporary Poet as Artist and Critic: Eight Symposia. Boston, Little Brown, 1965.

Parkinson, Thomas. "Some Recent Pacific Coast Poetry," *Pacific Coast Spectator*, IV (Summer 1950), 290–305.

Peck, Virginia. "Roethke's 'I Knew a Woman,'" *Explicator*, XXII, item 66 (1964).

Ramsey, Paul. "A Weather of Heaven," *Shenandoah*, XVI (Autumn 1964), 72–73.

Ransom, John Crowe. (Essay on "In a Dark Time.") "The Poet and His Critics: A Symposium," edited by Anthony Ostroff, *New World Writing*, XIX (1961), 191–201.

Rodman, Selwin. "Intuitive Poet," *New York Herald Tribune Book Review*, XXVIII (December 2, 1951), 32.

Rosenthal, M. L. "Closing in on the Self," *Nation*, CLXXXVIII (March 21, 1959), 258–60.

—— The Modern Poets. New York, Oxford University Press, 1965.

—— "The Couch and Poetic Insight," *Reporter*, XXXII (March 25, 1965), 52–53.

—— "Throes of Creation," *New York Times Book Review*, July 18, 1965, p. 4.

Sawyer, Kenneth B. "Praises and Crutches," *Hopkins Review*, V (Summer 1952), 131–32.

Schwartz, Delmore. "Cunning and Craft of the Unconscious and Preconscious," *Poetry*, XCIV (June 1959), 203–5.

Scott, Winfred Townley. "Has Anyone Seen a Trend?" *Saturday Review*, XLII (January 3, 1959), 13.

Seymour-Smith, Martin. "Where Is Mr. Roethke?" *Black Mountain Review*, I (Spring 1954), 40–47.

Shapiro, Harvey. *Furioso*, VII (Fall 1952), 56–58.

Sitwell, Edith. "Preface," The American Genius. London, Lehmann, 1951.

Skelton, Robin. "Poets' Ways of Speech," *Manchester Guardian*, February 4, 1958, p. 4.

Smith, William J. "Two Posthumous Volumes," *Harper*, CCXXIX (October 1964), 133–34.

Snodgrass, W. D. "Spring Verse Chronicle," *Hudson Review*, XII (Spring 1959), 114–17.

—— "The Last Poems of Theodore Roethke," *New York Review of Books*, III (October 8, 1964), 5–6.

Southworth, James G. "The Poetry of Theodore Roethke," *College English*, XXI (March 1960), 326–38.

Spender, Stephen. *New Republic*, CXLI (August 10, 1959), 21–22.

234   *Bibliography*

Stammler, Heinrich. "Dichter in Amerika," *Merkur*, X (November 1956), 1072–73.

Staples, Hugh. "Rose in the Sea-Wind: A Reading of Theodore Roethke's 'North American Sequence,'" *American Literature*, VI (May 1964), 189–203.

Stein, Arnold, editor. *Theodore Roethke: Essays on the Poetry.* Seattle, University of Washington Press, 1965.

Stoneburner, Tony. "Ardent Quest," *Christian Century*, LXXXI (September 30, 1964), 1217–18.

Sweeny, John L. "New Poetry," *Yale Review*, XXX (Summer 1941), 817–18.

Tate, Allen. "In Memoriam—Theodore Roethke, 1908–1963," *Encounter*, XXI (October 1963), 68.

Vazakas, Bryon. "Eleven Contemporary Poets," *New Mexico Quarterly*, XXII (Summer 1952), 224–25.

Viereck, Peter. "Five Good Poets in a Bad Year," *Atlantic*, CLXXXII (November 1948), 95.

——— "Technique and Inspiration," *Atlantic*, CLXXXIX (January 1952), 81.

Wain, John. "Half-way to Greatness," *Encounter*, X (April 1958), 82–84.

Walsh, Chad. *Saturday Review*, XLVIII (January 2, 1965), 28.

Walton, Edna Lou. "Bridges of Iron Lace," *New York Herald Tribune Book Review*, XVII (August 10, 1941), 4.

Willingham, John R. *Library Journal*, LXXXIX (September 15, 1964), 3320.

Winters, Yvor. "The Poems of Theodore Roethke," *Kenyon Review*, III (Autumn 1941), 514–16.

Index

Titles are those of Roethke's works unless otherwise indicated

"Abyss, The," 196–200, 209
"Academic," 29
"Adamant, The," 25, 35–37, 38, 46, 108; imagery of, 36, 41, 42
Adams, Léonie, 9, 19, 21, 24n, 222
"Advice, The," 157
"Against Disaster," 29
"All Morning," 202–3
"All the Earth, All the Air," 126–27, 128
"American Poet Introduces Himself and His Poems, An" (BBC broadcast), 1n, 2n, 79n, 106n, 108n
Anima, 113, 120, 126, 137
Animals: as spiritual symbols, 28, 92, 94, 117, 118, 127, 150, 161, 163, 177–78, 185, 201; as sexual symbols, 29, 71, 74, 75, 76, 80, 81, 83–87, 92, 118, 128, 184–85, 196–97
Anxiety, 15, 37, 147, 220, 224; vision and, 7–8, 140, 152, 207; sexuality and, 86–87; love and, 120–21, 125, 129, 133, 134, 137, 142; Tillich on, 132n
"Apparition, The," 192
Archetypes, 17, 59–60; the child-hero, 64, 66–67; the journey, 65, 159, 160, 167, 170, 176, 177,

180–81, 184, 197, 199, 208, 225; Joyce's use of, 68–69; of woman, 112–13, 120; sibyl and centaur, 136–37; of man, 186
"Auction, The," 29
Auden, W. H., 11, 144n, 158; quoted, 43; influence of, 9, 19, 22, 24, 27, 31–32, 222

Baldanza, Stephen, quoted, 43
"Ballad of the Clairvoyant Widow," 31
"Bat, The," 28
Bats, 28, 183, 184
Baudelaire, Charles, 101n
Bears, 6, 13, 117
"Beast, The," 147
Beatrice figure, 115, 120, 126, 195
Being, 127, 131, 136, 139, 141, 149, 156, 166, 169–70, 173, 185, 186, 188, 196–98, 205, 214
Belitt, Ben, 34, 37n; quoted, 35n
Bennington College, 9
Bible, 3, 67, 76, 87, 137, 138
"Big Wind," 51n, 53, 57
Birds, 111, 150, 155, 157, 163, 167, 184, 190, 198, 214–19; heron, 27–28; crow, 58–60; owl, 104, 187; swan, 128; wood thrush, 148–49; sparrow, 160, 162; lark,

Birds (*Continued*)
166, 202; gull, 179; kingfisher,
187; phoenix, 192
Birth: images of, 51, 52, 75, 76, 78,
95, 104, 179, 187, 190, 192; collective unconscious and, 63, 69*n*;
spiritual growth and, 69, 70, 73,
96, 105
Blake, William, 8*n*, 20, 80, 182,
183, 222; quoted, 25, 92, 93,
103-4; mystical tradition and, 65,
67, 76, 91, 102*n*, 103, 138, 152,
186, 187; Roethke on, 104, 203,
219
Bodkin, Maud, quoted, 59-60, 61
Boehme, Jacob, 96, 102-3, 138,
154*n*, 198; quoted, 94*n*, 102,
132*n*; "Pure Fury" and, 79, 131,
169*n*
Bogan, Louise, 19, 22, 222
Bollingen Prize, 14
"Bringer of Tidings, The," 22
"Bring the Day!" 80, 93
Buber, Martin, 13, 124; quoted,
169-70; "I-Thou" of, 127, 169,
174, 183, 198, 202, 217
Bucke, R. M., quoted, 139-40
Buddhism, 65, 100
"Buds Now Stretch, The," 21
Burke, Kenneth, 47*n*, 95*n*; quoted,
45*n*3, 101*n*, 106
Burtt, E. A., 100*n*

"Carnations," 55
Cats, 71, 74, 75, 81, 93, 184-85
"Centaur, The," 136*n*
"Changeling, The," 63*n*
Childhood, 24, 40, 42; the natural
world and, 1-2, 44, 47-48, 50,
162-63, 179, 183, 215; sexual
imagery and, 39, 52-53, 70-75,
77-78, 80, 81-82, 97-98, 126-
27; collective unconscious and,
60, 64, 69*n*, 147, 159-60; spiritual growth and, 66-67, 69*n*, 76-
81, 188, 197

"Child on Top of a Greenhouse,"
55
"Chums, The," 201
Ciardi, John, 1*n*, 2*n*, 4*n*, 63*n*;
quoted, 13, 65
Clare, John, 8*n*, 203, 222
Collective unconscious, 59-60, 63-
64, 68, 147; memory and, 73,
182, 188; death and, 99-100,
207
"Coming of the Cold, The," 27, 40
Correspondences, doctrine of, 26-
27, 33, 38*n*, 132, 138; imagery
and, 41, 58-59, 61, 101, 134-
35, 139, 176; human and vegetable, 48-50, 102-3, 221; joy and
terror in, 114, 165, 173, 208
Courage to Be, The (Tillich), 131,
132*n*, 134, 141*n*, 210*n*
Creation, 105; order and, 2, 3, 96,
186*n*; death and, 152-53, 158,
187; guilt and, 200-1
Creatures (poem sequence), 150-
51, 201
"Cuttings," 50
"Cuttings—*later*," 49-51, 53, 98
"Cycle, The," 61

Dance, 6, 13; symbolic use of, 115-
21, 130, 142, 143, 154, 212, 219
"Dance, The," 115-17
Dante Alighieri, 46, 47*n*, 65, 117,
118; imagery of, 87, 90, 97, 134,
135, 152, 188; Beatrice and, 115,
120, 126, 195
Darkness: as the unconscious, 64,
96, 99, 105; as disorder, 88-89,
118-19, 120-21, 126-27, 130-31;
the "night of the soul," 134-35,
137, 154-55, 197-99, 207
Davies, John, 116, 117, 118, 222
Death, 16, 23, 58, 108, 115; identity and, 14, 29, 55, 81, 98, 99-
100, 133-34, 135, 141, 148, 155-
56, 162, 163-64, 167, 168-69,
179, 181-82, 186-87, 199, 207,
208, 213-15, 220, 225; sexuality

and, 25, 27–28, 48, 55, 76, 78, 81, 85–86, 88, 91, 126, 154; imagery of, 42, 55, 75, 78, 82, 83, 88, 104, 123, 130, 134–37, 150, 160–62, 179, 187, 190, 193, 196, 208; in the elegies, 111–12, 146, 200; the mother figure and, 113–14; love and, 118–21, 129, 130, 133, 137, 158, 159, 168, 205–6; Stoicism and, 114–15, 122, 123; mysticism and, 123, 141–42, 149, 152, 169, 212, 214, 220; eternity and, 184, 186–87, 214

"Death Piece," 24, 35n

"Decision, The," 147, 215–16

Dickinson, Emily, 20, 29, 222

Dionysius the Areopagite, 154–55

Dogs, 86, 87, 93, 98–99, 110, 118, 181

"Dolor," 30, 57

Donne, John, 18, 19, 22, 36, 42, 76, 119, 128, 222

"Double Feature," 57

"Dream, The," 126

Dying Man, The (poem sequence): 102n, 124n, 126, 151–59, 162n, 209n, 218n; stylistic development in, 13, 222, 225; *Open House* and, 33; wall image in, 82n, 153–54, 208; "fury" in, 135; rose in, 183n; Proteus figure in, 186; "Her Longing" and, 193

Eckhart, Meister, 154n30, 169, 174, 198, 216n; quoted, 94n, 168

"Elegy," 146

"Elegy for Jane, *My Student Thrown by a Horse*," 111–12

"Elegy" (to Aunt Tilly), 200

Eliot, T. S., 10, 14, 18, 41, 90, 175, 180, 187, 208, 222–23, 225; quoted, 178, 185

Emotion: reason and, 25; restraint of, 40; archetypes and, 59–60, 67; Joyce and, 69; rhythm and, 108; vision of correspondences and, 114, 165, 173, 208

"Epidermal Macabre," 28, 37–38, 39, 41

"Eternity is Now," 152–53, 186

Eunice Tietjiens Prize, 11

Existentialism, 13, 124, 141, 185, 224; alienation and, 135; time and, 149; identity and, 198, 220

"Exorcism, The," 124n, 145, 147; quoted, 134, 152; introduction cited, 135n, 136; anxiety and, 7, 87n, 173, 207

"Exulting, The," 155

Eye, the, 39, 96, 181, 207, 219; as identity, 23–24, 25, 26, 29

Fall of Man, 161; birth as, 76, 86; sexuality as, 80, 87, 91

Far Field, The, 3n, 8, 11, 34, 172–219, 225; publication, 16, 172

"Far Field, The," 179, 184, 190, 210n

Father figure, 2–3, 24, 27, 105, 126; in "The Premonition," 40–41, 42; in "The Lost Son," 51n, 54, 85, 87, 88–89, 90, 91, 96, 152; in "My Papa's Waltz," 57; in "Where Knock is Open Wide," 71, 72, 73, 74, 75–79, 80, 98; in "Give Way Ye Gates," 81, 82; in "Sensibility! O La!" 83; in "The Long Alley," 93; in The Dying Man, 102n; archetype of, 113, 137; in "The Exorcism," 147; Yeats as, 151, 155, 158; in "The Wall," 154; in "Otto," 200–1; in "Infirmity," 214

"Favorite, The," 31

"Feud," 24, 30, 32, 83

"Field of Light, A," 63n, 93–95, 108, 165n

Fire, 80, 93, 97, 126, 127

"First Meditation," 160, 166, 167, 180

Fish, 80, 111, 177, 202, 219; father image, 73, 75–76, 81, 92, 93, 98

"Flower Dump," 55

"For an Amorous Lady," 29

"Forcing House," 51, 53
Four for Sir John Davies (poem sequence), 110n, 112, 115–21, 122, 126, 144, 225; "They Sing, They Sing" and, 156; "The Tranced" and, 205
"Fourth Meditation," 165–67
"Frau Bauman, Frau Schmidt, and Frau Schwartze," 45n, 54, 110n
Freud, Sigmund: influence of, 9–10, 24, 43, 65; "Freudian slips," 40; symbolism and, 48, 150; Oedipal triangle and, 76; on stages of development, 78, 81, 83

"Genesis," 28
"Gentle, The," 31, 40n
"Geranium, The," 163n, 202
Ghosts, 130, 153–54, 207; father image and, 75, 82, 83–85, 98, 147; as link between flesh and spirit, 118, 126, 137–38
"Give Way, Ye Gates," 69n, 80–81, 154, 163n
"Gob Music," 195n
God, 186n; father symbols of, 3, 54, 56, 76–80, 86–91, 93, 96, 137, 147, 200–1; death and, 131, 135, 146; man's relationship with, 168, 197–99, 209–12, 214–17
Godhead, the, 210–12, 214, 216
Greenhouse, the, 16n, 121, 150, 170, 221; symbolism of, 1–2, 9, 88, 123, 161–62, 188, 200; in *The Lost Son,* 44–57; in *The Waking,* 110n; in *Praise to the End,* 86
Growth: imagery of, 9–10, 49–51, 102, 103, 123; death and, 25, 55, 170; regression and, 63–64, 69n, 85, 86; spiritual, 65–67, 69, 76–84, 89, 105, 108, 221
Guilt, 53, 56–57, 77–78, 85; the Fall of Man and, 76, 80, 86, 87, 91; transcendence of, 88–89, 93, 98–99, 105, 126, 213–14; death and, 146–47; creation and, 200–1

Hands, 39, 75, 77, 81, 93, 97
"Happy Three, The," 194
"Heard in a Violent Ward," 8n, 203
"Her Becoming," 101n, 124n, 164–65, 167, 173
"Her Longing," 192–93
"Heron, The," 27
"Her Reticence," 192
"Her Time," 193
"Her Words," 192
"Her Wrath," 11, 195
"Highway: Michigan," 32
"His Foreboding," 194
"His Words," 152, 155
Holmes, John, 26; quoted, 23
Horses, 92, 118
"How to Write Like Somebody Else," 20n, 21nn, 116, 117n

I Am! Says the Lamb, 16n
"I Cry, Love! Love!" 104, 155
Identity: search for, 9, 10, 13, 14, 16, 28, 32–33, 42, 43, 64–65, 69n8, 123, 125, 170–71, 176, 182, 186n, 190, 197, 213, 220, 223; interaction with others and, 30, 33, 34, 67, 68, 79, 88, 94n, 127, 173–74, 188; formation of, 44, 55, 67, 69n8, 76–84, 155–56, 162–64, 188, 204, 218, 224; the natural world and, 61, 93–95, 127, 132–33, 139, 148, 165, 179, 185, 188–89, 198, 214, 217; failure to achieve, 98–99, 104, 105, 123, 135, 138, 146, 181; mysticism and, 140–41, 169, 86–87, 198, 207, 209–19
"Idyll," 32
"I Knew a Woman," 125–26
Imagery, 14; sexual, 4, 27–28, 39, 48, 52–53, 71–78, 80, 81, 85, 87, 88, 92–93, 96, 119, 150; archetypal, 17, 60, 61–62, 66–67, 112–13, 136–37, 147, 160–62, 167, 170, 176, 177, 180, 186; landscape, 22, 26, 27, 30, 32, 39, 91–92, 134–36, 160–62, 166, 175–

76, 178–79, 180, 182, 183, 185, 187, 190, 193, 194, 197, 217, 219; the eye, 23–24, 25, 26, 39, 96, 181, 207, 219; the hands, 39, 40–41, 75, 77, 81; of death, 42, 120, 130–31; father, 51, 52, 54, 56, 71–76, 79, 81, 82, 88, 147, 151; mother, 51, 52, 71, 72, 74, 79, 81–83, 95, 151; light, 64–65, 70, 88–90, 93–95, 99, 135, 136, 164, 198, 212; telescoped, 67–69, 143, 177, 191; regressive, 86, 87, 99; commercial, 87, 92; obsessive, 130, 134, 189–90, 225; of resurrection, 138, 187; pathetic fallacy in, 146; the abyss, 196, 197, 198–200, 205–6, 208, 216

Imagism, 41, 150

"I'm Here," 162–64, 167

In A Dark Time, 16, 36n, 41n

"In A Dark Time," 16, 20, 130, 155n, 217n, 206–11, 222; doctrine of correspondences and, 101–2, 173

Individuation, *see* Identity

"I Need, I Need," 78

"In Evening Air," 211–12

"Infirmity," 213–15, 222

"In Praise of Prairie," 27

Insanity, 7, 8, 13, 16–17, 203, 207–8, 220

"Interlude," 25

"In the Time of Change," 20

"I Sought a Measure," 22

"I Waited," 208n, 217

Jesus Christ, 98, 146, 187, 214

Job, 67, 87, 88

John of the Cross, Saint, 130, 135, 174, 207; quoted, 198–99, 209

Jonah, 176, 177, 199

"Journey to the Interior," 176, 202, 208n, 217n; landscape of, 179, 180–81, 189

Joyce, James, 12, 13n, 46, 68–69, 72

"Judge Not," 58

Jung, Carl G.: quoted, 59, 64, 113; influence of, 10, 64–66, 136, 207; on regression, 60–61, 63, 64, 73, 84, 176, 199; on the anima, 113, 120

Kierkegaard, Søren, 13, 124, 141, 174

Kramer, Hilton, 64n; quoted, 106–7

Kunitz, Stanley, 13n, 59n, 130–31, 168n; cited, 1n, 5n, 11n, 24n, 47, 124n, 207n, 222; quoted, 44, 49, 211; *Open House* and, 8

Lafayette College, 6, 23

"Last Class," 12

"Last Words," 58

Lawrence, D. H., 9, 47n, 55

Lee, Charlotte, quoted, 108

Levinson Award, 11

Light, 64, 65, 70, 88–90, 93–95, 99, 149, 164, 168–69, 179–80, 212; "dark path of the redeemer" and, 96–97, 105, 135, 136, 137, 198–99

"Light Breather, A," 111

"Light Comes Brighter, The," 26, 49

Lighter Pieces and Poems for Children (An Interlude), 124n

"Light Listened," 93–94

"Lines Upon Leaving a Sanitorium," 7n, 25n

"Lizard, The," 201

"Long Alley, The," 63n, 91–93, 118, 161, 213n

"Longing, The," 176, 178, 180, 181, 189

" 'Long Live the Weeds' Hopkins," 28, 66

"Long Waters, The," 181–84, 190

Lost Son and Other Poems, The, 44–62, 63, 64; publication, 9, 45; *The Waking* and, 10, 110n

"Lost Son, The," 3, 51n, 54n, 58, 63n, 84–91, 97, 138, 165n, 197n; on materialism, 77n, 87, 92; "A

"Lost Son, The" (*Continued*)
Field of Light" and, 94, 95, 108;
the rose in, 96, 152, 177
Love: anger and, 12–13; vision
and, 25, 32, 88–89, 120, 127–
28, 137, 140, 165, 205, 212; society and, 34; restraint of, 40,
92; order and, 118–21; meanings
of, 125, 128, 129, 142, 159;
union of contraries in, 128–29,
133, 139–40, 156, 191–92, 205–6
Love Poems (sequence in *The Far
Field*), 16, 33, 34, 191–95, 219;
(sequence in *Words for the
Wind*), 13, 34, 124n, 125–45,
150, 151, 156, 204, 225
"Love's Progress," 129
"Lull (November 1939)," 31–32
Lyrics, 38, 40, 175, 222; metaphysical, 9, 13, 26, 207, 215;
traditional, 9, 33, 44, 45, 57,
122n, 221; Yeatsian, 10, 16, 144,
151, 191; rhythms in, 143, 192,
193, 203, 206

"Manifestation, The," 172n, 204
"Marrow, The," 216–17, 222
Martz, Louis, 186; quoted, 175,
185, 223
Masturbation, 53, 77–78, 87, 88,
92–93, 97–99, 123
Materialism, 77n, 87, 92–93, 155,
161; Yeats and, 115; despair and,
176–77
"Meadow Mouse, The," 201–2
"Meditation at Oyster River," 178–
80, 189
"Meditations in Hydrotherapy," 7n
Meditations of an Old Woman
(poem sequence), 3, 124n, 159–
71, 222; organization of, 13–14,
33; North American Sequence
and, 16, 175, 176, 177, 180, 189,
197, 225; rhythms in, 122n, 155
"Memory," 127
Metaphysical poetry, 26, 125, 130,
141–42, 170, 221; twentieth-

century interest in, 9, 13, 18–19,
24n; style and, 19–20, 21, 22, 36–
37, 41, 138–39, 143; wit and, 23,
32, 65
"Mid-Country Blow," 27
Mills, Ralph J., Jr., 1n, 118n;
quoted, 172n
"Minimal, The," 61, 85n, 148n
Mixed Sequence (poem sequence),
16, 172n, 195–206, 219
"Moment, The," 172n, 205–6
Moon, 83, 87, 117, 130, 187
"Moss-Gathering," 53, 57, 87n
Mother figure, 2, 3–4, 24; in Medi-
tations of an Old Woman, 3,
159; in "Where Knock is Open
Wide," 71, 72, 74, 76; in "I
Need, I Need," 78; the natural
world and, 79, 82, 87, 91, 93;
Oedipal fantasy and, 81, 83; in
"The Shape of Fire," 95; in first
section of *The Waking*, 111, 112,
113, 118, 120; in the Love
Poems, 127, 156
"Motion, The," 213
Mouth, 78, 81, 100, 166
"My Dim-Wit Cousin," 30
"My Papa's Waltz," 3, 57
Mysticism, 13, 19, 65–67, 204; experience and, 16, 20, 138–39,
140–41, 169, 173–74, 198, 206–
10, 212, 213–19; vision and, 26,
89, 90–91, 94–95, 100–1, 117,
140, 152; collective unconscious
and, 73, 100; doctrine of correspondences and, 101, 102, 138;
extrovertive and introvertive distinguished, 90n, 105; Yeats and,
115, 117, 152; death and, 123,
141–42, 149, 152, 186, 220
Mysticism (Underhill), 102n, 103n,
168, 198n, 209n
Myth, 10, 24, 107, 147, 159–60; of
the growth of the spirit, 66–67;
Oedipal, 81

Narcissus, 92, 213

National Book Award, 14, 16, 170, 219

Negation: reality and, 28–29, 33, 154–55; love and, 32; life and, 114, 131

New Poems (poem sequence), 110*n*, 120–24, 170

"Night Crow," 58–60

"Night Journey," 32

"No Bird," 28

Nonbeing, 28–29, 33, 121, 131, 136, 141, 146, 156–58, 169–70, 197–98, 205; *see also* Death

North American Sequence (poem sequence), 16, 33, 122*n*, 172*n*, 173–90, 197, 204, 219, 222, 225

"Now We the Two," 22

O'Connell, Beatrice Heath, *see* Roethke, Beatrice

Oedipal fantasy, 4, 76, 81, 83, 85

"Old Florist, The," 54

"Old Lady's Winter Words," 112–15, 121, 153*n*

"O Lull Me, Lull Me," 83, 96, 197*n*

Onanism, *see* Masturbation

"Once More the Round," 104*n*, 219

"On 'Identity,'" 1*n*, 94*n*, 116*n*, 140*n*, 141*n*, 148*n*, 169*nn*, 173–74, 186*n*, 188*n*

"On the Road to Woodlawn," 29, 35*n*

"On the Quay," 203

Open House, 19, 22–43, 65, 68; publication, 8–9; *The Waking* and, 10, 110*n*, 123; *The Lost Son* and, 44, 45, 49, 50, 57, 58; *The Far Field* and, 172

"Open House," 23–24

"Open Letter," 1*n*, 51*n*, 52*n*, 53*n*, 84; on regression, 64*n*, 69*n*, 85*n*; on spiritual growth, 66–67; on childhood sexuality, 86*n*, 97, 99*n*; on God, 88*n*

"Orchids," 48, 53

Order, 2–3, 43, 50, 88, 186*n*; vision and, 91, 96, 120–21, 218; harmony concept and, 117, 118–19; the senses and, 175

"Orders for the Day," 25, 39

Ostroff, Anthony, 27*n*, 102*n*, 130*n*, 206–8, 210*n*, 211*n*

"Other, The," 127

"O, Thou Opening, O," 63*n*, 105–6, 110*n*, 128

Otter, 83–84, 85, 197

"Otto," 3*n*, 200–1

"Partner, The," 117–19

Party at the Zoo, 16*n*

"Pause, The," 22

Pennsylvania State College, 6

Philosophy, 10, 13, 36, 123; Roethke studies, 103, 124, 130, 174, 221; reality and, 121, 185, 186*n*, 220; love and, 142; the abyss and, 199–200

"Pickle Belt," 57

"Pike, The," 202

Pipes, 51*n*, 53–54, 88

"Plaint," 124*n*, 129

Plants, 111, 202, 219; symbolism of, 2, 9–10, 21, 26, 48–51, 52–53, 55, 76, 88, 93, 94, 102, 103, 197, 198; trees, 80, 81–82, 129, 143, 148, 189–90, 212, 216, 217–18; the mystic rose, 88, 95, 96, 152, 163, 164, 167, 177, 183, 187–88, 190

Plato, 65, 127, 131, 133, 136, 155, 167, 208, 212

Plotinus, 140; quoted, 139

"Poems of Theodore Roethke, The" (Winters), 35*n*

"Poet and His Critics: A Symposium, The" (Ostroff, ed.), 27*n*, 102*n*, 130*n*, 206–7, 210*n*, 211*n*

"Poetaster," 30

Praise to the End! 14, 33, 40, 65–109, 143, 222; publication, 10; *The Lost Son* and, 44, 56, 58, 60, 63*n*; *The Waking* and, 104–5,

Praise to the End! (*Continued*)
110n, 112, 113, 121–23; rhythms
of, 122n, 196; proverbs in, 145
"Praise to the End!" 71, 74, 77,
79n, 97–99, 110, 181n7
"Prayer," 25, 39
"Prayer Before Study," 30
"Premonition, The," 24–25, 27–28,
40–43, 55
"Prognosis," 24, 83
Psychology: Roethke's use, 9–10,
13, 14, 16, 24, 40, 43, 59–60,
68, 71, 76, 78, 81, 84, 107–8,
186n, 220, 221; mysticism and,
65–66, 139; guilt and, 88–89
"Pub Songs," 195n
Pulitzer Prize, 10, 11
"Pure Fury, The," 7, 87n, 124n,
129–36, 140, 155n, 157, 173,
212, 222; ghost in, 137–38,
208n27; philosophy and, 144;
"In A Dark Time" and, 207, 208

Raleigh, Walter, 116, 117, 118, 222
"Random Political Reflections," 30n
Reality, 6–8 16–19, 185, 198, 224;
death and, 14, 28–29, 123, 148–
49, 155–56, 164, 167, 197; senses
and, 25, 26, 32–33, 38–40, 45–47,
49, 90–91, 94–96, 105–6, 115,
117–22, 126, 127, 139–40, 142,
152, 163–67, 185, 212; identity
and, 29, 36, 43, 67, 84, 168–69,
198, 208, 220; symbol and, 36,
43, 48–50, 65, 67, 68, 101–3,
106–7, 221; doctrine of correspondences and, 102–3, 132, 165,
208; as conflict of opposites, 129,
132–33, 136–37, 164, 191–92,
205, 219, 221, 224
Reason, 10, 14, 25, 118; abstraction
and, 36, 107–8; illumination and,
89, 92, 101, 104, 168, 218; primary thinking, 107n, 221
Rebirth, 61, 63–64, 88, 96, 132,
137, 140, 150, 153, 156, 162,
179, 185, 187, 189, 192, 217

"Reckoning, The," 31
Regression, 70, 110; Jung on, 59–
60, 73, 84; Roethke on, 63–64,
225; in "The Lost Son," 85, 86,
87; in "The Long Alley," 91–92;
in "A Field of Light," 93–94;
vision and, 96; death and, 99–
100, 104, 123, 153–54, 197, 199;
in Meditations of an Old Woman,
159, 160–62, 167, 176, 197; in
North American Sequence, 176,
177, 180–81, 184, 197
Religion, 10, 13, 16, 19, 131, 185;
the father God, 3, 54, 56, 76–77,
79, 88–89, 214; the mother Virgin, 81; Roethke studies, 103,
124, 130, 209n, 220, 221; the
abyss and, 199–200
"Reminder, The," 31, 34–35
"Renewal, The," 7, 124n, 129–30,
136–41, 148n, 153, 173, 207–8,
212, 222
"Reply to a Lady Editor," 126
"Reply to Censure," 29
"Restored, The," 218
"Return, The," 58
Rhymes, 42, 177, 204; slant, 10,
117, 143, 158, 192, 200, 205;
rhythmic effects and, 194, 200;
stanza-linking, 206
Rhythm, 21, 122n, 222; naiveté of,
36, 116–17, 150, 175; in "Epidermal Macabre," 37–38; in
"The Premonition," 42; line
length and, 54, 56–57, 67, 71,
75, 108, 112n, 114, 144–45, 193,
196, 206, 218; in "Sensibility!
O La!" 83; in "The Lost Son,"
86, 95, 108; in "A Field of
Light," 94–95, 108; in "I cry
Love! Love!" 104; in "Advice,"
158; in "A Light Breather," 111;
in "An Old Lady's Winter
Words," 112, 114, 116; in "The
Waking," 122–23
Richard of St. Victor, 209–10
"Right Thing, The," 122n, 218–19

"River Incident," 60–61
Roethke, Beatrice (Mrs. Theodore),
    9–11, 120n, 124, 172n, 195;
    Roethke's collected poems, 13n;
    Roethke's reading, 59n, 169n
Roethke, Helen Marie Huebner
    (Roethke's mother), 2, 3–4
Roethke, Otto (Roethke's father),
    1, 2–3, 5, 27; "The Premonition"
    and, 40–41, 42; in "The Lost
    Son," 51n, 54; in "The Dying
    Man," 102n; "Otto" and, 200–1
"Roethke Remembers," 1n
"Root Cellar," 48, 51, 57, 86
"Rose, The," 178, 187, 190
Roses, 88, 95, 96, 143, 152, 163,
    164, 167, 177, 183, 187–88, 190
Rothberg, Winterset (Roethke
    pseudonym), 12

Saginaw, Michigan, 1, 5, 13
"Saginaw Song, The," 2n, 4n
"Sale," 32
Seager, Allan, 17
"Second Shadow," 38n
"Second Version," 21n, 38n
Senses, the, 43, 183, 221; imagina-
    tion and, 14, 47; dichotomy of
    spirit and, 37, 136–37, 138, 154,
    163, 166, 177, 193; reality and,
    39, 46, 47, 49, 50, 105, 118, 119,
    121, 142, 185, 213; transcend-
    ence of, 174, 205, 219
"Sensibility! O La!" 82–83, 111
"Sensualists, The," 126
"Sententious Man, The," 128–29
"Sequel, The," 212–13, 223
Sequence, Sometimes Metaphysical
    (poem sequence), 16–17, 33,
    130, 172n, 173, 174, 191, 204,
    206–19, 225
Sexuality: mother imagery and, 4,
    72, 74, 78, 81, 95, 96; death and,
    25, 27–28, 48, 55, 76, 78, 81, 82,
    85–86, 88, 91, 126, 154; atti-
    tudes toward, 30, 93, 125–26,
    127, 193; childhood and, 39, 48,

    53, 70–78, 80–82, 85–86, 97–98;
    vision and, 96–97, 118, 166, 205,
    213; dance metaphor, 119–21,
    126
"Shape of the Fire, The," 63n, 95–
    97
"She," 127
"'Shimmer of Evil, The' *Louise
    Bogan*," 146
"Shy Man, The," 195
"Signals, The," 25
"Silence," 29
"Siskins, The," 150
"Slow Season," 26–27, 49
Slug, 150, 157, 177
"Slug," 150
"Small, The," 148
Smart, Christopher, 8n, 70, 203,
    222
"Snake," 150
Society, 8, 57, 87, 92, 186n; the
    individual and, 29–34, 176–77;
    the natural world and, 48, 50, 87,
    91–93
"Some Remarks on Rhythm," 14n,
    56n; quoted, 112n
"Some Self-Analysis," 1n, 4n
"Song," 168n, 193
"Song" (in Mixed Sequence), 203
"Song, The," 147
Southworth, James G., 30n
Stace, W. T., 90n; quoted, 94n
Stanzaic form, 10, 205; of "The
    Adamant," 36; of "Epidermal
    Macabre," 38; rhythm and, 112n,
    143–44, 194, 196, 200, 212; of
    "The Dance," 116–17; villanelles,
    62n, 121–22; of "In A Dark
    Time," 211
Staples, Hugh, 175, 176, 178
"Statement," 7n
Stein, Arnold, 17
Stevens, Wallace, 175, 186, 222
Stoicism, 114–15, 122, 123, 204
Stones, 98, 104, 111, 190; as essen-
    tial unity, 93, 99, 110, 117, 130,
    194; correspondence doctrine

Stones (*Continued*)
    and, 101, 132, 139, 140; eternity
    and, 148, 183, 205
"Storm, The," 203
"Straw for the Fire," 169n, 216n
Structure: of *Open House*, 23–24,
    32–33; of *The Lost Son*, 45; of
    Praise to the End! 69; of *Words
    for the Wind*, 145, 170; of *The
    Far Field*, 191, 195, 206, 219,
    225
Style: Roethke development, 9–10,
    13–14, 35–36, 38–39, 40, 43, 45,
    46, 56, 58, 68, 106–9, 143–45,
    172, 191, 200, 206, 211, 215,
    217, 220–26; metaphysical, 19–
    20, 21–22, 26–27, 36–37, 41,
    138–39, 143, 170; Roethke on,
    34, 37, 46–47, 56, 67–68, 108–9;
    traditional forms, 121–22, 177,
    205, 218–19, 221; aphoristic,
    145, 215, 223–24
Sun, 87, 93, 187
"Surly One, The," 129
Surrealism, 68
Swan, 128, 167
"Swan, The," 124n, 128, 143
Swedenborg, Emmanuel, 102n
Symbolism, 1–2; reality and, 36,
    40–43, 48–50, 65, 67, 68, 101–3,
    106–7, 221
Symbolists, 101

"Teaching Poet, The," 11–12
Tennis, 6, 9, 11
Themes, 9, 18–19, 34, 205; alter-
    nation of, 14, 159; regression as,
    63–64; of "Where Knock is
    Open Wide," 78; of "O, Thou
    Opening, O," 105; of the later
    (1954–1958) poems, 125, 130;
    of North American Sequence,
    174–75, 178n; Roethke list of,
    186n
"Theodore Roethke Writes . . . ,"
    4n, 23n, 109n
"They Sing, They Sing," 156–57

"Thing, The," 202
"This Light," 20–21
Thomas, Dylan, 10, 46, 70n, 80,
    182n, 222; dream technique,
    68; "Elegy" for, 146
Tillich, Paul, 13, 124, 153, 174;
    quoted, 131–32, 134–35, 140–41,
    146, 149, 152, 210; influence of,
    136, 149, 169n, 197
Time: eternity manifest in, 19, 115,
    119, 121, 128, 147–49, 152, 157,
    168–70, 181, 183, 185, 187, 188,
    193, 202–3, 205–6, 212, 219;
    birth and, 73; death and, 133,
    153, 164, 168, 181, 184–85
"Tirade Turning, A," 12–13
"To My Sister," 24–25, 41, 43, 55;
    quoted, 38–39
"Tower, The" (Yeats), 144
Traherne, Thomas, 65, 67, 76, 91,
    222
"Tranced, The," 172n, 204–5, 216
"Transplanting," 54
"Tree, the Bird, The," 217–18
Trees, 80, 81–82, 129, 143, 148,
    189–90, 212, 216, 217–18

Underhill, Evelyn: cited, 102n,
    103n, 209n; quoted, 168, 198
"Unextinguished, The," 28
"Unfold! Unfold!" 99–104, 120,
    138, 153n, 165, 173, 185

Vaughan, Henry, 18, 19, 20–21, 26,
    65, 76, 80, 91, 138, 187, 222, 223
"Vernal Sentiment," 30
"Verse with Allusions," 30
"Vigil, The," 96n, 120–21
Virgin Mary, 81
Vision: identity and, 23–24, 29,
    32–33, 65, 125; reality and, 25,
    26, 38, 39, 45–46, 65, 94–95,
    100–1, 104–6, 115, 117, 120–22,
    126, 127, 139–40, 164–67, 212;
    of God as father, 88–89, 91; sex-
    uality and, 96–97, 118, 166, 205,
    213

"Visitant, The," 110–11, 112, 126
"Voice, The," 127
Voices and Creatures (poem sequence), 13, 124n, 145–49, 160, 170, 201

Waking, The, 13, 45n, 62n, 63n, 110–23, 124n; publication, 10–11, 224, 225; *Praise to the End!* and, 104–5, 110n
"Waking, The," 61–62
"Waking, The" (villanelle, 1953), 62n, 105n, 121–23, 144, 196, 204, 218
"Walk in Late Summer, A," 145, 148–49, 184
"Wall, The," 153–55
Wall, 82, 130, 137, 147, 153–54, 196, 208, 213
Washington, University of, 6, 9
Water, 178–79, 182, 183, 185, 187, 190, 193, 194, 197, 217, 219
"Weed Puller," 52, 86
"What Can I Tell My Bones?" 167–69, 214
"What Now?" 153, 154n

"Where Knock Is Open Wide," 54n, 69n, 70–78, 80, 98
Whitman, Walt, 176–77, 187–88, 196, 202, 222,
Winters, Yvor, quoted, 35
"Wish for a Young Wife," 11, 195
Wit, 23, 29, 30, 32–33, 37–39, 65
Woman, 110–15, 117–20, 126, 135–36, 142–43, 156–59
Words for the Wind, 7, 8, 11, 89n, 124–71; *The Waking* and, 10, 110n, 124n; publication, 13–15, 124n; *The Far Field* and, 16, 193, 204, 217, 225
"Words for the Wind," 11, 127, 128, 129, 143–45, 152, 222
"Wraith, The," 119–20
Wylie, Elinor, 20–21, 24n; influence of, 9, 19, 26, 104n, 222

Yeats, William Butler, 223, 226; quoted, 128, 153n, 215n; influence of, 10–11, 13–15, 54, 115–18, 144, 188, 191, 207, 222; The Dying Man and, 13, 102n, 151, 152, 154, 156–58
"Young Girl, The," 191–92